Anima as Fate

The Jungian Classics Series

serves to make available again works of long-standing value in the tradition of C. G. Jung's psychology:

ANIELA JAFFÉ
Apparitions
An Archetypal Approach to Death Dreams and Ghosts

JAMES HILLMAN
Insearch
Psychology and Religion

MARIE-LOUISE VON FRANZ
The Passion of Perpetua

VICTOR WHITE
God and the Unconscious

EDGAR HERZOG
Psyche and Death
Death-Demons in Folklore, Myths and Modern Dreams

ANIELA JAFFÉ
Jung's Last Years and Other Essays

ROBERT STEIN
Incest and Human Love
The Betrayal of the Soul in Psychotherapy

LINDA FIERZ-DAVID
The Dream of Poliphilo
(forthcoming)

Anima as Fate

Cornelia Brunner

translated by
JULIUS HEUSCHER

edited by
DAVID SCOTT MAY

Preface by
C. G. JUNG

Spring Publications, Inc.
Dallas, Texas

Published by Spring Publications, Inc.; P.O. Box 222069;
Dallas, Texas 75222. Printed in the United States of America

This translation is based on Cornelia Brunner's German language work
Die Anima als Schicksalsproblem des Mannes, published as a study from
the C. G. Jung-Institute, Zürich, in 1963 by Rascher Verlag, Zürich,
Switzerland, and with the assistance of the Swiss National Foundation.

Cover: The cover photograph "Sprite," originally a Polaroid Land print,
was taken by Rosamond W. Purcell and appears by courtesy of the artist,
who exhibits at the Marcuse Pfeifer Gallery in New York City. Design
assistance and cover production by Jimmie Paroline Hudson.

International distributors:
Spring; Postfach; 8800 Thalwil; Switzerland.
Japan Spring Sha, Inc.; 1–2–4, Nishisakaidani-Cho;
  Ohharano, Nishikyo-Ku; Kyoto, 610–11, Japan.
Element Books Ltd; Longmead Shaftesbury;
  Dorset SP7 8PL; England.

Library of Congress Cataloging-in-Publication Data

Brunner, Cornelia.
  Anima as fate.

  (The Jungian classic series ; 9)
  Translation of: Die Anima als Schicksalsproblem des
Mannes.
  Bibliography: p.
  1. Anima (Psychoanalysis) 2. Haggard, H. Rider
(Henry Rider), 1856–1925. Ayesha, the return of She.
3. Haggard, H. Rider (Henry Rider), 1856–1925.
4. Novelists, English—20th century—Biography.
5. Novelists, English—20th century—Psychology.
6. Dreams—Case studies. I. May, David Scott.
II. Title. III. Series.
BF175.5.A52B7813 1986   150.19'54   86–14264
ISBN 0–88214–508–8

Contents

PREFACE BY C. G. JUNG   *ix*
PREFACE TO THE ENGLISH TRANSLATION
  BY CORNELIA BRUNNER   *xv*
EDITOR'S PREFACE   *xvii*
ACKNOWLEDGMENTS   *xx*
INTRODUCTION   *xxi*

FIRST PART: THE ANIMA IN RIDER HAGGARD

  I. *The Adventurous Life of Rider Haggard*   3

  II. *Psychological Interpretation of Haggard's* She   31
      Psychological Hypotheses of the Novel   *31*
      The Story   *32*
      Holly   *33*
      Vincey   *37*
      Leo, the Sun-Child   *39*
      Job, the Servant   *41*
      The Message in the Trunk   *41*
      The Twin-Heroes   *46*
      The Night Sea-Journey   *48*
      Mother Nature   *49*
      The Ethiopian Head   *51*
      The Animals   *52*
      The Swamp Belt   *55*
      The Old Wise Man Billali and His Tribe   *55*
      The First Crater   *58*
      Ustane   *59*
      The Incandescent Pot   *61*
      The Mummy   *66*
      The Land of Fever   *69*
      The Mandala of the Heart: Kor   *69*
      She   *71*
      Benoit's *Atlantide*   *76*
      The Reverse Side of the Heart   *81*
      The Feast of the Animal Masks and Epiphany   *85*
      The Temple of Truth   *89*
      Transitus   *92*
      The Death in the Fire   *105*
      Later Continuations of She   *110*

  III. *Summary of the Symbolism and of its Explanation*   116

153165

SECOND PART: THE DEVELOPMENT OF THE ANIMA
PORTRAYED IN A SERIES OF DREAMS

I. Introduction to the Series of Dreams   125

II. The Dreams and Their Interpretation   135

Dream One: Bugs   *135*

Dream Two: The Crash   *137*

Dream Three: Sunrise   *137*

Dream Four: The Image of the Royal Couple   *138*

Dream Five: The Royal Couple in the Country of Blacks   *139*

Dream Six: Old Man   *140*

Dream Seven: The Wedding Did Not Take Place   *140*

Dream Eight: The Hand-Spun Coat   *142*

Dream Nine: The Horses Bolt   *143*

Dream Ten: Riding   *143*

Dream Eleven: The Heath-Cock   *144*

Dream Twelve: The Bathing Suit   *145*

Dream Thirteen: Young Hart, Poacher, Earth-Mother and Variegated
Field   *146*

Dream Fourteen: Mouse and Corn-Hawk   *149*

Dream Fifteen: The Circus Athlete   *150*

Dream Sixteen: Rotary Motion   *150*

Dream Seventeen: Spanish Riding School   *152*

Dream Eighteen: The Anima Warns against the Eleven Crows   *152*

Dream Nineteen: The White Bull and the Three Girls   *156*

Dream Twenty: The Woman-Commander   *159*

Dream Twenty-One: The Sword of the Ancestors   *162*

Dream Twenty-Two: The Little Daughter with the Ball   *164*

Dream Twenty-Three: Bow and Arrow   *166*

Dream Twenty-Four: The Chinese Girl in a Blue and White Dress   *167*

Dream Twenty-Five: The Runner   *169*

Dream Twenty-Six: The Rats   *170*

Dream Twenty-Seven: I Overtake My Mother   *171*

Dream Twenty-Eight: The Church Collapses   *172*

Dream Twenty-Eight A: The Bomb   *173*

Dream Twenty-Nine: The Field on the Mountain Slope   *176*

Dream Thirty: The Eagle   *180*

Dream Thirty-One: The Woman in the Furrow   *182*

Dream Thirty-Two: Divine Service in the Grotto   *183*

Dream Thirty-Three: The New Church   *184*

Dream Thirty-Four: The Tabernacle   *184*

Dream Thirty-Five: The Sapphire Ring   *185*

Dream Thirty-Six: Brandy   *187*

Dream Thirty-Seven: The Transition   *191*

Dream Thirty-Eight: The Lay Priest and the Three Wart Fellows   *194*

Dream Thirty-Nine: The Woman in the Violet Dress   *196*

CONTENTS • vii

Dream Forty: The Explosion of the White Powder   *197*
Dream Forty-One: Volcanic Eruption   *197*
Dream Forty-Two: Faust and Mephistopheles   *197*
Dream Forty-Three: Aida   *200*
Dream Forty-Four: Three Priests and a Priestess   *201*
Dream Forty-Five: The Adoration of the Queen   *203*
Dream Forty-Six: The Convent with the Throne Room   *204*
Dream Forty-Seven: The Round Church   *206*
Dream Forty-Eight: Four Speeches   *208*
Dream Forty-Nine: Riding Lesson   *211*
Dream Fifty: The Hart   *213*
Dream Fifty-One: Your Will—Your Way   *215*
Dream Fifty-Two: Deliverance from the Water Tank   *216*
Dream Fifty-Three: Imprisonment in the Rocky Cliff   *219*
Dream Fifty-Four: The Taming of the Anima   *223*
Dream Fifty-Five: The Communion Rail   *225*
Dream Fifty-Six: Church or University   *227*
Dream Fifty-Seven: The Bird Griff   *228*
Dream Fifty-Eight: The Cormorant   *229*
Dream Fifty-Nine: The Flying Hart   *231*
Dream Sixty: The Picture of the Ancestors   *233*
Dream Sixty-One: The Church of the *Magna Mater*   *234*
Dream Sixty-Two: Betrothal   *240*
Dream Sixty-Three: End of the World   *241*
Dream Sixty-Four: Arrogance   *248*
Dream Sixty-Five: Baggage   *249*
Dream Sixty-Six: The Giantess and Her Child   *250*
Dream Sixty-Seven: The Oversized Farmer   *250*
Dream Sixty-Eight: The Oversized Couple   *251*
Dream Sixty-Nine: The Chapel in the Vatican   *252*
Concluding Remarks to the Series of Dreams   *253*

III. *Summary*   *256*

NOTE TO THE READER   *264*
NOTES   *265*

Preface

This book is based on some important presuppositions. The lack of familiarity with these could give rise to misunderstandings. I would, therefore, wish to draw the reader's attention to the fact that the material of the second part represents a therapeutic dialogue extended over an eight-year period. From the very beginning, the partners of this dialogue committed themselves to be as open, accurate, and complete as is humanly possible. Such a commitment can naturally be followed only to the limits of the influence of consciousness. Recognizing this limitation, the partners set themselves the additional task to give consideration to any unconscious reactions that accompanied their conscious statements. This demanding endeavor, however, could only be fully accomplished if all the unconscious reactions of both partners were recorded. Such a "biographic" dialogue represents something totally unique and could be realized only under exceptionally favorable circumstances. Considering the extraordinary difficulties and obstacles in such a task, the author deserves our appreciation and thanks for having recorded at least three-fourths of the dialogue with all the required thoroughness and detail. Her successful attempt will gain the recognition of all those who are interested in the authentic life of the soul, especially since she makes use of her clinical experience and extensive mythological and literary material when illustrating a problem common to men. Each case history of this kind follows some basic archetypal pattern. However, the value of any particular case consists, in the first place, in its uniqueness. The author's focusing upon its uniqueness becomes a positive criterion for the objectivity of the presentation. The true carrier of reality is the individual, not the schema of the "probable" or "typical." Thus, the author manifests her genuine appreciation of facts by restricting her descriptions to two persons. The live personality has its meaning and worth only in his/her uniqueness, not in collective or statistical qualities. The latter are but properties of the human species and thus unconditional requirements of superpersonal nature. Restricting the description to two personalities may leave the impression of an unscientific atmosphere of subjectivity, yet it signifies psychological objectivity: this is how it stands with the real life of the soul; this is what truly happened. Whatever aspect of all this that can be grasped theoretically belongs to the general principles of the psychologic process and could also be observed under different circumstances and in other individuals. Scientific insight is largely a side-product of personal psychological dialogue. The latter gains its required freedom of expression by this very fact. True and untrue, right and wrong are ethically related concepts but are not measured by a universal truth or correctness. True and correct comment in this situation only on whether or not what is happening is experienced by the subject in the same way.

Thus, the reader becomes the invisible listener in a serious dialogue between two educated human beings of our time, dealing with questions that arise between them. Both offer freely and to the best of their abilities their contributions and remain faithful to their commitment throughout the dialogue. This deserves special commendation. In fact, it is in no way assumed that conversations are adequately pursued. Often they end prematurely, as one or the other or both partners, for good or bad reasons, terminate them. Frequently, they walk away from each other as soon as some difficulty presents itself.

It is the author's additional merit to have recorded the content of the long discussions on two planes. The sequence of thoughts and events which she describes constitutes an extremely instructive human document. Yet, because of its uniqueness it is exposed to the danger of being misunderstood and rejected as overly subjective or fantastic. In fact, we deal here with those aspects of human relatedness which Freud summarized with the concept of *transference* and characterized as infantile fantasies. Such depreciation caused these aspects of human relatedness to fall prey to the rational prejudice which obscured their considerable importance as events or phenomena of transformation. This scientific sin of omission is but a link in the long chain of underestimations of the human soul; underestimations for which no adequate proofs can be adduced. The fact that it has largely lost sight of the extraordinary importance of the soul as the basis for human existence is a grave symptom of the nearsightedness, nay unconsciousness, of the natural-scientific era. What use are technical improvements when humanity must still tremble in the face of ridiculous, childish, terrifying tyrants similar to Hitler? Such persons owe their power exclusively to the frightful immaturity of today's human being, to his/her spiritual poverty and his/her barbaric unconsciousness. We can no longer afford the underestimation of the psychic factor in world events nor the disdain of soul-processes and of the efforts to understand them. In fact, our one and only hope is that the masses will awaken to genuine humanness. We have, however, not yet reached the point of being able to see clearly where in *us* the defect is. This dialogue then represents but an attempt; yet all true experience arises from such attempts. Without concrete, specific, personal experience, there can never be any valid general insight.

The author has done well in presenting first, almost as an introduction, a widely-known case in literature, namely Rider Haggard, who evidenced a similar Anima-problem. Rider Haggard is without doubt a classic example of a writer dealing with the motif of the Anima, which appears, consciously, already with the humanists of the fifteenth or seventeenth century. Thus, the *Ipnerotomachia* of Francesco Colonna; it also appears as a psychological concept in England's Richardus Vitus von Basingstoke or as a poetic figure in the *fedeli d'amore,* which is in accord with *The Divine Comedy.*

The literary work of Rider Haggard is an excellent introduction to the main purpose of this book inasmuch as it offers an almost exclusively pictorial presentation of the Anima-Symbolism and Problem. His book *She,* though, is but an initial step without continuation, since the ground of reality is never reached. Everything remains suspended in fantasy and stuck in symbolic anticipation. Rider Haggard did not know of his spiritual ancestors. Therefore, he was unaware of confronting a task which not only philosophical alchemy had dealt with but which also the last of the great masterpieces, Goethe's *Faust,* was able to sketch as "accomplished" only in the afterlife of the protagonist.

For Rider Haggard the significant motif of the Anima unfolds in the purest and most naive fashion. Throughout his literary production he never tires, remaining faithful to his dialogue with her. As if committed to his name, he was an abstemious knight of his lady, a late-born troubadour or Knight of the Holy Grail. As if from nowhere, he had fallen right into the middle of the Victorian era. He enshrines it, is captured by it, and serves as its typical representative. Nothing was left for him to do but to shape his wonderful tale of olden times into the contemporary, somewhat mediocre form of a "yarn." Nevertheless, he is a true heir of the bards and poets who were the delight of the knightly twelfth and thirteenth centuries. Not nearly as harmless was the romantic project of his German contemporary, Richard Wagner. Then a dangerous genius, Friedrich Nietzsche, became involved in the project, and through him it was Zarathustra, lacking a wise woman to converse with, who raised his voice. This powerful voice originated in a bachelor, who—six thousand feet beyond good and evil—met his "Dudu and Suleika" only after he became insane. To Dudu and Suleika he made the confessions which his sister tried to cover up so completely that only traces of them have been left in his medical records. They may sound neither good nor beautiful; but it is part of being grownup to hear and to integrate within the picture of reality the horrible dissonances produced by one's actual life. Truth and reality, indeed, are not heavenly music but beauty and horror of nature. Unfortunately, psychological understanding cannot make allowances for aesthetic needs. Thus the greatness and significance of a motif, such as that of the Anima, are not determined by its relation to the form of its expression. If Rider Haggard makes use of the modest literary form of the "yarn," this does not curtail the content of his statements. He who looks for entertaining literature or artful use of language can easily find something superior. He, however, who seeks understanding and insight will find rich fare in *She*, just because of the simplicity and naivete of the views which lack deliberate psychological implications.

Richest, naturally, is the harvest in the second part of the book, the harvest of the dreams which—neither invented nor imagined—are a spontaneous product of nature. In the dreams the psychological process expresses itself directly, without being significantly altered by one-sided, impulsive, or arbitrary tendencies of subjective consciousness. One might say, however, that this richness discloses itself mostly to him who understands the language of animals and plants. There is truth in this thought, and yet any intelligent human being may also gain understanding and insight as long as he possesses a modicum of intuition and some healthy resistance against common doctrines. Intuition follows the flow of images, joins them, and empathically transforms them until they begin to speak and to manifest their meaning. They present, but do not prove, themselves. Intuition accompanies the images, instinctively sensing their truth. Trusting the presentiment of ancient times, intuition rediscovers forgotten or obliterated paths upon which already many have walked long ago, upon which maybe even one's partner in the dialogue has traveled. Recognizing the traces of the path, the partners walk side by side. Thus they learn to follow the natural structure of the psyche.

The author has been successful in bringing forth within the dreamer the kind of intuitive attitude which he needs for following the traces of his unconscious developmental process. Interpretation is not based on any theory but responds to the symbolically viewed hints of the dream. Whenever psychological concepts are introduced, such as Anima, we must not see this as a theoretical presupposition, since Anima, in this case, is meant to be, not an abstract idea, but an empirical concept or name designating an array of observable and typical events. In such an extended dialogue we find that interpretations are but passing phases and tentative formulations which eventually would have to prove themselves within the whole. Whether they have accomplished this becomes evident only in the end result. The latter will show whether one was on the right path or not. Such an ongoing dialogue is always a creative risk-taking where one must offer, at each and every moment, the best one knows. Only then can the great work of transformation—God willing—succeed.

C. G. Jung
April 1959

Preface to the English Translation

I'm deeply obliged to Julius Heuscher and Scott May for the careful translation of my book which deals with Rider Haggard's novel *She* and with the development of the Anima as portrayed in the dreams of a young physician. The latter had served in the Army during World War II and spent a brief time in Russian captivity.

Rider Haggard's bestseller *She*—not unlike Benoit's novel *Atlantide*—portrays the unconscious Anima's abysmal dangerousness and her insatiable demand for power. As the "feminine soul of the man," she compensates for his Christian consciousness and his gentleman-ideal.

The series of dreams points to the fact that *fascination* and *being-in-love* are, in part, projections from one's own soul. The interpretation of these projected contents and the resulting broadened consciousness make possible the gradual withdrawal of these projections. This unburdens the relationship and can lead towards a genuine friendship. One must not, however, forget that this has nothing to do with finding a new marriage partner but aims at an inner evolution. In the man this evolution manifests itself in his feelings and relatedness, nourished by the example of the woman. In the woman, on the other hand, it manifests itself in the development of her thinking and spirit as a result of the dialogue with the man. It is important not to neglect in such stormy periods the concrete, everyday tasks and obligations. Only then can even one's relationship to one's family gain in reliability.

As a result of such an evolutionary process, spirit and soul—Animus and Anima—become mediators for a new personal and transpersonal sense-perception and moral commitment.

Several young men have told me that they happened to hit on this book just at the right moment, namely when—not unlike Rider Haggard—they found themselves faced with a painful choice between their marriage and a new friendship. Thus, I hope that this book will continue to serve in our confused times as a signpost on man's inner journey.

Cornelia Brunner

Editor's Preface

What would possess a thirty-four-year-old American-born and -trained psychiatrist who was about to begin two additional years of psychiatric training to voluntarily collaborate on a three-year project to translate a 330-page book originally written in German twenty-five years ago? I was obliged to answer this question not only for the preface to this book but also on many weekends during the past several years.

My answer to this question, and the reason that I hope many of you will engage with this book, is that the fate of the Anima for men is an emerging and critical issue at the personal, social, and political levels for us all. Through the impact of women's liberation and the relaxation of previously stereotypic masculine and feminine roles, the conscious exploration of a man's own Anima is more available to him and no longer restricted to a few visionary or "deviant" males. Additionally, the traditional rewards of an Animus-dominated life—material rewards and comforts, power, outward adventure—even when substantial, are no longer seen as being enough by a number of "successful" males. Instead, there remains a vague premonition that something in a man's psyche is calling forth to be known and explored. Perhaps the so-called "Midlife Crisis" for a man is really the rumblings of the long-imprisoned Anima seeking a valued position and expression in his life. The ever-present danger of nuclear self-annihilation is a further reminder of the pressing need for men to integrate their Anima. No doubt, should a nuclear war get started, the orders will be given and the buttons pushed by men whose contact with their Anima is largely if not exclusively unconscious.

Yet even if all this is true, the question remains, why this book instead of another, perhaps more recently written. The answer as I came to see it is the distinctly imaginative, lucid, and open manner in which Cornelia Brunner brings a man's struggle with his Anima into focus. Ironically, it is her womanly vision and wisdom that allows a man to understand his hidden struggle. Additionally, Cornelia Brunner's close association with Carl Jung and his ideas over many years is a strong, illuminating force that runs through this book. Had she attempted a strictly logical, linear, scientific examination, she would have instead created a simple reflection of the Animus looking back at itself rather than her softer, yet more penetrating view revealing the Anima. Thus, her ability to illuminate the issues through the life of the writer H. Rider Haggard, through Haggard's literary figure and powerful Anima projection "She," and through the series of dreams of an outwardly successful yet questing man allows the reader to see into man's struggle with his Anima, much as one has to look through a window at an angle with soft light if he is to see anything other than his own reflection.

My sense is that, along with H. Rider Haggard, the thirty-nine-year-old physician whose dreams are analyzed, and myself, many of the readers of this book share a nagging if not haunting sense of incompleteness, despite our strivings and achievements. This volume brings into focus from various angles the elusive, frightening, and seductive qualities of a man's connection with his Anima, tracing the way that the Anima can gradually become conscious to a man rather than remain a shadowy, projected force. At times as I was working on this project, I found myself reconsidering my heavy reliance on Animus-based forces as I experienced relationships that withered, illnesses that did not respond to my most thoughtful analysis, and emotionally empty times that stubbornly refused to yield. It was at these times that I could begin to recognize my excessive reliance on power and logic and the relative limits I had placed on love, soulfulness, and relatedness—all manifestations of my own Anima.

Here, Cornelia Brunner has both clarified a number of the obstacles common to men as they make contact with their Anima and revealed the unfolding process of a man eventually befriending his Anima. Cornelia Brunner is guide, teacher, and priestess as she traces the movement of the Anima through nearly seventy dreams as it is transformed from wild and alien to known and integrated.

Julius Heuscher, M.D., a mentor while I was in training and the man responsible for the majority of this translation, demonstrated the possibility of a balanced Anima/Animus existence as he artfully transformed the German to English while preserving its original depth.

Working on this book required a certain amount of energy and initial suspension of judgment, just as reading it most likely will; however, the depth and integration that follow from the experience make it well worth the effort.

Scott May

Acknowledgments

I would like to thank the following for their assistance in the preparation of this book:

Julius Heuscher, M.D., for this thoughtful and conscientious translation;
Jean Bolen, M.D., for her inspiration and insight into these issues;
The Northern California Analytical Psychology Club and Jungian Institute for their professional and financial support of this project;
Tovah Hollander, for her intelligent and painstaking typing of this manuscript;
Ken Igarashi, for his valuable editorial assistance.

S. M.
Los Angeles, 1984

Introduction

This work originated at the suggestion of C. G. Jung, the eminent psychiatrist who again and again occupied himself throughout his life with the Anima, the feminine soul-image of man, and with the Animus, the masculine soul-image of woman.[1] This relentless interest grew not from theoretical considerations but from the vital necessity to deal with unconscious contents within his patients as well as within himself. Unconscious forces and complexes have a determining—and often disturbing—effect upon consciousness. An erroneous orientation of consciousness can, therefore, be changed only when the causes rooted in the unconscious are known. The unconscious forces and complexes tend to be personified in dreams and fantasies, whereby they become accessible to personal insight. One of the most important personal complexes is the countersexual soul-component. In the dreams of men, this unconscious feminine soul appears as an unfamiliar woman. The Anima embodies the man's feelings, his eros; negatively, his fears, moods, and touchiness. While she is unconscious, the Anima appears to him in the form of a projection. Whomever he loves or hates, this inner image of the woman—as anticipation, as a wish-fulfillment image, as fearfulness—squeezes itself between him and the real person he encounters. His soul-image is first constellated by the mother, since she is the first recipient and carrier of the projection. As he once related to his mother, so the man later relates to his Anima and to women. And he will appreciate or despise women, depending upon his estimate of his own Anima.

The Anima determines man's relationship to women, and in the encounter with a woman, man experiences and recognizes the essence of his own soul.[2] Wherever he projects his soul upon a woman, a kind of magic identity is established. This expresses itself in the guise of overwhelming emotions, especially with the intense feeling of "falling-in-love." Thereby the Anima becomes fate-shaping. When one's own soul is projected, one feels unable to separate oneself any longer from the object of the projection. When one believes he has found, at long last, one's complement, one does not want to lose this "other half." Thus the Anima drives the young man towards the realization of his yearnings.

The Anima projection does not terminate with marriage. The preconscious soul-image contains, as a germ, all the original experience of the man with the woman as a collective, inner, archetypal image. The longing for this image drives the man to seek ever further, until he recognizes that he cannot acquire his soul by falling in love with every new woman. Only when he recognizes the projections as such, when he tries to understand what it is that attracts him so much to this or that woman, and only when he endeavors to develop these qualities within himself can he find that part of his being whose spell gave him no rest. Yet he is not capable of understanding and developing the Anima by himself. For this he requires an encounter with a woman who portrays and lives for him that which corresponds not to his conscious experience but to his feminine soul-image. Only in the encounter with such a woman does the Anima awaken for him. In the second half of life, the meaning of such a relationship consists primarily in the *symbolic* experience of the feminine rather than in the actual possession of a concrete woman. It may then become possible to reclaim piece by piece the Anima projections. Thus by renouncing the projection, and by combining into an inner wholeness the masculine with one's relatedness towards the feminine, the man achieves a realistic spiritual orientation.

The concept *Anima* was devised by C. G. Jung. He utilized it to describe and develop a reality which occupied him and many poets before him, to mention but the feminine figures in Goethe's *Faust* or the "mistress soul" in Spitteler's *Prometheus* and especially Spitteler's *Imago*.

In his writings Jung refers repeatedly to the Anima description in Rider Haggard's *She*. This fantastic novel was published in 1866. Haggard thereby became famous almost overnight, because—like Pierre Benoit in *Atlantide*, published in 1900—he describes man's soul. The striking similarity between She and Antinea is explained by both authors' hitting upon the same inner fact, upon a truth that concerns everyone. Because of this, *She* and *Atlantide* were so universally and enthusiastically accepted. The enthusiasm was in no way due to literary or poetic perfection. Haggard is not a poet but rather a narrator. It was his ability to evoke the wish-fulfillment image of the man, to elicit the goal of his longing, that brought the book's success. The enthusiasm was born out of the unconscious knowledge about the inner reality of the Anima.

It was Jung, later on, who put it in words—that She, the goddess, was the personification of man's soul. As godly imago dwelling in the unconscious, She still retains the original, paradoxical, and ambivalent quality of the wholeness of a great goddess. Her being simultaneously wonderful and abysmal makes the encounter with her both a desired and dangerous adventure. Such an adventure awaits every man as he turns inward. Should he, however, fail to undertake this quest, this voyage of discovery for the sake of becoming conscious of his soul, the Anima remains just as active in his life, even though he does not know anything of her. As the maiden of wishes, she spins his wishes; and as the goddess of fate, she weaves his destiny by means of the light and dark threads of his feelings.

In *Aion* Jung tells of the Anima and Animus. As shown by practical experience, both archetypes possess at a given time a fatality that expresses itself in tragic dimensions. They are quite properly father and mother of all hopeless, fateful entanglements, and as such they have been known all over the world. They are a pair of gods of whom Animus is characterized as Pneuma (Spirit) and Nous (Knowledge) because of his Logos-Nature, resembling the variegated, sparkling Hermes. The Anima—because of her Eros-Nature—carries the characteristics of Aphrodite, of Helen, of Persephone, and of Hekate. Animus and Anima are unconscious powers, indeed gods, as which they were viewed quite "correctly" in earlier times. By this designation they are accorded the central position in the psychological scale of importance, a position they occupy whether consciousness acknowledges this pivotal importance or not; in fact, their power grows in direct proportion to the degree of unconsciousness.[3]

The interpretation of Haggard's *She* aims at discovering the being of the Anima and at understanding psychologically the relationship to her of the various stations of the journey.[4] Haggard wrote the story feverishly, as if possessed, within six weeks and changed almost nothing from his first draft. He drew a lively and scintillating image of a soul-mistress which can greatly help the understanding of a man's actions and reactions when dictated by feelings.

As a spontaneous fantasy, the novel expresses itself with the same images as we see in a great dream. Therefore, the method of interpretation of the novel can be similar to that of dreams. We may then seek the meaning as compensation for the current level of consciousness, or we may illuminate the meaning with similar images from religious history, from myths, and from fairy tales.[5]

Our interpretation of the novel is preceded by a portrayal of Haggard's life in order for the reader to shape his own picture of this author's personality. A fantasy of such compelling power presented in a novel cannot be an accidental phenomenon. It is the answer to a dangerous situation. Whenever there are seemingly hopeless difficulties, whether internal or external, the soul announces itself—either in a dream, in a fantasy, or a vision—by means of an archetypal image which is linked to past tradition and forgotten cultural heritage. Such images let us see personal difficulties as universal human problems and help us change our attitude by widening our spiritual horizons. Dreams and fantasies that arise from the unconscious and assume shapes must be recognized as an answer to an all too narrow consciousness as well as to the one-sidedness of the current culture. We must, therefore, also explain the historical limitation of the author. In its effort to compensate for a particular consciousness, fantasy brings forth those traits which were lacking or are being suppressed deliberately. It is thus important that we get to know the attitudinal and functional type of an author. In the case of Haggard, we notice the introverted, intuitive type in whom the extroverted sensation remained developmentally backward as the fourth function.[6] Haggard's life offers a clear image of the introverted, intuitive individual. It shows what catches this type's attention, what attracts him, what distinguishes him, but also what is difficult for him and what he lacks.

After completing my work concerning Haggard and his *She*, I obtained the dreams of a modern, educated man whose profession dealt with the natural sciences. In his dreams many motifs could be found which were strikingly similar to the ones in *She:* the fight between confronting animals; the sunrise; the journey to Africa; the Anima as a nature-being and, later on, as leader of an army and as Queen. Thus, the opportunity presented itself to use a contemporary dream sequence containing images reminiscent of those of Haggard and to make it the starting point for an exploration. This exploration intends to show how the Anima can develop and change as a result of a conscious discussion of life's problems and of the accompanying dreams. After the initial projection of the Anima upon mother and sister, we see appear various feminine dream-figures which the dreamer recognizes as belonging to him, with whom he establishes a relationship, by whom he is taught, and for whom he must establish proper limits. Inasmuch as the dreams deal with the daily problems, they represent also a critique of the everyday comportment or a supplement and widening of the habitual, immediate attitudes towards life and its daily encounters. If the meaning and purpose of the dreams are understood, and if an attempt to correct one's comportment follows, the new effort shows its genuineness when subsequent dreams take on new, qualitatively different problems. However, when there is not a sufficient understanding nor a true realization in one's life, development comes to a halt. Conversely, if one tries to integrate in one's life what one has seen, thought, and felt, the new insight can become one's lasting possession. In this case the Anima that had been longed for and sought as a distant wish-fulfillment image establishes itself as one's own spontaneous feelings, manifesting itself as the capacity for empathy towards one's neighbor.

My thanks go at this point primarily to my venerated teacher C. G. Jung, because of his untiring participation and help in preparing this book. It was his work, the publications from the circle of his students, the speakers in the Psychological Club, and the teachers at the C. G. Jung Institute that gave me access to the mythologic and cultural-historical materials that were required for the interpretation of the novel and for the understanding of the dream sequence. Several friends have assisted me with counsel and action during the reading of the manuscript. All of them I must thank for their patience and collaboration.

Cornelia Brunner
Zürich, December 1961

FIRST PART
The Anima in Rider Haggard

I. The Adventurous Life of Rider Haggard[7]

Rider Haggard, his life, and his work interest us here exclusively from a psychological vantage point. Literary questions are not explored. We are not concerned with Rider Haggard the scribe but with Rider Haggard the human being, with his personality, his insight, and his internal journey. His work is of particular interest since his early novels, especially *She,* are not delicately chiseled creations but raw material which allows the underlying psychological process to become directly visible.

Henry Rider Haggard was born in England on the twenty-second of July, 1856. His family originally came from Jutland, and their name at that time was Guildenstjerne. An ancestor who assumed the name of the Danish family dwelling, Aagaard, emigrated in 1420 to England where he attained great wealth and fame. William Henry Haggard, Rider's great-grandfather, bought Bradenham Hall in West Norfolk, a beautiful estate with excellent oak groves, where Lady Hamilton lived for some time when it was leased to her relatives. It was on this property that little Rider was born. His great-grandfather, a gifted, lovable gentleman, occupied himself, not only with his business ventures, but also with literature. In 1781 he married Frances Amyand, the daughter of a stubborn, irritable, and brilliant man and the granddaughter of Claudius Amyand, the surgeon of George II. From this time on the Amyand traits became predominant in the Haggard family. According to Lilias Rider Haggard's biography, the Haggards retained much of their intelligence as well as their large noses, but they lost their business acumen. Known for their courage, they lacked endurance and thoroughness when it came to business enterprises. Long and lean, they had red or blond hair, sharp blue eyes, and a dangerous charm. They loved traveling and yet were just as passionately attached to their homeland. Whereas their ancestors were merchants and bankers, they now joined the army or the navy and went to India or wherever there were adventures to be had. People shook their heads when telling of their daring exploits, of their extravagances, and of their wild love affairs.[8]

The eldest son of William Henry Haggard and Frances Amyand, Rider's grandfather, was sent to a banking business in Leningrad where he met and married a Russian woman, Elisabeth Meybohm. Her family originally came from Bremen and had some Slavic and probably Jewish blood as well. Rider's father was born in Russia but grew up in Bradenham in Norfolk, England. Rider's mother, Ella Doveton, spent her youth in Bombay, India. Her family had lived on the island of St. Helena and in India for several generations.

The ancestral heritage of Rider Haggard is thus an extraordinary mixture of contrasts, the sedentary nature and the love of their land of the early Danish Haggards crossed with the irrepressible joy of adventure of the Amyands. The ancestors were shaped, not only by the cultures of Jutland, England, Germany, and Russia, but also by India where Rider's mother was born and grew up. The Indian culture, with its pantheon of gods and its ancient traditions, extended beyond the conscious and the unconscious of the mother to her son. To create a whole out of such contradictory ingredients was a difficult task that shipwrecked more than one of Rider's brothers.

Rider's father, William Meybohm Haggard, was a unique character. Good looking and well-liked, he was known widely on account of his powerful voice.[9] At times exceptionally pleasant, he was also capable of frightening temper outbursts. When he argued with one of his seven sons, he would leave the house, slamming at least five heavy doors. But then he would re-enter through another door and sit down peacefully at the table, especially if the involved son had also left the house, in another direction, slamming other doors. The mother, meanwhile, would sit in the midst of all this uproar, looking like an angel who had lost her way. When a daughter-in-law once asked her how she ever managed to get herself heard in all this turmoil, she answered, "Only by whispering." Rider was quite attached to his mother. Even twenty years after her death he still thought every night of her, and it seemed to him that their mutual relationship was continuing to grow in a wonderful, concrete way. He states that she was not beautiful but rather distinguished-looking, charming, and gentle. She had talents for drawing and music and was especially gifted in literature. She managed to remain current in literature and politics, in spite of bearing ten children and contending with many worries and sorrows. Rider quotes some of her beautiful, religiously tinged poems. It was she who taught him that love was immortal and that Christ was the kernel of faith. This religious seed planted in him by his mother grew into a tree that was to bear rich fruits. What especially distinguished his mother were her conversational skills. She knew how to draw from each person the topic he/she was most interested in and in which he/she could participate best. All her children loved and admired her, and all survived her.

With his Slavic heritage, the father played his role like an ancient god radiating and thundering. At moments he would suddenly remember his sons and interfere in their destinies. For example, he had Rider interrupt his studies and go to Africa, where he had the opportunity to experience a piece of history and become a man. While basically a male personality, the father had nevertheless some marked feminine traits, being given to many moods, emotions, and sudden ideas. The father was not a stabilizing influence nor a spiritual example. The mother compensated for this deficiency with her gentle pleasantness, her faithful acceptance of her duties, and her profound religiosity. Her reliability offered Rider the type of support which the father was unable to give.

The favorable and caring influence of this "dearest" mother established in Haggard the basics of a positive mother-complex.[10] This mother-complex expresses itself later on in his life, in his novels, and in his steady and deep attachment to her. Such a mother-complex drives a son towards finding in his life that which the mother had signified earlier for him in his childhood. It can turn him into a Don Juan-type, an adventurer who continues to seek without satisfaction, since he can never reach that bliss contained in the memories of his earliest youth. These memories are tempting and so utterly unreachable, since they are glowing inner images, fueled by the mother in the soul of the little boy. These images forever promise more than reality is able to deliver. A son who is so strongly determined by the mother remains attached to her. In such a case the tie to the mother may become pathological, especially if the son finds little support for his masculine side in the father or if the mother claims the son for herself because of her own unsatisfied wishes. The mother-complex may injure the masculinity in the man and cause an effeminate response. However, when there isn't such a pathological extreme, the mother can exercise a refining influence upon the being of the man. In this case the son becomes open to feelings, to the soul and its internal images. He develops an ability for empathy, a sense of beauty, and religious longings. What can negatively become the Don Juan-type can positively become an insatiable desire which never settles for the ordinary, everyday life but seeks to find and realize those paradises of which the mother reminds him and which he now pursues all over the world and into all spheres of the spirit.[11]

The initial result of young Rider's mother-complex was the partial suppression of the conscious, masculine side and the resulting intensification of his fantasy and dream world.

Haggard was the eighth of ten children and the sixth of seven sons. He was a quiet child. He seemed leaden to his mother. Since he knew he was viewed as the dummy of the family, Rider kept his thoughts carefully to himself. He was slow in school, where he thought of everything else except school work. Though he rarely forgot anything essential, he was incapable of memorizing most things. Desperate, his father was of the opinion that this son was only capable of becoming a greengrocer. At the same time, his father was spending a fortune on the education of the many bright sons in Oxford and Cambridge. Considering the hopeless lack of talent of little Rider, it didn't seem worthwhile to send him, too, to a good school. Thus Rider was the only son sent to an inexpensive grammar school. Mathematics was a nightmare for him, and he was utterly bored by geometry. On the other hand, he once wrote an excellent poem in Latin, and his teacher could not believe that he had composed it himself. In school Rider experienced the typical difficulties of an introverted, intuitive person, which have been described before in children of this type.[12]

The little Rider felt somewhat lost amongst his noisy brothers. He was neither one of the older ones nor was he the pampered youngest, since he was soon pushed aside from being the cared-for, central figure by the births of a younger brother and sister. This evidently had a weakening effect on him, further reinforcing his natural inclination to daydream. His receiving insufficient attention at home was probably a factor in his poor school performance. However, it was also the result of his mother-complex which drew him away from the exterior world and attracted him towards the dream world of the unconscious. This reinforcement of unconscious influences exposes the mother-bound son more strongly to external dangers. In fact, Rider, as a child, nearly drowned on several occasions and later in life placed himself numerous times in serious danger.

The seven brothers owned two horses, and each had his own rifle. Rider with his rifle not only killed a brooding thrush, a misdeed that plagued him for a long time, but also a pheasant and the tenant-farmer's best laying duck. Hunting, he rode his brother's horse until it became lame. Once he almost shot himself in the face, and on another occasion he nearly shot one of his brothers while they were hunting rabbits. Undoubtedly, he suffered at some preconscious level from jealousy towards his brothers. This fits in with a dream which he had when he was about nine—at a time when the thought suddenly confronted him that he, too, would have to die sooner or later. In the dream he was in hell, being eaten alive by rats. It seems that in this death-fantasy he experienced his own being assailed by his own hungry instincts.

One day Rider was taken unexpectedly out of the grammar school. Now he was to go to London in order to study foreign languages and to prepare himself for a job in the Foreign Office. Whereas his brothers at that age were well-cared for in college, he now found himself at eighteen in London, totally responsible for himself and exposed to all types of dangers. At first he lived in an unsavory boarding house and later within a spiritistic circle with an outlandish reputation.

This was the time when the Enlightenment had opened all the doors for materialism. Reason was about to change religion into pragmatic ethics. Natural science simply declared the soul to be nonexistent. Yet, as a reaction against this growing rationalism came a true epidemic of the Ouija board. Originating in the United States, it moved via England to continental Europe and led to the establishment of innumerable spiritistic circles which gained the attention not only of the bourgeoisie but also of many scientists. In 1873 a small circle of "Cambridge friends" came together. In 1882 this circle founded the Society for Psychical Research, with the intention of rediscovering the soul by means of experiments and by careful, factual observations.[13] The famous standard work *Phantasms of the Living* originated from this group.[14] Blavatsky's *Isis Unveiled* and Haggard's *She* were published in the same year. The young Haggard had joined this high tide of Spiritism in London in 1874, and he reportedly experienced many unbelievable things that are rarely reported now that the interest in Spiritism has waned. Haggard himself seemed to have considerable talents as a medium, and great hopes were placed on him in this regard.

The predisposition for these qualities can be found in his attitudinal and functional type. As a type, as we already mentioned, he was an introverted, intuitive person. In his youth he unquestionably was oriented more inwardly than towards the world. His main function, intuition, thus gave him access to the pictures within himself and led him to find interest more in the past and in the future than in the present. As a school boy he made few efforts to develop his ability to think; and even later, in his novels, he is less interested in logical abstractions and conclusions than in religious meanings and wisdom of life. From this we can conclude that he trusted, besides his intuition, also the value-shaping function of his feelings; whereas thinking and sensation remained more primitive or underdeveloped in him because they were his unconscious functions.

It becomes clear also from his daughter's account that sensation, the function of reality, was the least developed function in him. Thus, she reports that he almost always left behind his baggage during some phase of his many voyages. This would result in his having to appear at receptions in a borrowed evening suit which usually was too small. As further evidence of his poorly developed sensation function, his baggage tended to swell gradually because he was unable to repack properly the myriads of things he took along on his journeys. Indeed, he was so clumsy that he was incapable of making a suitable package.[15] What on the surface appeared as lack of skill, however, may simply have been the impatience of the intuitive person who dislikes spending time caring for his things and who therefore ends up having to cope with them all the more. As an introverted-intuitive type whose reality function was poorly developed from the beginning, Haggard was inclined to feel attracted by all kinds of modern and unusual fads of his time and to participate in them much more than another psychological type would have done. His presence in the spiritistic circle may well have contributed to the intensification of the phenomena produced there.

At a later date Haggard still accepted Spiritism as a field of research, while rejecting its widespread use, so that at his family table no one was to utter a word about it. In his novels, however, he could not avoid inserting, again and again, his experiences with Spiritism and mediums. In this way he is a child of his time, not unlike Edward Carpenter, Hall Caine, Oscar Wilde, R. L. Stevenson, and the poets of Celtic Renaissance—W. B. Yeats, Fiona Macleods— and others who allowed themselves to be impressed by the reality of the unconscious.[16]

A first love, with far-reaching impact, belongs also to this London period. On the occasion of a garden party in Richmond, Haggard met an exceptionally good-looking young lady whom he names Lilith. When, a few years later, Haggard wanted to return from Africa in order to become engaged to her, he was prevented from coming home because of a very irate letter from his father. He was never thereafter able to fully forgive his father for this interference with his freedom. The beloved lady married another man with whom she soon became unhappy. It took Haggard a long time to overcome this loss, and only much later did he recognize that a friendly fate had protected him from a union with this rather weak and not all too clever woman.

According to Jewish legend, Lilith is the first, demonic wife of Adam. This cover-name which Haggard used for his beloved points meaningfully beyond his lady friend towards the man's inner experience of his soul's demonic aspects.[17] He portrayed the story of this love in one of his first novels, *The Witch's Head*. Many years later he felt called upon to help his former beloved with counsel and assistance; however, while she was still young, she died from a serious illness, destitute and unhappy. Then, when he—accompanied by his wife—followed her casket to the cemetery, suddenly everything seemed strangely familiar. The door, the carpet, the scent of the flowers—it all was exactly like the time when he first met his beloved at that garden party in Richmond. He reached her grave quite dazed by this extraordinary experience; however, we have gotten ahead of the story and must return to the London period.

Haggard, in London as earlier in his life, was unable to take his examinations. For, when his father's friend, Sir Henry Bulwer, was nominated to become Governor of Natal, father Haggard saw in this a favorable opportunity for one of his many sons. He decided that Rider should accompany the governor to Africa as his private secretary. Haggard found himself, therefore, at nineteen in South Africa, where he was not only the governor's secretary but also official host. During the many official receptions, he was responsible for the household, the dinner preparations, and the comfort of the guests. On these occasions Haggard could find the company of respected, capable men whom he looked up to and who liked him. He became particularly close to Sir Theophilus Shepstone, secretary of native affairs. He traveled with him into the interior of the country and watched the war dances of the Zulus and the performances of the medicine men. Shepstone, who had grown up in Africa as the son of a missionary, was for many years the most popular white man among the blacks. Once when Haggard lost his way in the deserted countryside, he was able to make himself understood by a black man by simply mentioning the name of Shepstone. Right away the local natives helped him find his way back to the lost caravan. The Zulus not only venerated and loved Shepstone; they also attributed to him kingly powers.[18]

In 1876 Shepstone was nominated special commissioner of the Transvaal with the power to take the land by force if he deemed it necessary to protect the colonies of the whites—the English and the Boers—against the invasion of Cetewayo with his thousands of Zulus. Thus Shepstone inquired of Sir Henry Bulwer whether Haggard could accompany him to Pretoria along with his own staff of fifteen people. He liked Rider and saw that the young man understood the indigenous population. Shepstone knew he would be able to teach Haggard a great many things. One of the members of the staff was Umslopogaas, an old Zulu, son of Mzwazi, king of Swaziland, of whom Haggard later speaks frequently in his stories. During the trip Shepstone and his companions would sit around the campfires and tell of their adventures. These were the people who probably had the profoundest knowledge of the Zulus. Many of the unbelievable adventures in Haggard's hunting stories are either his own or those he heard about from these friends.

The commission was received with open arms in Pretoria. Even the Dutch mayor was desperate about the situation and offered no serious objection against the annexation. Only Shepstone had the power to stop the impending invasion of the Zulus by placing Transvaal under the protection of the English crown. The written message of Cetewayo, rendered verbatim by Haggard, is quite clear in this respect.[19] From Pretoria, Haggard was delegated as Secretary of two English negotiators to Secocoeni, a Basuto chief in a town of native people where whites had rarely been seen and where an uncanny, barbaric atmosphere prevailed. Returning from this mission, Haggard and the two negotiators arrived one evening, just as the moon appeared, at a crossroad. The two older companions wanted to continue on the upper road, but Haggard had the fixed idea that the moonlight was going to be more magnificent in the valley than on the crest. He did not let up until his superiors agreed to take the lower road. Rider's romantic urge saved them from an ambush by the Basutos that was planned on the upper path and which would have meant the certain demise of the three Englishmen.

On the day celebrating the annexation in Pretoria, Haggard was the one to raise the English flag. However, the Boers from the surrounding area were unable to maintain a broad view of the situation and soon assembled near the city. Thus the commissioners were continually in danger of their lives and continually challenged to demonstrate their courage in the face of the dissidents. Once, shortly before the annexation, Haggard had dared to ask Shepstone whether it might not have been better not to annex the land, since in that case the Boers and the Zulus would have ended up killing each other, so that the land would fall like a ripe apple into the hands of England. This one time Shepstone retorted angrily that such a policy would cause the death of thousands of white men, women, and children by the spears of the Zulus and assure wars between the whites and the blacks. Eventually, this war which Shepstone had so farsightedly tried to prevent was provoked through the negligent politics of Britain which did not recognize the full extent of the danger.

Shortly after the annexation, the Master and Registrar of the High Court died. Though lacking any formal legal education, Haggard was elected, first to fill in for him, then to become his successor, since there were few dependable persons in Africa to assume such a post. As the youngest head of a department, without experience or training, he had to find his own way and to cope with the opposition of the lawyers, of whom many were corrupt. In addition, he had the responsibility for the administration of all the assets of widows and orphans. He succeeded in remedying some bad conditions and in creating order—and even became popular. The range of his duties included his taking long and lonesome trips, together with the twenty-seven-year-old judge, Kotze, into the interior of the land, where he also had to be present as a witness at executions.

In the fall of 1868, when the new English High Commissioner, Sir Bartle Frere, declared war on the Zulus, Haggard joined the troops and—without any prior combat experience—became a staff lieutenant. However, he regarded this declaration of war a mistake, committed because of a lack of familiarity with the situation by this politician who had only recently arrived in South Africa from India. Military service, with all its dangers, delighted Haggard. When England sent additional, regular troops, Haggard's regiment of voluntary soldiers was discharged. Now he made a seemingly crazy decision: he resigned his government position and, together with a friend, acquired an ostrich farm in Newcastle in Natal. Yet, had he stayed in Pretoria, he would have had to endure, two years later, the bloody siege by the Boers and would have lost his position under much more difficult conditions.

First, he returned to England where he married a friend of his sister, Louisa Margitson. He calls this the wisest and best act of his life. He is full of admiration for his wife's abilities and courage during the dangerous times in Africa where they returned, planting corn on the farm, raising ostriches and—something new in Africa—growing hay. In addition they baked tiles and operated the first steam-engine-driven mill. As characteristic of the intuitive type, he undertook many things at one time, and the Boers were surprised to see him and his friend actively at work in every project.

Meanwhile, Transvaal was in open revolt, and even in Natal one felt steadily surrounded by danger. The English troops suffered some bloody defeats quite near Haggard's farm. Since the Royal Commission happened to be lodged in his house, the return of the Transvaal to the Boers was signed under his roof.

He now became witness to the exodus from Transvaal of the English and of the anglophile Dutch farmers. He also saw all the misery brought on for the blacks by the failure of the British government. It is here that his passionate belief in the responsibility of the British Empire became deeply rooted. Later on, often with all his heart and even to his own disadvantage, he would stand up for his responsibility.

The course taken by the Conservative Party in England was weak and dangerous for the African colonies. This influenced Haggard's decision to return to England with his family where, now a father of two small children and with hardly any means, he had to start over. Taking leave from Africa was painful, but most painful was having to separate from his horse and from his faithful servant Masooku who had saved his life on several occasions. In *The Witch's Head,* we find Masooku's words of good-bye, "Just a word, my father, and I shall no longer bother your ears, since my voice will forever be silent for you. When your time comes to die and you will go, as the white man says, to heaven, and where, then, you regain sight and you'll again be a man, then turn around and shout with a loud voice, 'Masooku, son of Ingolura of the tribe of the Maguilisini, where are you, oh my dog? Come and serve me!' And if I'm still alive I will hear your voice and rattle in the throat and die in order to come to you; yet if I'm already dead, I shall be by your side as soon as you call for me."[20]

Thirty-three years later, when Haggard visited the African Crown colonies in the capacity of a royal commissioner, the old Masooku appeared in front of his hotel in Pretoria in order to again serve him.

Africa was for Haggard "the great experience." There he encountered primal nature, unchanged, as it was on the day of creation. There he found the space to unfold his strengths and his aptitudes, and there he learned to cope effectively with reality. He experienced himself as a man amongst men and established life-long friendships. He had to face perils and to carry responsibilities. In Africa he shared in the high points of the empire. He was drawn into the battle and power, into the intoxication of the empire, but he did not remain a blind follower. He saw what errors were made and expressed critical opinions. Because of this he became unpopular with many. He felt the great responsibility that the rulers have for the subjected tribes and had major reservations about the long-range policies.

Once he had returned to England, Haggard had to catch up with his schooling and pass his examinations in Greek, Latin, and History in order to be admitted to law school. He did all the preparatory studies at home. Now he learned easily and quickly and worked tirelessly. Meanwhile, he also wrote his first book, *Cetewayo and his White Neighbours,* dealing with his experiences in Zululand, Transvaal, and Natal. The book brought him to the attention of Lord Carnarvon, who at that time was Secretary for the colonies, and of Lord Randolph Churchill. He was critical of colonial politics, and later developments proved his dark prophecies to be correct.

At twenty-seven he wrote his first novel, *Angela,* or *Dawn,* after seeing in church a peculiarly beautiful, sympathetic lady whom he and his wife decided to turn into the heroine of a novel. His wife soon abandoned the task, but for Haggard this decision began his literary lifework. While in Africa he had filled several diaries with notes and had written some articles for the newspapers. But now when he was again confined to the schoolbench, when he was restricted by finances and narrowed by the insular, middle-class life, his innermost self called insistently for expression. The good-looking, gently-sad lady in the church turned into the symbol of the soul to whom he now wanted to dedicate his attention.

His first attempts to write novels are reflections of his earlier life. Looking back upon this phase of his life, he reshapes it in order to resolve it, to understand it, and to grow beyond it. *Dawn,* which he himself describes as a somewhat humorous, old-fashioned, Victorian novel, deals with obvious youth conflicts painted in white and black. He reveals in it his resentments towards his father and brothers, as well as his own shadow-sides and his uncontrolled despair after the loss of his first beloved. From the psychological point of view, this book must be seen as an attempt to deal with the shadow.[21]

Yet in the next novel, *The Witch's Head,* we already find the Anima in the foreground.[22] Here his first beloved (whom Haggard named Lilith in his autobiography) is Eve, whereas in the first novel, *Dawn,* the women were given idealized Christian names, Maria and Angela. Eve has a dark, intelligent, artistically talented sister who jealously interferes with the plans of the lovers. Thus, we find that the Anima-projection has been split into a healthy, earthy, maternal figure and a jealous, scheming figure who is also capable of portraying artistic and spiritual values.

In this novel, Eve fishes from a cemetery—that is half submerged in the sea—an old suitcase which contains the mummified head of an Irish witch. Behind the two young women appears the archetypal image of the feminine. This witch-like projection is of a sunken and distorted goddess. In the novel, the head of the witch affects the course of events in a catastrophic manner. Its presence causes the dark, evil thoughts, hidden in the depth of the soul, to become realities. It is indeed one of the functions of the Anima to push the man, both in the good and in the bad, towards action.

The witch's head, a feminine, demonic nature-spirit, arises from the sea, that is, from the collective unconscious. It is a reaction against the rationalism of the patriarchally determined spirit of the times. That which in the Celtic Renaissance was tuned to gentleness and national rebirth reveals here a different face. This change has validity not only for Haggard but also for the entire Western culture. The overly conventional, Victorian concept of the woman calls for a reaction that initially expresses itself in the negative form of the witch who spreads destruction. When an archetype emerges from the unconscious, it often reveals itself first in its negative-destructive side and continues in this way as long as the prevailing consciousness confronts it with hostility. Extended conscious dialogues are frequently required before such an archetype seems to change and can be assimilated in its positive form through one's consciousness. Haggard began these intense discussions or dialogues in his novels. However, if an archetype confronts weak egos and then takes over the masses, as happened in Nazi Germany, it may be assimilated in its negative, and thus destructive, form. For any one nation it is of the utmost importance that as many separate individuals as possible manage to become conscious of the archetype that is latent in their unconscious and to battle against its negative aspect.

In Haggard's first novel *Dawn,* a somewhat weakly hero, Philip, loses his inheritance to a scheming cousin. Philip then tries to regain what was due to him by offering his own daughter to his antagonist (psychologically to his shadow), whereupon the daughter's dog (instinct) kills the deceiver. In the death of the cousin, who had been favored by the father, we can recognize the theme of fratricide. This motif is picked up again in *The Witch's Head,* where the hero kills in a duel his cousin who has arrogated the right of inheritance. Haggard had first to overcome his older and favored brothers before he could hope to break through with his own personality. After a long struggle and after a long period of atonement and suffering, the hero eventually obtains his inheritance and title. By shaping his internal problem in writing, Haggard succeeded in overcoming his resentment. Later in life he attained possessions and title through his own efforts.

In *The Witch's Head* Ernest Kershaw, the sun-hero, is no longer alone. The dog, which resolved the dilemma in the first novel, is now replaced by a human friend, a clumsy, good-hearted, reliable companion with enormous strength, who remotely resembles Enkidu, the beast-like companion of the sun-hero Gilgamesh. This friend gradually changes in the course of the novel from hunter to farmer. He represents in the form of the shadow (as greed, jealousy, as victim of moods) Haggard's inferior function, his clumsy, unwieldy sensation. Now the shadow no longer interferes with the aims of the sun-hero (namely with the primary function, the intuition), as was the case in the first novel. The inferior function has changed from dog to hunter. As such he is oriented towards nature; and later, as a farmer, he takes on the role of cultivating the earth. Thus the shadow-friend recapitulates a step in the evolution of mankind, the transition from the nomadic hunter to the tiller of the earth. This transformation occurred in Haggard's own life when he left his governmental service in Africa and became a farmer.

After the loss of his beloved, the hero—representing the primary function, intuition, and thus also the ego—throws himself into wild adventures. His friend, representing sensation, however, does not abandon him. At the end he is struck by lightning. We know from Martin Luther that this "being struck by lightning" is an experience of vocation. The hero becomes blind as a result. Ernest Kershaw is now a marked person, gazing into his interior, but eventually he marries the courageous, dependable friend of his beloved. She is not an Anima, nor is she beautiful; but she is a clear-thinking, prudent, well-adjusted, sisterly person. With these images Haggard relates and works through another segment of his own life. The hero who is blinded and is forced to look within himself represents the introverted intuition which now, after all kinds of adventures in the outside world, turns towards its genuine goal—the contemplation of internal images. Eve-Lilith, the lost beloved, now becomes the bridge to this subjective world, to an internal spiritual reality; she becomes the inner Anima over against which Dorothy stands, as wife, in the external world.

It is quite consistent, then, that in the following novel, *King Solomon's Mines,* Haggard's intuition would turn towards the richness of the unconscious. The later is portrayed by South Africa with its gold and diamond mines, the history of which allegedly goes back all the way to the time of King Solomon. Thus Africa, with its unspoiled nature and its dark past, becomes for Haggard the treasury of the collective unconscious. The three men who are out for adventure bring back only a few valuable gems. Yet their discovery is sufficiently precious for them to be able to live from it indefinitely.

Similarly, Haggard himself literally lived off the treasures that linked him to Africa and to his unconscious. They enabled him to write over fifty novels that earned him enough money to support a large family and to return to serve his country without pay. In all this he also followed external constraints since, after passing the bar examinations, he came to the realization that there was no future for him in the legal profession. At one time he had hoped to become a respected judge. Yet as he was listening during a trial to the argument of the defending lawyer, another attorney recognized him, asking, "Are you the Rider Haggard who wrote *King Solomon's Mines?* What in the world are you doing here? What are you doing in court?" An Englishman would never trust a writer of adventure to have any real, solid, scientific knowledge. Haggard himself shared his compatriot's derogatory opinion of his literary career; yet there was nothing else for him to do but to write and to yield to the necessity of giving form to his inner images. Now he silently hoped to become an immortal poet. He was misled in this pursuit by the power of the inner images he tried to shape. Indeed, he did eventually become famous, not as a poet, but, rather indirectly, as the interpreter of the archetypes, as the mediator for the urgent, yet still unconscious, problems of his time.

King Solomon's Mines was followed by *Allan Quatermain.* In its preface, we find Allan grieving over the death of his only son. The author dedicated this book to his own little son. Thus, in tragic anticipation, he wrote for him an early lament, because fate took from Haggard his only son six years later.

The same three men who in *King Solomon's Mines* had gone on the search for diamonds penetrate in *Allan Quatermain* into the interior of Africa, into the distant kingdom of two white queens.

The hero, Sir Henry, has Haggard's first name, is also of Danish ancestry, and is thus the genuine hero-ancestor. He gains the hand of one queen and battles against the sister. Yet as prince-consort and father of a little son, he finds himself trapped in Africa. He cannot return from the faraway, dark realm of the unconscious. There is an old legend in the family of the two queens: one of the ancestors was given the task of linking two open stairs with a building. The solution to this task was brought to him by a beautiful woman in a dream. We find here the dawning of a pre-sentiment. The true task is the bridging of the contrast represented by the two queens, and it is the Anima who holds the key to the solution.

The next book, *Jess,* begins at this point.[23] John, the hero, finds himself again between two women, but this time he is unable to choose between them. At first he becomes engaged to the attractive, extroverted Bessie. Yet Jess, the more mature and mentally gifted one, exerts an equal fascination for him. Thus he hopes to marry Bessie without losing Jess and that Jess eventually would live with them. "He was not himself aware how large a proportion of his daily thoughts were occupied by this dark-eyed girl or how completely her personality was overshadowing him. He only knew that she had the knack of making him feel thoroughly happy in her society. When he was talking to her, or even sitting silently by her, he became aware of a sensation of restfulness and reliance that he had never before experienced in the society of a woman. It was the shadow of that utter sympathy and perfect accord which is the surest sign of the presence of the highest forms of affection, and which, when it accompanies the passion of men and women . . . raises it almost above the level of the earth. For the love where that sympathy exists, whether it is between mother and son, husband and wife, or those who, whilst desiring it, have no hope of that relationship, is an undying love, and will endure till the night of Time has swallowed all things."

However, John is eventually overcome by his passion for Jess. He confesses his love to her, and she would like to yield to it, but she reminds him, "You forget that you will marry Bessie."[24]

The igniting flame really comes from Jess or, rather, from a spirit which blows like the wind and which drives her. And her eyes have "a near spiritual intensity." A spiritual wind, a "pneuma," affects the woman, and thus her now awakened Animus awakens the soul, the Anima, within the man. This spirit, says Haggard, was aroused in the conversations in which the highly educated man had turned towards the unschooled, but truly talented, woman.

At the time Jess is seized by her feelings, she is sitting in a lonely valley under a blossoming bush beside a cave. These same details reappear in *She*. The lightning strikes an ancient, natural stone tower near her, which collapses into a smoking pile. This is the primal, natural form of the pillar of fire, of the fire of life, which in *She* becomes the central, archetypal symbol. Jess feels that her own life would only remain a smoking pile, like the stone pillar destroyed by lightning, if she were to steal her sister's bridegroom.[25]

In Jess the Animus, the male spirit of the woman, is aroused, and this in turn arouses in the man the Anima, his feminine soul. The contact between these two supra-personal figures[26] is experienced as lightning, as an eruption of cosmic power, as the danger of a destructive fire.

Jess and John renounce their love, sacrificing it out of decency towards Bessie. They could not conceive how faithfulness to Bessie could ever be harmonized with faithfulness to the other, given the inner reality of their feelings.

However, the sacrifice of these powerful feelings does not solve the conflict; rather, the conflict becomes all the sharper. Jess and John know that their renunciation was basically a lie.[27] It is significant that, right after this book in which Haggard speaks of the forceful suppression of feelings, he felt compelled to write a novel about an immortal woman and about an immortal love. Jess says of her love that it is like the Stone of the Philosophers: it is almost as difficult to find; yet once found, it turns everything into gold. The sacrificed love, then, equals the lost Stone. Because of this, the following book, *She,* must deal with the search for the lost life and the lost love.

Haggard wrote *King Solomon's Mines, Allan Quatermain, Jess,* and *She* in a year and a quarter. At the same time he continued his law studies and cared for his family and for his wife's farm. When he had finished *She,* his eyes and his nerves failed him. Thus, the approaching precipice seen in *Jess* was reached in *She* as well as in Haggard's own life. By expressing in *She* his personal inner turmoil as a portrayal of impersonal, universally valid problems, Haggard powerfully illuminated the backstage of modern history. During this period, his intuition reached an apex with a view of the future.

He not only matured but also became a contemporary, concerned with the present and willing to build towards the future. However, the full interpretation of his fantasy, over which he puzzled all his life, was left to the following century. For in this next century where psychology is so central, it was C. G. Jung who explained the Anima as soul-image and the Self as supra-personal human wholeness.

As a literary success, *She* was the high point in Haggard's life. It remains to show what came of him in his later years. After the publication of *She*, Haggard made a trip to Egypt. Ever since his early childhood, he had felt drawn to that country and read whatever he could find about it. In fact he had long intended to write a novel titled *Cleopatra*.

At one time a friend who believed in reincarnation brought him a list of his prior incarnations. Twice he was alleged to have lived in Egypt, once around the year 4000 B.C., and later as one of the minor pharaohs. His third incarnation was presumably as a Norman of the seventh century. Though he made some fun about this, and in spite of his Christian convictions, he did believe in reincarnation. Haggard admitted to having had a predilection for the Normans of epic times but explained this on the basis of his Danish ancestry. Yet not knowing of any Egyptian ancestors, he wondered why he felt even more at home with the ancient Egyptians than in his contemporary England. Haggard had said, "I can transport myself into the thoughts and feelings of the ancient Egyptians and understand their theology; and I venerate Isis and always feel tempted to bow before the moon." He also felt deep respect in the face of the Nordic gods Thor and Wotan. Yet he added that he similarly felt deep sympathy for the African natives, having always gotten along quite well with them, especially the Zulus, and that, therefore, his mystically inclined friend had probably forgotten to put a Zulu incarnation on the list.

Brugsch Bay showed him the Boulak Museum in Egypt. He also attended some excavations, near the pyramids of Gizah, of the pre-mummification period. In Thebes he visited the temple and royal burial chambers. Here, during a visit to a grave he once again nearly lost his life. Some large caves had been discovered near Aswan, and so he crawled through a small opening—the sand extended almost to the top of the door—into one of these burial chambers. Here he found hundreds of skeletons alongside the painted sarcophagus of a noble lady. Haggard then remembered that Aswan had experienced a plague-like epidemic near the time of Christ's birth and that someone might have opened this burial chamber in order to get rid of the innumerable dead as quickly as possible. Having heard that the germs of such plagues could remain virulent for a long time, Haggard called to his companions outside the chamber that he was exiting immediately. He began to crawl out, but the echo of his voice had started the sand into motion. From every crack the sand began to trickle down on him. Haggard realized that he would be completely buried within seconds. Only by using all his strength in the last moment was he able to escape. He describes this experience in *Ivory Child* but gives it a bad ending.

Another episode which made Haggard shudder even when he retold it is the one he described in *Queen of the Dawn*. Here one of his companions had recklessly climbed a pyramid up to the polished point. He then grew dizzy during the descent and had to cling precariously to the steep wall until the "sheik of the pyramids" suddenly rushed in and rescued him without ever saying a word. During a second trip to Egypt, Haggard, along with its discoverer, was one of the first to enter the burial chamber of Nofertari, wife of Ramses II.

While returning from this trip, Haggard learned that *She* had made him famous. Almost everyone on the boat was reading either *She* or *King Solomon's Mines*. It was at this time that he began to write *Cleopatra,* dedicating the book to his mother who had always shown a deep interest for the marvels of Egypt. It was also at this time that Haggard and his friend, Andrew Lang, a journalist and writer of fairy tales, bought twin rings that had probably belonged either to the queen Teje or Nefertiti.

In 1888 he visited Iceland and carried with him the Icelandic Sagas. He traveled extensively through those famous and forlorn regions, which in those days were rarely visited by foreigners. From there he returned on an old schooner that was used for transporting ponies. Because of overloading and terrible weather, many of the ponies died. At one point the ship landed at a remote island but had to continue the trip in spite of the heavy fog as there was no food available for the horses. Shortly after this the ship ran upon some rocks, and it was discovered that the lifeboats were too defective to be of any use. Haggard finally spotted a fishing vessel from the island which was not approaching because of the rocks and the heavy surf. He asked the captain whether or not to hail the vessel and received the reply, "Yes, Mr. Haggard, do everything you can to save yourself." Only then did Haggard realize how imminent the danger was and managed with his powerful voice to gain the attention of the people in the fishing boat. They approached and saved the passengers of the sinking ship, taking them to the island. Meanwhile, the inhabitants of the island had congregated; amongst them was the schoolteacher, who came towards Haggard, tipped his hat, bowed politely, and, with the best Scottish accent, said to him, "Are you not the author of *She?* I'm pleased to meet you!"[28]

In 1889 Haggard wrote *Nada the Lily,* the story of a dying people. In it he told of the Zulus, their battles, and their medicine men. The preface is a memorial to his old friend and mentor, Sir Theophilus Shepstone. It was one of the scenes from *Nada the Lily* that led Kipling to write his Wolves tales.

In 1891 he visited Mexico, accompanied by his wife. He intended to write about Montezuma and to dig with a friend for the hidden treasure of Guatemoc, a venture which only an intuitive type would have undertaken. As he took leave from his son, he had the distinct feeling that he would never see him again. Convinced that he would not return from this trip, he put all his papers in order. While he was traveling, the presentiments recurred more and more strongly, until he received the news of the death of his only son. He never fully overcame this loss. Even twenty years later he thought every day—often every hour—of this son. On his last journey to Egypt, shortly before his own death, he was asked by an Egyptian soothsayer, "What is this thing about the son of whom you constantly think?"

The treasure hunt through the interior of Mexico was full of adventures and perils. This, in addition to the grief over his son, affected his physical and mental health. Only when a third daughter was born to him did he improve.

When at home, he often tired of his life as a gentleman-farmer and author. He longed for greater and more useful activity and would have preferred to write about more "useful" themes. Yet to do this would not have enabled him to support his family. Finally, this inner dissatisfaction was dispelled by a repetitive, visionary dream. Here Haggard found himself in the hereafter, where he saw distant mountains, a sacred lake, and a river which—like the Nile—flooded the earth periodically so that it bore hundred-fold fruits. The river eventually reached a plain and a white city with palaces and domes. Yet his guide would not lead him there. From the east, a shadowless light fanned out over the sky all the way to some golden guardians high upon the distant rocks. At night this sky was covered with stars shining in all colors. In the foreground stood a house in the midst of a blossoming garden where everyone he loved and had ever loved walked in and out. Then he saw himself youthful and in white clothes sitting before a desk. This picture filled him with horror, as he sensed that this was the Purgatory in which he was condemned to write fantasy tales forever and ever. "What am I doing here?" he asked this guide, who stood beside him with a serene glow. "You are writing the history of a world, or possibly the history of the world." At this Rider sighed in relief and awakened.

Haggard's books contain more history than one would expect at first, in more than one sense. He experienced important segments of the history of the British Empire and wrote about them with exceptional clarity, always endeavoring to have personal interviews with the eyewitnesses from Zululand. And the very boys who were to shape history later on enthusiastically read his adventure novels.[29] Finally, he also dipped widely into the unconscious and thereby brought innumerable readers in touch with this germinal layer of future history. He was convinced that fantasy had its own kind of insight. Haggard would frequently describe places, people, and their destiny, believing it was pure invention, only to learn later on that some of these things had actually occurred, even down to small details, either before or sometimes considerably after he had written them down.

In *Maiwa's Revenge,* for example, Haggard gave a detailed account of Allan Quatermain's flight before the pursuing savages who reached him just as he tried to climb a steep rock and held him fast by a leg. Allan shot along his leg towards them and managed to free himself. A few years later an Englishman came to Haggard's home. He had come to Norfolk from London to find out how Haggard had ever heard of all the details of his flight from the savages, since he had never spoken to a soul about it. Haggard was able to convince himself that the experience of this Englishman and the adventure in the novel corresponded point for point.

In *The Way of the Spirit,* a tale of modern Egypt, Haggard invented five native musicians, whom he calls "The Wandering Minstrels." Three played the flute, two had drums. Rupert Ullershaw, the hero, met them three times in the Sudan desert yet was never able to talk to them. They would appear and disappear. Their melancholy music was always a preannouncement, for Rupert, of a mishap. All this was pure invention. Haggard had never heard or read that there were such spooky apparitions in the desert. He wrote *The Way of the Spirit* in 1905. In 1909 he received from Sir Gaston Maspero the latter's *Notes de Voyage* and discovered this passage: "Are these four possibly related to the four demons, of whom two play the flute and two the tambourine or Darabouka, and who in those areas spook the desert? They play for the travelers who come along, and it is invariably a bad omen to meet them." Maspero had been able to extract this legend only with great difficulties from the natives. In his autobiography Haggard notes that Maspero mentions four such demons, while he himself had created five. [30]

The idea for his next book, *Joan Haste,* came to Haggard while visiting an old church in Suffolk. One day an acquaintance visited him after reading the book, to let him know that a certain family B. was not likely to be pleased with it. Evidently, a certain episode in their family history of which they rarely spoke paralleled a story from *Joan Haste.* This acquaintance felt uncomfortable, since this family might assume he had divulged this story which had been told to him in confidence. It turned out that the graves of this family B. were exactly in the cemetery in which Haggard had been struck with the idea for this book and that the relatives owned most of the surrounding land. [31]

These are but a few of a large number of instances which show Haggard's intuitive talent. Similar episodes have been told in regard to other writers of adventure stories.

In the years preceding 1900, Haggard was at times active, politically and in business, in London. He was nominated as a member of Parliament, yet after he failed by only a few votes during the first election, there was not enough money left for a second try. It was probably his remarkably progressive views that interfered with his being successful as a politician. He was in favor of general conscription, of old age pensions, and of active support for agriculture over industry. He was also in favor of land reform and of relocating some of the industrial proletariat from the metropolitan areas to the country. Unsuccessful in the elections, he now tried his hand, together with an unreliable partner, in some financial dealings, from which he fortunately was able to extricate himself. He was president of the community council and of the writers' association.

He spent several years in intensive studies of rural England. After informative trips lasting many months, he composed his detailed accounts of the agricultural conditions in twenty-seven English counties, uncovering many deplorable conditions. Later he wrote a similar report about Denmark, where he found solutions that he considered appropriate also for England—for example, an agricultural reform giving land to small farmers who would then assist each other. His work did not achieve the hoped-for practical success. However, it caught the attention of the Secretary for Colonial Problems, who sent Haggard to the United States to study the settlements of the Salvation Army. The Salvation Army had made the first attempt to relocate in the country uprooted families from the large cities. This trip helped Haggard gain the friendship of President Theodore Roosevelt and of General Booth of the Salvation Army. Later he was a member of the royal commission for coast erosion and reforestation. Again the recommendations of his commission had little success because of the prevailing party structure. Yet Haggard's efforts and generous dedication to the welfare of the country were eventually recognized. In the midst of a wintry night, much to his surprise came the news that he was elevated to the rank of "Sir." Even more happy news for him was that he was elected to serve in the Royal Commission for the Dominions. With five other Englishmen, he visited the overseas possessions of the crown and gathered information concerning commercial and other matters that were relevant to England and the Crown.

At this point Haggard's autobiography ends. In 1951 his youngest daughter, Lilias, published a biography which continues the story and conveys a direct and vivid picture of Rider's personality.

Lilias was the daughter born shortly after the death of little Jock. Ever since that tragedy, Haggard was overly concerned about and overprotective of his children. On his trips he suffered from homesickness and fear for his family. Lilias inherited the literary talent from her father. It seems that she was in some respects closer to him than even his own wife. In fact, his wife, as a result of her strong prudence, often worked as a counterbalancing force to Haggard. It was Lilias to whom Haggard confided his new ideas. In later years she assumed to a large extent the role of his Anima.

In 1912–13 Haggard traveled to India, where he joined the Royal Commissioners with whom he was to visit Australia and New Zealand. In 1914, accompanied by his wife and Lilias, he went with the commission to South Africa. In Pretoria he was received warmly not only by the British but also by the Boers. He met old friends and felt rejuvenated. He criss-crossed the country and even reached Rhodesia, where he visited the fabulous ruins of the abandoned city, Zimbabwe. It was here, to his utter surprise, that the curator blamed him for having spread numerous erroneous observations about this city when, in fact, he had known absolutely nothing about these ruins at the time he wrote *She* and *King Solomon's Mines.*

He was presented to the Zulu chiefs as "Sompseu's Child" (as the child of Shepstone) and was greeted enthusiastically by them. Thus the power of Shepstone's name had continued for a second and third generation. Haggard listened to their complaints and wrote a report to the government, with an urgent appeal that England help its colored subjects, that it educate them and meet their hunger for knowledge. He stressed that only in this way could they become important members of the Commonwealth, rather than eventually take revenge for all the mistreatments which they had endured for many generations.

In July and August of 1914, the commission visited Canada. Because of the beginning of the first World War, the commissioners were not to make any speeches. Yet the people present demanded to hear Haggard. Finally, asked by the president of the commission, Haggard rose and spontaneously presented a memorable speech, stressing to the audience the gravity of the situation and the responsibility of each and every citizen.

Upon his return to England, he raised his warning voice in order to prepare for possible food shortages, but as so often before, no one listened. He offered himself for public service but was initially bypassed. Yet in 1916 he was asked to win permission in the Dominions for relocating discharged soldiers and their families. In spite of failing health and of having to bear the entire cost of the trip, he went off and traveled across the mine-infested oceans. Wherever he went, he first met rejection if not enmity; yet, thanks to his personality, his name, and his connections, he managed to sway the various governments. At that time, Canada named one of its mountains "Mount Sir Rider" and one of its glaciers "Haggard Glacier," to which he responded by quoting the proverb about the prophet in his own country.

He lost his money during the war and was compelled to sell his farm and to write additional novels in order to be able to finance his wife's country estate. As the war years ended, it seemed that Haggard also had found a peaceful harbor. The depressions from which he had suffered periodically on account of himself and on account of the Empire finally left him. He regained his humor, his joy of life, and his sociability.

Many of his friends had died, but he had made a new friend in Ronald Ross, the discoverer of the cause of malaria. Once more he visited Egypt where he felt even more at home than in his own country and whose history he knew better than that of his own people. When he died in 1925, at the age of sixty-nine, his son-in-law, an otherwise rather sober person, is said to have exclaimed: "By God, an old pharaoh!"

The last book to appear during Haggard's lifetime is *Queen of the Dawn,* whose title refers to that of his first novel *Dawn*. It is one of his few novels in which the contrasts seem temporarily reconciled. At the birth of the Egyptian princess, Nefra, two goddesses, Isis and Hathor, appear as benevolent fairies. In the hidden secrecy of the pyramids, Nefra is raised by the old wise man to become a priestess of Isis and simultaneously the successor to the throne. These are her inner and outer tasks. The sheik of the pyramids teaches her to climb them. One day she is observed by Prince Khian who, in the name of his father Apepi, is to ask for her hand in marriage. He sees her appear, ghost-like on the tip of the pyramid, accompanied by the sheik and his two sons. After long, drawn-out battles, Nefra, the heir to Upper Egypt, is married, not to the old pharaoh Apepi, but to her lover, Prince Khian. This unites the two kingdoms, Upper and Lower Egypt. Nefra herself, queen of Dawn, is a symbol for the union of wisdom and beauty, spirit and nature. She brings about a brief period of peace, followed, after her death, by the splintering of the kingdom.

In *Allan and the Ice Gods* the man tells the Anima: "In every group someone walks faster than the others." She replies, "In that case he will find himself alone." "No," says the man, "he must turn around in order to guide the others." Yet the woman answers, "But then night will overtake them before they reach the peak." And he, "When someone reaches the peak alone, what can he do for himself?" And now the Anima answers, "He can see the plains before him, and die! It suffices to have been the first one to see the New; and one day his bones will be found by those who follow his footsteps."[32]

We find here Haggard's profound ethical respect for those who are weaker; but we also see how he has hurried ahead with his intuition, without being able to set foot in the new plains he envisioned.

His last speech dealt with imagination. In it he mentioned that the human spirit seemed to him like those Arctic icebergs which hide four-fifths below the water, that it was those hidden forces of the spirit that linked the visible with the invisible, and that they were capable of hearing the softer voice from the infinite. Imagination, he said, was the source and origin of all great scientific discoveries, and the English were inclined, to their own detriment, to understate imagination. Imagination meant vision, and where vision is absent, the people perish.[33] Haggard finishes his autobiography with the words: "One boon, from infancy to age, has been showered upon me in a strange abundance, pressed down and running over—the uncountable, peculiar treasure of every degree and form of human love, which love alone, present or departed, has made my life worth living. But if it is all to cease and be forgotten at the borders of the grave, then life is not worth living. Such, however, is no faith of mine."

Haggard was an original, significant individual, who caught the attention of the people in the rural areas, as well as in London. During his travels for the Crown, he was exceptionally well-liked for his oratory skill, his humor, and his boylike exuberance, not only by his fellow commissioners, but also by the people in the countries he visited. He conversed with equal poise and expertise about literature, agriculture, history, and politics. He had the skill of gathering quickly an enormous amount of information. For many years he worked for the Empire, whose responsibility he sensed deeply. He risked his entire strength, his health, and his life for public tasks, without pay and often without due recognition.

Of the seven brothers he was the only one to develop enough stability during his life to be able to repeatedly come to the aid of others. In spite of the touchiness and jealousy of his brothers, there were always several of their children eating at his table. Besides many others, he also assisted his first love, Lilith, and her children when they were in need.

One of the old peasants of Norfolk once said to Lilias, "When your father does the reading in the church on Sunday, and when the text speaks of the angels with golden trumpets walking in the glory of God, and when I see him look up from the text, then I sit there and think, he sees them, the angels."

The dreamy boy became a sensitive, ambitious, enterprising youth. The intuitive young man managed step-by-step to develop his sensibility and thus to find a multi-dimensional relatedness to reality. He learned to control his wild temper that had overcome him occasionally in South Africa. Freely he assumed difficult tasks. With ever new efforts he developed his fantasy, so that it grew to be a fine instrument for accurate inner perception. His thinking became a tool for self-reflection, for reflecting about the world and about circumstances that point beyond this life. His existence was lively, filled with productive labor, and rich in insight and love. Viewed from the conscious vantage point, his life was dedicated to the gentleman's ideal. Viewed from the unconscious vantage point, it was dedicated to the Anima. True, this dialogue with his "mistress soul" was conditioned by his time. Nevertheless, like Carl Spitteler in *Prometheus and Epimetheus,* he was able to penetrate down to the timeless archetype and to give it a living form. The tragic aspect of his life consisted of his not being able to find a future-oriented solution to the conflict. What is missing is a dialogue with the Anima that both is conscious and that leads to the type of concrete realization in life which eventually causes a change and integration of the whole personality. The psychological knowledge that would enable such a progress was lacking in his time. As a precursor of this knowledge, he remained overly attached to the Anima and to the unconscious and thus could not fulfill himself completely as a conscious personality. It may have been this incomplete development of the self that was the basis for his prolonged and frequent grieving, until his own death, for his little son.

II. Psychological Interpretation of Haggard's She

Psychological Hypotheses of the Novel

Rider Haggard started to write *She* in 1886 and finished the book in six weeks. The manuscript went to print almost without corrections. He himself states, "I remember that my ideas concerning the development of the action were quite vague. My only clear image was that of an immortal woman inspired by an immortal love. Everything else shaped itself around this figure. And it came, it came more rapidly than my poor hand was able to write it down. As a matter of fact, it was written in the white glow of passion, without hardly any interruption."[34] At one time, waiting in his publisher's office, he asked for paper and wrote the scene in which She immolated herself in the fire of life.

Where does this intense eruption originate, this super-pressure of the unconscious that powerfully forces its way? This question is answered by a poem of his friend, Andrew Lang, which Haggard placed at the end of one of his later editions.

A love was buried because she contradicted, as the poem says, "some divine decree." The unconscious responds to this with the vision of an "immortal woman" and of an "immortal love." Ayesha,[35] or simply She, is this immortal woman; yet "She-who-is-to-be-obeyed"[36] was initially the name of a rag-doll used by a nanny to scare Rider and his siblings and to make them behave. She, the goddess, was first a demon in a closet, a child's phobia, an autonomous complex forcing the ego to obey. This portrays *She* as a continuation of the motif of *The Witch's Head*.

Not only *She* but also the previously completed book *Jess* speaks of a buried love. *Jess* is the more realistic novel, partly but not consistently autobiographical. As was mentioned, John wanted to marry Bessie but also fell in love with Jess, the spiritually more gifted sister of his bride.[37] Jess compares her love to the philosophers' stone and therefore attributes to it the highest, indestructible value. Yet both Jess and John feel obliged to sacrifice their overwhelming feelings for Bessie's sake. Only two months after completing this book Haggard was possessed by the fantastic vision of the immortal woman and her immortal love. Thus *She* deals with the search for the lost treasure, for the feeling that is living in the caves of Kor, in the city of the heart. There in darkest Africa she lives among the dead and calls out for redemption.

In his autobiography, Haggard avoids revealing the real background of this story. However, the white glow of passion with which *She* was written allows us to surmise that something analogous was happening in his own life at that time. Possibly, out of consideration for his wife, he sacrificed his love for another woman who meant a great deal to him spiritually. In any case, we find both in *Jess* and in Andrew Lang's poem how intensely Haggard dealt with such a conflict at the time he wrote *She*. His unexpressed suffering evoked the mythologic vision of *She*. The archetype he evokes draws his attention to the transpersonal significance of this conflict, revealing his own destiny and his sacrifice under the guise of a universal-human experience. In the background of the personal experience appears the image of the "Eternal Feminine"; it emerges from the unconscious of the man in the form of his inner, seductive, wonderful, and perilous soul-image.

The Story

Holly, an Englishman, is about to enter as a Fellow in a college; yet his terminally ill friend, Vincey, convinces him to change his mind. Vincey asks Holly to take care of his five-year-old son, Leo, and to hand over to Leo, upon his twenty-fifth birthday, an old trunk. Inside it is a message from Amenartas, an ancestor of Vincey's, addressed to her son or some later descendant, asking him to journey to Africa and to find the white queen secretly guarding the fire of life. The message also asks him to extract from the white queen the secret of immortality and to wreak vengeance upon her for having killed Amenartas's husband in a fit of jealousy. When Leo turns twenty-five, he and Holly begin the journey. They first reach a tribe of primitive natives, one of whom, Ustane, desires Leo to marry her. But Leo and Holly are nearly murdered by the malevolent natives who kill foreigners by covering their heads with red-hot metal pots. She, the white queen, sees to it that they are saved and brought to her. It emerges that Ustane is the reincarnation of Amenartas, the Egyptian princess, and that Leo is Kallikrates, Amenartas's husband, who died so young. Amenartas-Ustane has waited two thousand years for his return. When Ustane refuses to let go of Leo, She kills Ustane without any hesitation. Then She insists that Leo place himself within the Fire of Life, in order for him to also acquire, by means of the flames, eternal life, beauty, and power. Only in this way can she receive him as husband without endangering him with her superhuman essence. Leo hesitates in face of the awesome power of the blazing pillar of fire. To encourage Leo, She places herself for a second time into the flames and turns into a pitiful and grotesquely aged figure. Only after many difficulties can the horrified Englishmen find their way back home.

Holly

The novel begins in Cambridge where Ludwig Horace Holly, the narrator, is about to take his examination in Mathematics, in order to be accepted as a Fellow in the college. Thoughtfully, he stands before a mirror. Saddened by his apelike appearance, he suffers because all women turn away from him. He cannot rely on his external appearance, but he can trust his strength and intelligence.

The English College is the starting point of the narration: Haggard had also attempted to withdraw, because of his conflict and suffering, into the solitude of resumed studies. Yet the college displays an impersonal aspect. Cambridge not only stands for knowledge and education but also for the Victorian perspectives, which, having become overly narrow, are in dire need of broadening. We find a situation like that in the story of the Holy Grail that starts in a wasteland or, as in the beginning of many fairy tales, that portrays a state of deficiency. The scientific and spiritual orientation of the Victorian period, while endowed with the power to rule the world, excludes or turns away from the feminine principle, Eros, the soul.

Holly, by necessity, is a misanthrope and woman-hater. In the story, the natives call him "Baboon" on account of his long arms and hairy ugliness. Though he speaks in the first person, we must not mistake Holly for the ego of Haggard. The latter was married, and the Zulus called him "Indanda," which translates as "He who walks on the heights" or "tall and agreeable." Furthermore, Holly is a positive shadow-figure, an aspect of Haggard which he had failed to develop in his youth, namely, the functions of sensation and thinking. Holly is that friend and companion who appears in Haggard's earlier novels, the comrade of the sun-hero: first the dog, later the strong but naive friend, and subsequently the farmer.

Upon his return from Africa, Haggard turned, by means of his reality and thinking functions, towards those studies for which he had mustered very little interest as a boy. Inasmuch as he lets Holly speak in the first person, Haggard renounces his own identification with his overly dominant primary function, intuition.[38] He reflects upon the other side of his being, and with Holly he creates for himself a new ideal, just as he had with Allan Quatermain in an earlier novel. Holly, as a compensatory inner figure, is largely in opposition to Haggard's basic inclinations. He embodies reasonableness, the matter-of-fact Englishman, the attitude which Haggard requires in order to be able to adjust himself again to England. Whereas the young Haggard loves women, Holly, his other side, runs from them. Indeed, he fears them more than a rabid dog. The more Holly tries to rely on reason, the more dangerous this other side appears to him. The split-off feelings turn into an uncontrollable emotional force which could attack and infect him just like a rabid dog would. He wishes to flee this danger by going to college, the equivalent of a modern male convent. Frequently, the most "normal" and "reasonable" men are the ones most afraid of their unconscious side.

Holly is the personification of the Victorian gentleman, the ideal image of the Englishman: conservative, reasonable, Christian, and a passionate hunter and sportsman. Haggard hoped to educate the British youth towards this gentleman-ideal and tried himself to live it. He tried to protect himself against his shadow, against the unstructuring power of the unconscious and the danger of "going black." However, the identification with this conscious ideal established all too narrow limits for his inner development.

Holly is called "Charon"[39] by his comrades at Cambridge. He is an extraordinary human being, since he has an archetypal quality. Haggard himself relates Holly to Thoth, the Scribe-God, who in his role of the God of Justice confronts the dead with their heart and with their sins.[40] Thus, Thoth represents a perceptive self-reflection, a godly conscience, the inner judge. Charon, Thoth,[41] and his Greek heir, Hermes, are all guides of the soul. Charon ferries the souls across the river Styx to the "other," sorrowful, somber shore. Thoth guides the dead through the ritual of the dead and towards rebirth in the starry sky. In the guise of Hermes-Mercury, he leads the souls into the underworld from which he returns a few, exceptional heroes back to the light of day.

In his role as companion and guide, Holly portrays the reflective consciousness of the hero. He promotes consciousness, and in this capacity he sees to it that the hero is not swallowed by the underworld, namely the unconscious, but finds the way back into the light. In other words, the reflective consciousness helps to prevent the ego from dissolving in the unconscious. Holly has a role analogous to that of Virgil in the *Divine Comedy*. Like Virgil, he has the name of a poet, Horace. Horace sings in his odes of love, but he is also the voice for a reasonable, simple, ethical life. Holly likewise is both a lyric poet and a warning voice. His first name, Horace or Horatio, furthermore calls to mind the friend of Hamlet; and we find a quote from *Hamlet* in *She:* "There are more things in heaven and earth, Horatio, than are dreamt of in your philosophy." This quote also applies to the conceptual limitations of the person Holly, whose philosophy proves insufficient to understand the miracles and terrors he is about to endure.

In addition, Holly is the Celtic name of a thorny tree or bush. Holly himself explains to She that he is a knotty, prickly tree. She answers that behind the knotty exterior was hidden a good, reliable kernel. As an evergreen plant that weathers the winter, the holly tree is a promise of spring's return. In England it takes the place of the Christmas tree. As a plant-symbol related to the Christmas tree, it represents the inward, natural spiritual growth striving out of the earth towards the light. Holly represents the probability of spiritual growth in the presence of inner turmoil. The holly tree has been viewed as the refuge for spirits, because it is green during winter. The English have always lived in their old houses and castles in company of all kinds of spooks or ghostly phenomena. And even after the age of enlightenment had declared them nonexistent, these phenomena were easily pulled out of a drawer after a brief period of hibernation. In England the term "holly" designates also the habitual storyteller, the braggart. As does the holly tree or bush, he has a relationship to a spiritual world which one would like to negate, about which one tells "false stories," but which nevertheless is connected to the life experience of the Englishman.

Holly represents restraint and control to the intuitive Haggard. Holly stands for reflection and simultaneously for relationship with reality, thus for thinking and sensation, Haggard's primitive and least developed functions. Whereas the intuitive person continually focuses upon the future and upon meaningfulness, his inferior function, sensation, is characterized by sober reasonableness and conservatism. Yet wherever enough attention is given the inferior function that it is allowed to unfold in its own way, it can develop into the "transcendental function."[42] The inferior function can then become the bridge linking consciousness with the collective unconscious, with the ancestors, with the secrets of the soul. It is for this reason that Holly is like Charon who ferries towards the land of the dead or like Thoth who records the messages of the gods and their unimpeachable judgments. It is for this reason that the holly tree is a refuge for the spirits. The story begins with him, since in the guise of Haggard's "inferior function" Holly perceives and transmits the messages of the unconscious.

In spiritistic circles, Haggard received a strong push to develop this archaic, transcending aspect of his inferior function. Later, as already mentioned, he shunned the occult, even though many respected and educated persons dealt with this subject at that time. Spiritism became taboo for him, since in his youth in London it had nearly proved calamitous. The significant and creative aspect of Haggard's inferior function subsequently emerged in his callously suppressed love affair. Still later, it re-emerged in his literary friendships and, most of all, in his writings.

Vincey

Shortly before midnight, while Holly is engulfed by melancholic reflections, someone knocks at his door. Should he open? But he then recognizes the cough of his gravely ill friend, Vincey. Vincey beseeches Holly to assume care after his death of his son Leo and to give Leo, upon his twenty-fifth birthday, the trunk which he has brought with him. "Ah, Holly," he states, "life is not worthwhile without love, at least not for me; but maybe it is for Leo if he has courage and faith." With these words he takes leave, and the next morning Holly gets word that Vincey has killed himself.

It is midnight, just before Holly's examinations, an important moment of transition. Is this to become the final withdrawal into the intellectual world of men? Holly opens the door reluctantly. He would rather refuse admittance to this other side of his which announces itself. His friend Vincey is outside. In many ways, Vincey represents Haggard's ego. He is the impulsive youth which hoped to conquer the world with intuition and feeling. Yet this one-sided youthful orientation perishes, since a life without love no longer seems worthwhile. Also, it is impossible to venture towards one's soul and one's self by relying solely on one's primary function. Challenged at an earlier time by the trunk's contents—of which more will be said—Vincey had undertaken a journey to Africa but was shipwrecked. He subsequently married a Greek woman who was as beautiful as the mystical ancestor described in the document preserved inside the trunk. Yet Vincey's young wife dies shortly after Leo's birth, and Vincey now feels that he cannot continue living without her.

Vincey is a representative of the pioneer spirit, an explorer of Africa. His ancient trunk holds the hidden secret, the driving force behind all colonization and conquest: it is the quest for the "hard-to-find treasure."[43] Seen from the psychological perspective, all such adventures imply the winning of the soul and the discovery of the fire of life—life's crucial adventure by means of which one finds one's way through the world to oneself. This quest leads to knowledge of the world around us as well as to the mysterious city of Kor, the innermost core of one's own heart. Haggard, having returned from his journey in Africa to the narrowness of his homeland, is now driven by his own suffering to find the transition from the external to the inner adventure.

To Vincey, his Greek bride and wife was the ideal of the feminine. In his bride, a man encounters the picture of his own feminine soul, the sought-after image he carries within. In everyday life this image is rarely projected for any length of time upon the spouse. Once she has turned into a wife and mother, the bride is no longer the faraway love, the unknown princess. Instead, she becomes a concrete, well-known, and not always agreeable companion. Once she becomes a mother and is experienced as a definite, delimited, human individual, she no longer embodies the archetype of the eternal-feminine and of the virginal bride. She can no longer portray the lofty spiritual priestess as well as the dangerously demonic, vixen-like traits of the feminine archetype. And it would be wrong for her to play out the glittering possibilities of the Anima. Besides, as a young girl she can more easily correspond to the images which the man carries within himself of his yet undeveloped feminine side. Marriage, therefore, is a marriage of death, not only for the young girl who dies in order to become a woman, but also, and mainly, for the soul-image of the man which disappears, only to reappear elsewhere. The death of Vincey's Greek wife is such a death of the ideal image.

After the wedding, the man has to adjust to an everyday marriage with bills and crying children. Much of what he had longingly and vaguely hoped for from his intimacy with "the bride of his soul" remains unfulfilled. This ideal image then becomes the hope of the son who is to achieve one day all that slumbers as the longings in the father.

However, the despairing Vincey places his son into the care of someone else. Grieving over the past, he cuts himself off from any hope for the future. He looks back on the lost love and is unable to continue to live without the values he projected upon the lost wife. Nevertheless, he tries once more to prepare himself for the voyage by learning Arabic. Yet his life-fire is diminishing; his lungs are diseased. Since love died, his contact with the spiritual life is disrupted. Thus he loses the courage to live and commits suicide. Like many other fathers, Vincey leaves the quest to his son, since this most crucial task is a family problem that poses itself repeatedly until finally one in the line of descendants solves it. Vincey portrays Haggard's attitudes as a young man. He dies in order to make a place for his son Leo, for a renewed and more consciously aware attitude in which to approach this task.

Leo, the Sun-Child

With Vincey's death, the world-conquering energy flows back into the unconscious where it enlivens forgotten as well as new contents. Therefore Leo, the five-year-old child, appears on the horizon, a child the same age as Haggard's son Jock, who was still alive at that time. If Holly accepts this child, this new inner possibility, and cares for it, he too will receive part of Vincey's fortune. In other words, a part of the energy which earlier flowed to the primary function becomes free and strengthens the inferior functions.

Little Leo with his golden curls is a sun-child. He shares with many heroic children in myths and fairy tales the fate of being abandoned by his parents.[44] Later he receives out of the trunk of the ancestors a scarab carrying the inscription "Royal Son of the Sun." Just as a young pharaoh, he is the reborn Horus-Harmachis, the rising sun on the eastern horizon. Horus, like so many child-gods, grows up without a father. According to the myth, Isis conceived Horus only after the death of her husband Osiris. Like Horus, Leo Vincey is a Vindex-Tisisthenes: a powerful avenger. Horus has the task of avenging his father, the dead Osiris, and of regaining during the fight his rightful inheritance. This battle is portrayed in the pictures of the temple of Edfu.[45] Horus and Seth are warring brothers. Again we find an allusion to fratricide which played a significant role in Haggard's prior novels. Yet with Horus the battle is raised to the level of the gods, upon an inner, ethical plain. Osiris represents goodness, whereas Seth represents the searing heat of the desert, impulsivity, violent passion, and darkness.

Seth embodies the base, animal nature, over against Horus, the falcon with the sun and moon eye, who floats over the earth as spiritual consciousness.

The Egyptian seal, the scarab, which Leo received from the trunk, establishes his task. He must be more thoroughly prepared with knowledge than was his father if he is to succeed in his mission. As a new Horus, as a rejuvenated Sun, he is to bring forth a better epoch and a new consciousness. To this effect Leo is given a second spiritual father in the person of Holly. Holly can be likened to Bes, the Egyptian dwarf, or to the cripple Harpocrates, the educator of the hero-child.[46] With his simian features, his intellectualism, and his rejection of relations with women, Holly reveals himself as the mother's Animus.[47] This ties in with Haggard's inheriting from his mother his predilection for Egypt as well as prudence, clarity, and form. Her spirit or Animus becomes his guide through a period of need and suffering.

It is his father's wish that Leo study mathematics. He is to learn formulas through which the life processes can be divested of personal features and instead ordered and reviewed. Thus, the intuitive individual who tends to be satisfied with approximations is to acquire from his inferior side abstract thinking as well as knowledge of precise categories and immutable laws of nature. In addition he is to study Greek and Arabic, languages which represent keys to the pre-Christian and non-Christian worlds.

The child entrusted to him prevents Holly from moving into the College. Similarly, Haggard's own studies gained a new purpose, that of the development and the renewal of consciousness. He had returned from Africa to the bourgeois narrowness and materialism of England. Haggard suddenly found himself, not at the end of a youthful adventure, but at a new beginning. He succeeds in detaching his view from the past to look forward to a new goal.

Holly hires, not a woman to care for little Leo, but the servant Job, who had previously worked with horses. The reason why the care was not entrusted to a woman seems thus: the hero *must* be detached from the mother, who primarily represents nature, in order to turn his love entirely to Holly and to the spiritual quest, the spiritual adventure.

Job, the Servant

The servant Job whom Holly hires for the little Leo reveals by his name that he is a servant of God, a suffering human being striving towards consciousness.[48] Haggard describes this servant as a rather unsophisticated spirit whose education consisted in working in a horse stable and whose interest was limited to the care and training of the body. Culture and empathy are replaced in him by rules of law. Haggard's novel describes him as the shadow-aspect of a narrow, puritanical Protestantism, based largely on the Old Testament and its Ten Commandments. Job thus brings with him a strengthening of the masculine, legalistic viewpoint; he is a rigid, simple-minded spirit who now joins Holly and Leo, the "father" and the "son." In his role of servant to the heroes, he portrays the limitedness of the human ego or, more specifically, the negative shadow-aspect of Holly's gentlemanly, conventional view of life. Expressed more concisely, Job is the body-person, the body-ego, which previously had served the instincts (symbolized by the horses) but which now assumes the task of caring for "the heavenly child," for the germ of a new wholeness.

The Message in the Trunk

Leo's youth passes inconspicuously. As is the case with other "heavenly children," it evolves in one instant. Suddenly the young hero is grown. For a god, twenty-four years are like one day. On his twenty-fifth birthday, the trunk, his father's legacy, is brought forth.

A second trunk made of black wood is found inside this outer iron trunk which the dying Vincey had given to his friend Holly. Inside this interior trunk rests a still smaller one made of silver with four sphinxes as feet and a fifth sphinx on the curved cover. Within this silver trunk is a fragment of a Greek amphora, covered with ancient Greek writings. Next to the Greek text are found a Latin and two English translations, one of the latter by Leo's father. In addition there is a picture of Leo's mother, a beautiful Greek woman, and a scarab with the Egyptian seal "Royal Son of the Sun."

The inscription narrates that Amenartas, princess of Egypt and spouse of Kallikrates, a priest of Isis, had bequeathed the contents of the trunk to her young son Tisisthenes (the powerful avenger). It further tells of her flight with Kallikrates, whom she induced through her love to break his priestly vows, into the interior of Africa, during the days of Nectanebes. It clearly describes the path they had to follow, starting from a rock shaped like the head of an Ethiopian, on the east coast of Africa. The path led them to a white sorceress-queen, who fell in love with Kallikrates and wanted to kill Amenartas. A sorcery-charm possessed by Amenartas prevented it.

Thus the white sorceress-queen led Kallikrates and Amenartas into the cave containing the pillar of life, the fiery column of life. She then placed herself within the flame and emerged unscathed and more beautiful. Thereupon she promised Kallikrates that he too could become immortal on the condition that he kill his wife Amenartas. When Kallikrates refused to obey her, she murdered him with her magical power. She subsequently mourned his death and sent Amenartas away. The latter eventually reached Athens where she bore a son. This child was enjoined to discover the queen's secret of immortal life and then kill her. Should he fail in this task, the obligation would pass on to all his descendants, until one day a courageous man was found who would dare to bathe in this fire and would later ascend the throne of the Pharaohs. Further notations on the amphora indicated that Vincey's ancestors had moved from Greece to Northern Italy and, around 1400, to England, thus alluding to important transitions within Western cultural history.

Twenty-five years have passed but only one day for the gods. This day started with the first appearance of the "heavenly child" in the form of a vaguely recognized but often ignored inner birth. The acquisition of the knowledge necessary for the recognition of the task and the attempt to meet it gradually emerged from this inner birth.

Opening the trunk and removing the external wrappings portray a progressive penetration into a mystery which, unknown to the grandson, had become an ever-recurring problem to the ancestors. Yet the latter remained without a satisfactory answer to this fundamental question of every human life.

First the iron trunk is opened. Iron is the metal of Mars. It symbolizes the forcefulness of the ego, strife and aggressive daredevilishness, force and sexuality in its primitive form. This is the rough outward wrapping, while the hidden treasure, the Anima's message, is contained within. One is not allowed to stop with such youthful, inconsiderate aggression but must penetrate further into the meaning of the task. The middle, wooden trunk is like a small coffin which hides within it a silver trunk with its curved cover and five sphinxes. The initial black gloom with which Haggard started to write the book brings forth a shiny vessel. This trunk is not of gold but of silver, not like the light of the sun, but more like the cool moonlight which illuminates the African nights. It is connected with the night, the moon, and the feminine principle. The sphinx is winged like the birds and has the same relationship to the air and the spirit as does the dove. This birdlike aspect is linked to a female upper torso, a lion's body and, sometimes, in the Hellenic period, a dragon's tail. In Egypt the sphinx guarded temples and graves; in Thebes her name was Phix, analogous to the nearby mountain of which she was the worthy mountain-goddess. She is a dreadful, man-eating monster, a frightening, deadly mother, related to the Gorgons.[49] Hera places her upon the road that leads Oedipus to the city of his parents where, as half-animal and half-feminine unconscious, she confronts him with her riddles.

Not without reason does the sphinx stand at the beginning of the "quest." Like Oedipus, Haggard descends from a family of red-haired, hot-blooded strongmen. Like Oedipus, he remains a "mother's boy." Haggard himself mentions that there was never a day on which he did not think of his mother. To her he dedicated his novel *Cleopatra,* the one following *She.* Nor was Haggard ever able completely to suppress his rancor towards his father. In the novel, Leo is pondering, like Oedipus, the question of the sphinx, namely, the dangers of his yet undifferentiated and unconscious instinctual side. The silver trunk is a valuable container. In the shape of a cube it points towards the realization of the feminine principle in the world. The curved cover symbolizes, like the sky, the encompassing view which culminates in a fifth sphinx, the quintessence of the feminine, instinctual soul. Yet all this is but an unrealized possibility, a mysteriously dangerous question and challenge.

The valuable silver container holds a clay fragment with a guiding inscription, concluding with a sphinx with two feathers. Holly had previously seen this symbol but only with kings or with bulls. Jacobsohn[50] illuminates the meaning of this inscribed sphinx. On a banner he had seen was a sphinx with a double-feather crown which represented the Royal Ka. This "Ka," he states, links the king with the gods and ancestors during festivities. For Jacobsohn, the Ka is the power of the Pharaoh's soul.[51] It is incarnated in the Apis, the live and spiritually creative principle which, emerging from the god Horus, disperses itself in the world and its creatures.[52] The guiding inscription is an appeal that originates in the spiritual and creative power of the soul, in the principle which Leo would have to integrate before becoming a "Horus" or, in more modern terms, a "god-man."

The inscription is written upon a fragment of clay, a broken amphora. The amphora is a vessel to collect and store water, the greatest treasure of arid countries. Vessels are always symbols of femininity, symbols of nourishing, enveloping, receiving, and rebirth. In many cultures, the vessel symbolized the mother.[53] Leo receives only a fragment of this symbol. This underlines the fact that once again the feminine aspect is lacking. Two thousand years before, the feminine principle had lost dignity and power as a result of the decline of the great goddess's cult.

We can assume that the inscription is a message from the unconscious, directed not only at Leo but also at the writer Haggard himself. It alludes to the conflict between two women, to the fight between two queens, and thus also between two principles. Kallikrates, which in Greek means "mighty through beauty," is the priest of Isis in Egypt and is hopelessly caught between his wife Amenartas, the daughter of the Pharaoh, and the priestess of Isis, "She," who represents the goddess here on earth. Thus the external queen stands in opposition to the internal one. The outer material world stands against the inner world of the gods and of the soul. On one side stands the love for and faithfulness to the mother of his unborn child, respect for conventions, and obedience to the external law. On the other, there is the promise of inexhaustible vitality and of unimaginable creative energies.

The inner queen, however, demands Kallikrates' exclusive love as the price for this gift of interminable superhuman power. The goddess does so with considerable justification, since Kallikrates, as priest of Isis, had made marriage vows to her priestess prior to his marriage to Amenartas. Thus right opposes right; duty opposes duty; the external, concrete obligation conflicts with the inner, religious one. The situation is further complicated by the fact that the priestess demands the priest for herself, inasmuch as she represents the goddess here on earth. Amenartas, however, will not let go of Kallikrates. She cannot allow herself to deliver him to the priestess for absolute possession, since as his wife she must defend marriage, the other pole of the feminine principle she represents, i.e., the external demands of life. Yet Kallikrates himself shies away from the priestess-goddess and refuses to murder his wife. When he does not relinquish her, the flame of wrath flares up in the priestess, and she slays her beloved. Neither of the two women grants him to the other. Neither is willing to relinquish any of her claim, and thus he is lost to both of them. Just as Isis and Nephtys grieve over the dead Osiris, so "She" and Amenartas mourn over their dead lover. He is torn from both, though he continues in his yet unborn child.

The message on the clay fragment modifies the drama of Isis and Osiris. It is a drama of the gods, an archetypal conflict. As mentioned, the wife, Amenartas, embodies worldly station and renown in her role as daughter of the Pharaoh. "She," on the other hand, is the incarnation of the goddess and simultaneously the "mistress soul" who promises superhuman happiness, glory, and powerful spiritual creativeness. Her legal claim on Kallikrates is older than that of his wife. In the guise of his soul she was, like Isis with Osiris, united with him in heaven before their births. Haggard points this out in one of his last books, *Wisdom's Daughter*.

Carl Spitteler, the Swiss poet, found himself confronted with this same dilemma some time before Haggard. He chose unequivocally his "severe mistress soul," thereby renouncing much natural, human happiness.[54] The Greek Kallikrates stood, like Haggard, for consideration, law, and outward respect, renouncing glory and immortality because of the justified fear of the demands of the impulsive, heathen soul personified by "She." Two thousand years ago her powerful urges had to be denied and overcome, for the sake of a higher, spiritual law, namely, the Christian ideal of morality and humanity. This goal became a universal value as the result of the Christian influence on consciousness. Kallikrates had to make a one-sided decision. However, the longing for completion through the Anima, the longing for inner unification with the natural soul, continues to live and eventually reaches Leo by means of the message of the clay fragment. Leo then begins his quest for the lost treasure.

The trunk contains, in addition to the message, the picture of Leo's Greek mother. It is his mother's picture that summons him to search for the Anima, the image of the soul.

As evidence of his mission, he obtains the scarab with the inscription "Royal Son of the Sun." The scarab is a dung-beetle that rolls a black sphere through the sand. This characteristic made it into an Egyptian symbol of the black sun's nightly sea journey. The black sun travels in the form of a scarab on the sun-boat from west to east where it rises again. Thus the beetle also becomes the symbol of rebirth. Leo is challenged by his scarab to bring about a new consciousness by means of a sea voyage. Confronted with both death and resurrection, he will have to find his wholeness, his inner balance, within this conflict.

The Twin-Heroes

Holly remains skeptical in the face of the clay-fragment message, but Leo is immediately ready to accept the task and to leave in search of the queen and the swirling column of life. This reveals the basic difference between the two. Leo is the active hero, bursting forward in quest of adventure and renewal. Holly, on the other hand, is the prudent individual who hesitates and reflects; yet he is too close to Leo to let him take this voyage alone. Holly decides that, even though there may be nothing to the message, he will at least have a fine opportunity to hunt. Job, the servant, does not want to remain behind when his masters face grave risks, though he has forebodings about this affair. Thus Job represents the human being who is drawn, half-willing, half-resisting, into the adventures of gods and heroes, whenever the time arrives for the transformation of consciousness. We have viewed Leo and Holly as archetypal figures, representing, as it were, the sun and its shadow.[55] Shadow here is not meant in a moral sense but in the sense of orientation and attitude. Leo is youthful optimism and conquering spirit, Holly aging, moderation, moral reflection, and depressed-saturnal mood. In short, Holly is that aspect which Haggard grew to know only too well in the course of the advancing years. As a youth, Rider had a lot in common with Leo, but the aging Haggard prefers to identify with Holly. Even so, the older Haggard could at times be more youthful and radiant than many others and additionally had known periods of depression in his youth.

The friendship of Leo and Holly has many precursors in mythology and fairy tales. Kerényi points out the hidden link, if not identity, between Zeus and Hades, between the illuminated god and the hidden, concealing god.[56] He mentions an analogous hidden identity and relationship between Apollo and Dionysus who are, respectively, light and underworld aspects of the deity.[57] The identical, and later the dissimilar, twins date back to the period of the astrologic religions.[58] Margarete Riemschneider found symbols of the twin-god and of the twins as far back as Susa and Ur.[59] The two symbolical eyes of the Eye or Twin-God are interpreted as sun and moon. Gilgamesh and Enkidu are equally a pair of friends belonging to this series. Like Leo, Gilgamesh is the new sun, the regenerator of consciousness, and Enkidu, his hairy, animal-man companion, has striking similarities to Holly.

Yet, considering the more advanced cultural evolution which affects the relation of the opposites, we find that Holly is, not pure instinct like Enkidu, but also knowledge and reason. He can be seen as related to Mephisto, the animal-human shadow-brother of Faust, who is intellectually quite sophisticated. Only his hoof and his whispered suggestions recall his rootedness in animal instinctuality. Yet Haggard himself, the hero's companion, developed from animal to hunter to farmer, and he eventually succeeds in turning these energies towards the humanities. Thus he recapitulated human evolution. In college he reached the contemporary limits of science and then faced a challenge to further widen his consciousness, lest he remain stuck in Victorian rationalism. Usually at this point in development, the ancient pair of twin-gods appears showing that deeds are in the making, and a new phase of life opens up. As an example, we learn that the Asvins, the Indian twin-gods, carry in their chariot "Ushas," the dawn, as their shared bride.[60] Sons of the sun, they are the precursors of a new day, rescuers and healers. At one and the same time, they create in the world and augment consciousness. At this point Haggard conceives of Leo and Holly as rescuers and helpers. As such, they are the complementary aspects of their culture: Leo portrays the Englishman's self-confident, individualistic spirit of enterprise; Holly represents the conservative, ascetic, sober tradition.

The Night Sea-Journey

Holly and Leo, accompanied by Job, begin their journey. They sail along the east coast of Africa and plan to reach this shore in their own "whaleboat." At the moment of their arrival, in the middle of the night, they are hit by a violent hurricane. Only Leo, Holly, Job, and the Arabian steersman, Mohamed, survive. Risking their lives, they overcome the heavy surf and reach the quiet waters of the mouth of a river.

This storm is a sign that the foursome has lost contact with the conscious world of controllable, rational choices and is ready to deliver itself to the unconscious with its "perils of the soul." As if out of a clear sky, they are caught by the uproar of the elements, by wild emotions erupting from primitive depths. The large boat, their last link with England, and the crew, their human partnership, become victims of these emotions. Commonly, the first approach to the unconscious goes hand in hand with a sudden, dangerous commotion during which old values and relationships perish. At such a moment, it is essential to have a friend and guide like Holly. Once the hurricane has torn the heroes away from the security of their traditional world view, they must pass the trial of water. This is their first engagement with the unconscious.[61] Without Holly, that is, without a reflective consciousness, Leo, the young sun, would be lost. He would be swallowed by the darkness back into the primitive, undifferentiated universe. Leo is unconscious when he is rescued from the raging waters and is carried through the surf to shore in a small boat. This is the characteristic image of the night sea-journey of the sun which descends into the ocean in the west in order to re-emerge in the east. According to the text of the Egyptian book of the dead, the deceased Pharaoh also travels in the sun-boat towards his resurrection. Similarly, the dismembered Osiris floats down the Nile River in his coffin, as did Moses in a woven basket.

Mother Nature

With the destruction of the large ship, the heroes have also lost the soil of Europe as well as the foundations of Christian tradition. Fortunately, they have their own little boat in which they now begin their separate quest. Only four men are left. Of them, as is implied by their names, Holly represents the Nordic ancestors, Leo the Greco-Roman inheritance, and Job the Old Testament. They form a trinity widened by Mohamed, the representative of Islam, into a quaternity. Mohamed joins them as delegate of the dark continent which they are approaching. This male quaternity might create the illusion of a self-satisfied, self-contained masculinity.[62] Yet for complete wholeness, they are lacking the "feminine" and the "shadow." Admittedly, Job and Mohamed are shadows of the heroes, Job because of his conventional limitations and Mohamed because of his connection with the dark continent. Yet what is lacking, what would be truly complementary, announces itself for the first time in the vision of a woman in the sea, torn by suffering:

> Presently the moon went down, and left us floating on the waters, now only heaving like some troubled woman's breast. The moon went slowly down in chastened loveliness, she departed like some sweet bride into her chamber, and long veil-like shadows crept up the sky through which the stars peeped shyly out. Soon, however, they began to pale before a splendour in the east, and then the quivering footsteps of the dawn came rushing across the newborn blue, and shook the planets from their places. Quieter and yet more quiet grew the sea, quiet as the soft mist that brooded on her

bosom, and covered up her troubling, as the illusive wreaths of sleep brood upon a pain-racked mind, causing it to forget its sorrow. From the east to the west sped the angels of the Dawn, from sea to sea, from mountain top to mountain top, scattering light with both their hands. On they sped out of the darkness, perfect, glorious, like spirits of the just breaking from the tomb; on, over the quiet sea, over the low coast line, and the swamps beyond, and the mountains beyond them; over those who slept in peace, and those who woke in sorrow; over the evil and the good; over the living and the dead. . . .

The shipwreck corresponds, as we mentioned, to the loss of security within the European realm. Inasmuch as a ship is a technological instrument built by human beings for crossing the sea, it may also symbolize one's habitual world-view which offers security against the sea of the unconscious. In *Psychology and Alchemy* Jung states, "The ship is the vehicle which transports him/her across the sea and the depths of the unconscious. As human construction it has the meaning of a system, of a way, of a method (e.g., Hinayana and Mahayana = little and large vehicle: the two forms of Buddhism)." Our Nordic churches were built according to the model of a ship, which is the reason for their lateral entrances and for naming the long structure "ship."

In place of the collective security afforded by the protective ship as well as by the Mother-Church, we now witness the emergence of an older mother-image. The heaving ocean becomes a symbolic image of the all-encompassing Mother Nature's suffering. Wasn't the great goddess originally also the mistress of the waters?[63] Her suffering is more than the personal suffering that drove Vincey to his death. It is the suffering and enduring as passive, feminine principle far removed yet from consciousness. Because of the emergence of the great goddess, the archetypal myth of the youthful god's rebirth out of the original maternal waters resounds. The storm's turbulence gives way to a wonderful, cosmic vision. The torment of the Great Mother subsides. The god rests in her womb from which he must be born again. The moon resembles the chaste bride who hurries into her chamber, to the *Hierosgamos,* to the holy marriage, while the angels of dawn bring forth the new day. The exclusively masculine consciousness which is about to enter the realm of the unconscious meets the vision of a multiplicity of feminine figures who are supposed to give birth and bring forth the new day. In the story this vision remains like a poetic foreboding, vague and unreal, a cosmic image still unreachably distant for the human being.

The Ethiopian Head

With the break of day, the men discover the omen of the land, the rock with the Ethiopian head. Job, frightened at the sight, exclaims that this is the portrait of the devil.

In early Christian usage, the term "Ethiopian," like the term "Egyptian," was used for the devil.[64] In alchemy he is the black "prima materia"[65] with which the alchemistic opus begins. The first and most important task of any dialogue with the unconscious is becoming aware of one's own blackness, of the shadow, of the dark reverse side of our self-satisfied consciousness. We dislike seeing our own inadequacies, our selfish motives, our evil impulses and thoughts. Of the shadow Jung says,

> It is a moral problem which challenges the entirety of the Ego-personality, inasmuch as no one is capable of confronting the shadow without a great amount of moral decisiveness. In fact this confrontation demands that we recognize the dark aspects of our personality as being unquestionably present. This is the unavoidable basis for any genuine self-knowledge and meets, therefore, considerable resistance. If psychotherapy aims for such self-knowledge, considerable difficult work is needed which may require a long time.[66]

The evil which we ignore reappears as a projection, as a "splinter in the brother's eye."

In the head of the Ethiopian, not only do the three white men see a dark, hostile, dangerous consciousness, but also Job perceives the quintessence of evil. Laurens van der Post, in *The Dark Eye of Africa,* states: "It is because the whites in Africa see in the blacks their own nature, that the prejudice against the black skin has become so entrenched. . . ." The Ethiopian's threatening head anticipates that which our heroes are to expect in terms of primitive cruelty from the depths of their unconscious, from the abyss of human nature.

The Animals

The morning after the storm, the men row between swamps up the river and tie their boat to a magnificent magnolia tree with reddish blossoms.[67] The pendulum has quickly swung from the black devil towards the other side, the rose-colored tree. Flowers and blossoms symbolize feelings, and this is particularly true of a reddish color. The dark, evil world which the men enter contains not only evil but also the delicate miracle of naturally growing feelings.

They find an ancient port, which indicates that once there had been a commercial route. Later they navigate between hippopotami, hundreds of crocodiles, and thousands of swamp birds. The first animal they shoot is an unusual wild goose with two spurs on its wings and a spur on its nose. No one had seen one before, and Job names it a unicorn-goose.

The unicorn-goose has three spurs; it (in German "she") is a unity and a trinity.[68] Jung's extensive writings about the unicorn explain that it personifies a demonic–divine nature-power, which has connections with the "holy spirit." The horn on its forehead is a creative, spiritual quality. As a white bird, the unicorn-goose belongs to the same category as the swan or the dove. In contrast to the dove, the symbol of the holy spirit, the goose is a nature-spirit. Yet like the dove, the goose is sacred to Aphrodite and thus belongs to the world of femininity.

The natural spirit is projected into the wild nature of Africa. Leo had met it once before in the sphinx. Now, when the waters have calmed, Leo kills the goose as their first hunting booty. His ability to hit it ("her") indicates his intuitive understanding. He has somehow captured the bird-aspect of the sphinx from the otherwise still unknown nature-connection. Through this nature connectedness, Leo will be involved in a primitive, fundamental passion, in a non-dogmatic form of spiritual experience, in an instinctual, vital state of mind which is to compensate for the intellectualism of Holly and the spiritlessness of Job.

Shortly thereafter, Job attempts unsuccessfully to shoot a water buck. Holly must then kill it. As a buck it is related to the wild stag and therefore also to Leo whom Haggard describes in the book's introduction as a wild stag. Leo cannot grasp or understand his own stag- or buck-like nature; hence, he needs the help of Holly, the reflective spectator. An alchemical picture shows the buck as soul, over against the unicorn as spirit.[69] The "natural" spirit and the "natural" soul, in contrast to the spirit of the church and to the Christian soul, must be brought back from their projection into nature and re-integrated. The task is to become aware of and to assimilate fleeting, seemingly aimless longings and ideas, of barely conscious wishes and of subconscious thoughts. Such impulses and feelings live hidden in the unconscious and, like shy, fleeing game, are hard to hunt down. The buck is found near open water to which he is driven by thirst. So it is that thirst and hunger give body to the impulses and drive these feelings that are hard to grasp towards a clearing, towards the edge of consciousness where we can comprehend them.

During the night, the four men are awakened by a lion and lioness. Leo kills the lioness; in the next instant a crocodile grabs the remaining lion by its paw. A life and death struggle ensues, and both animals succumb. The lion and lioness are royal animals. The lion passes as the king of the virgin forest. In the horoscope, as *domicilium solis,* he indicates the zenith of the sun and confers royal bearing and the power to rule. The lioness is companion to the God-Mother of Asia Minor. Lions pull the chariot of Cybele and serve her as throne. Margarete Riemschneider points to Sumerian seals and reliefs on which lions carry the goddess.[70]

The attitude and symbolism of the lion represent strength of the body, heroic attack, self-assuredness, and royal rule. Yet they also stand for rapacity and voracity. As an animal sacred to the mother-goddess, the lioness combines royal nature with maternal tenderness. Power and rapacity serve her primarily for the care of the young. Obviously, the lion portrays the animal nature of the sun-hero Leo. Thus by killing the lioness, Leo separates the animal-parents. By killing the mother-animal who tenderly cares for her young, he surmounts his own longing for security near mother.[71] Later on, the lioness reappears in a new form, as the Royal Anima.

The lion and the crocodile are not killed by the heroes but rather fight and kill each other. They symbolize contrasting and conflicting forces within the unconscious. In Africa the crocodile stands for a lurking, great danger. Whoever receives the crocodile in an oracle is doomed to die.[72] Just as the lion is connected to Leo, the crocodile has a secret relationship to Holly who had the Cambridge nickname of Charon, death's ferryman. The lion is the hero's victory, while the crocodile is the evil outcome, the "No," the being pulled back into the unconscious. The two animals represent opposing life forces. Deriving from the animal-nature of the hero are the hot-blooded rapacity and greed for power of the lion, as well as the cold-blooded goal-directedness of the crocodile and serpent. Lion and crocodile embody life and death, progress and annihilation.

Yet, in which way are they related to Haggard himself? At twenty years of age, he was already viewed by the African natives as representative of the queen. As "Sompseu's child" and master of the highest court, he was given royal honors. When he traveled to supervise the execution of judgments, he sometimes brought death. This power that descended on him at such an early age awakened his "power soul" without his becoming aware of it. Crocodile and lion are not shot in the novel. The battle of these opposites remains a natural drama. This tension between unconscious opposites, parallel to the tension within the heroes themselves, remains hidden to them at this juncture. As a result, a certain amount of instinctual forces remains unrecognized and unavailable.

Haggard's inadequate insight into the instinctual aspects of human nature results in a frustration of his goals. It is important to keep in mind that Haggard was truly a pioneer. He did not have available, as we do today, any orientation to the unconscious as offered by modern psychology. Still he went a long step beyond the insights of his time. In this story, however, the absence of a conscious confrontation with the lion and crocodile diminishes the effectiveness of the hero's instinctual nature.[73]

The Swamp Belt

The following day, the four men row upstream and reach a man-made canal. Rowing against the current characterizes the journey as a struggle against the river. Not a life that devolves unconsciously and effortlessly, this is an undertaking in opposition to the ordinary course of things. The attempt to extract its secret from the unconscious, a heroic task, goes against nature. Yet the man-made canal which they reach and to which they must entrust themselves reveals that they are now following a path traveled in earlier times. In fact, there are ancient ways to penetrate into the hidden realm of the unconscious.

The swamp belt along the coast which they must traverse is one of the natural formations in that region. It also serves as a symbol of the chaotic condition of the initial state, well-known in alchemy. It is the initial period of the inner journey, when the firm ground of conscious orientation is left behind and when the conscious and the unconscious are no longer distinguishable. Here the unconscious threatens to flood the conscious human being with its contradictions. So the individual is repeatedly in danger of remaining stuck or of drowning in the inner disorder and disorganization.

The Old Wise Man Billali and His Tribe

After four days on the canal in this miserable region, our exhausted heroes awake one morning under the frightening gaze of savages who would have killed them instantly were it not for their queen. "She-who-is-to-be-obeyed" has ordered her people to spare the lives of the white men rowing up the river and to bring them into the interior.

The savages are good-looking, but their expressions are indescribably cruel. Their leader, an ancient white-haired man named Billali, brings the strangers in sedan-chairs to his tribe which lives in the fertile grassland of an extinct crater. The people dwell in caves which, in fact, are ancient sepulchral vaults. They call themselves "Amahagger," the people from the rocks, and are matriarchally structured. This elicits Holly's comment that morality seemed to be a function of geographical latitude, since much of what is viewed as good and decent in one place turns out to be false and indecent in another.

Morality's becoming relativistic is the normal consequence of a clash with a different cultural group. Many people thereby lose the moral strength that they would otherwise have maintained in their own culture. Like the hero of *The Witch's Head* after his disappointment in love, they start drinking, gambling, or running around with women. Yet others try to cling all the more tenaciously to inherited standards, which leads to a progressive inner emptiness since the external behavior corresponds neither to the environment nor to the subjective truth.

The collision with another culture and another morality—a difficult problem and one that is very timely for many—demands a dialogue not only with the foreign consciousness but also with the contents of one's unconscious. The unconscious has mysterious connections with the environment and will be influenced directly by the instinctual patterns of a differently shaped environment. In order to achieve a viable adjustment to the new environment, one must seek a satisfactory position between one's traditional, conscious way of life and one's unconscious, which is being stirred up powerfully by the different culture and the subconscious instincts within it. Dealing with dreams and with spontaneous fantasies furthers understanding of the unconscious processes stirred up by the new environment and helps prepare for a new synthesis.

Haggard's position towards other cultures was open-minded. Yet in terms of himself and of the English youths for whom he wrote, he held fast to a strict, denominational Christian position and to the gentleman-ideal. The Christian example which he held up against an invasion by the unconscious prevents the breakthrough of Antichrist forces, as occurred later in Germany. However, his one-sided attachment to the gentleman-ideal so limits consciousness that the shadow cannot be integrated but continues to be projected, thus manifesting itself as an external peril.

Leo and his companions, representing a penetrating consciousness, are met by a commotion coming from the very center of the dark continent, of the unconscious. Though previously confronting anything foreign with murderous intent, the unconscious now responds to this new approach with a sense of anticipation. The right "knights," with the right attitude, are arriving. They have unconquerable curiosity and are willing to die in order to discover the secret of the white queen. The lonely queen's deep longing to be redeemed supports their firm purpose. Thus she sends out her servant, Billali, so he can safely escort them to her.

Billali has a long, white beard, a hook-nose like that of an eagle, and eyes as sharp as those of a serpent. His behavior is instinctive, with partly bitter and partly wise humor. In contrast to academic knowledge, he personifies an instinctive insight and ability to deal with primitive nature. Without this quality, it is impossible to advance either into the inner Africa or the virgin forest of the unconscious. Billali is a nature-spirit, helpful but not dependable. That which the heroes met first in the sphinx and later in the hunted animals, namely, their unconscious impulses and instincts, returns now in a transformed way, as instinct-bound, helpful, unfamiliar knowledge.

Billal is the name of Mohammed's first *muezzin* or prayer-leader. In Cambodia all prayer-leaders are called Billal. Thus, Billali reveals himself to be a descendant of a Mohammedan in whom the recollection of the meaning of prayer and submission to Allah has remained alive. In the novel, however, Allah's servant has become the servant of the goddess who is banished to the unconscious. He has regressed to pre-Islamic matriarchy.

From the second novel concerning She—*Ayesha, The Return of She*—we learn that Holly is the reborn Noot, the wise, long-deceased, Egyptian priest and teacher of She. Yet only a limited amount of Noot's wisdom is reincarnated in Holly: knowledge, worldly prudence, morality, without priestly piety and wisdom. In modern human beings, piety as a basic attitude has become largely suppressed, and therefore unconscious and primitive, as a result of increasing technological acquisitions and greater, sharper knowledge. For modern humans the wise priest has died.

On the other hand, anthropologists are profoundly impressed to find in Africa genuine piety as an expression of the human being's dependence upon superordinate powers.[74] The European encounters in Africa this lost part of his being, namely, piety as a natural instinct; here it is permeated by the sense of one's dependence, something that is still contained in the Mohammedans' concept of destiny. Without regaining some of this attitude, the European cannot become whole or wise. Billali and his long white beard embody another part of the heritage of the ancient wise man Noot. Job speaks of Billali sarcastically as "he-goat," underscoring the impulsivity of his spirit, his unpredictability, and his relatedness to the buck-hoofed Pan. As servant of She, Billali is subordinated to the feminine principle and conveys knowledge about instincts as well as the skill of dealing with nature within and about us. By means of this nature-piety, he offers a significant compensation for European intellectualism. Holly addresses Billali as "father." Billali possesses the older knowledge from which our own pragmatic science has evolved.

The First Crater

As head of his tribe, Billali lives in a small, extinct crater. The edge of the crater that surrounds the buried opening, which at one time reached the interior of the earth, is circular. This circle enclosed by high rocks is a first symbol for the "roundness," the "wholeness" that is grounded in itself, which comprehends the opposites and which Jung designates as Self.[75]

In the earlier phases of humanity's evolution, the wholeness does not realize itself in the individual but in the tribe with its complementary halves. Layard referred to this in his *Stonemen of Malekula,* and the same has been observed among the Pueblo Indian tribes. The four "quarters" of ancient cities also reflect the subdivision of the collective wholeness. The city of Kor where She waits for the heroes is similarly situated in a still larger crater surrounded by rocks. The crater of the "Amahagger," the rock-people, is a preliminary form, a barbaric shadow-aspect, of the Self's wholeness. Here it is achieved on a primitive level, whereas Leo's task is to achieve this wholeness, in conjunction with She, on an individual level.

Both Billali's crater and that of She are also gravesites: the heroes enter a realm of the dead. The Self includes generations, in numerable layers of an impersonal past, all of which may announce themselves again in dreams and fantasies. The first encounter with the Self is often experienced as compensation for the Christianity of consciousness, as an encounter with evil. The crater shelters greedy, cruel, beastly human beings. Additionally as compensation for the patriarchal orientation of our consciousness, we find here matriarchy, which is common to many African tribes.

Ustane

At the first welcoming, a distinguished young woman kisses Leo, whereupon Job mutters, "The hussy—well, I never!" Surprised and hesitant at first, Leo then returns the embrace, commenting that obviously some early Christian customs must still be valid in this region. It turns out, however, that the greeting is a marriage-ceremony of the Amahagger which is initiated by the women and which a woman can dissolve at her discretion. Another woman approaches Job with the same intention, but he fends her off. His clumsy righteousness cannot tolerate such a thing. Yet his rigid attitude will bring forth a bitter revenge. Not only the rejected woman, but also the entire tribe, feels dishonored and plans vengeance.

What Leo took for early-Christian brotherliness is in fact a marriage-ceremony. While in his native country women are expected to behave passively, we find that here, in the unconscious, activity originates in the woman. That which in England is unalterable, i.e., marriage-law, is determined here by the variable emotions of the feminine eros.

Leo's returning Ustane's kiss characterizes the harmlessness of the sun-hero who sends his rays to all creation without allowing himself to be impeded. Yet, as Leo returns what to him seems a non-binding greeting, he consents to a different, local custom. It becomes evident that his gesture is understood by feminine feelings as a commitment. By returning the kiss, the sun-hero unexpectedly finds himself tied in marriage to a black woman. In *King Solomon's Mines*, Haggard couldn't yet conceive of a marriage between a black woman and a white man; yet here it occurs, against knowledge and will, even before Leo knows what has happened.

The male thinks he is to choose or to reject. He identifies with the sun-hero who strives towards his faraway goal: the white queen of his ideals. Yet things are decided differently in the unconscious. Unexpectedly, he succumbs to the embrace of his dark Anima. Thus marriage reveals a feature which men do not intend and do not wish to see, but of which some become painfully aware just before the wedding—namely, that viewed superficially he has been caught in a woman's net but that at closer view he has become a prisoner of his own nature. This occurs even more drastically in the colonies: consciously the white man thinks he is caught in a woman's trap. Yet in truth, the dark-skinned woman gains power over him only because he no longer is able to resist the dark side of his own nature which has been strengthened by the environment. Ustane's tie to Leo is primitive, the type of marriage people commonly live as long as no spiritual partnership is built upon it. Ustane cares for Leo, she offers him her feelings, nurses him during his illness, shares the nights with him; but missing is a genuine relationship based on mutual understanding.

Marriage as a binding but still primitive relationship is a preliminary form of the Self. Through the union of man and woman, marriage portrays an initial wholeness. It is the necessary basis for a relatedness to the feminine principle, a first step in helping the man to get closer to his nature and his soul and eventually to unite with it. At this point Leo gains a new experience of the "unconscious nature" which had appeared to him in the vision of the sea as a suffering woman.

Yet, in this layer of the unconscious, primitive impulses predominate. These impulses can become dangerous for the relationship and for consciousness. The feminine element which has been lacking in these heroes approaches them from the inferior, primitive, rejected side, thus bringing with it other contents. The young men clad in leopard skins also belong by nature to the matriarchal level. In Greece they are known as Corybants who, armed with swords and shields and clad in animal skins, dance around the newborn child of Rhea, the first mother.[76] Elsewhere, the Kabires and Daktyles belong to the mother-goddess's entourage: a large number of young men, warriors, dwarfs, phallic creatures, or skilled blacksmiths. Here the male element is an anonymous, impregnating force, a universal, generative force, an energy which begins to differentiate itself by bearing arms and learning artistic skills. These are fervent, ardent men who have learned how to deal with and to use fire. On this level impulses begin to change into will; more accurately, here will is still composed primarily of impulse, and the essence of will shows itself in the form of spontaneous and sometimes destructive fire.

One evening, as Leo, Holly, and Ustane sit around a fire, the woman begins to sing: "You are my chosen one—I've waited for you since the beginning." But the song ends by telling how She, the white queen, proves herself the stronger and that something horrendous will separate Ustane from her chosen husband. Here, in the realm of the unconscious, Ustane may be free to take the initiative towards a man, but she does not have the rights that civil law grants a spouse to protect her against rivals. In "She-who-is-to-be-obeyed" she runs into a rival who is stronger and more beautiful.

The Incandescent Pot

Billali has visited She for five days in order to receive her instructions. Once within her sphere, the heroes are no longer free to act according to their own will. They have entered the soul's field of forces. Primary decisions now originate in the innermost center to which they are drawn as if by magic. They only retain the freedom to respond to the orders coming from within, according to their own insight.

The threatening thunderstorm comes to a head on the fifth day after Billali's departure. The two friends are invited along with Job to feast; and even Mohamed, the Arabian steersman, is brought in, trembling and pale, by the woman whom Job had rejected. An enormous fire lights the hall, and brandy is passed around in jugs upon which love-scenes are depicted in strangely childlike simplicity and frankness.

Naive simplicity and freedom in matters of love, but behind this sits intoxication from brandy, and a great peril. "Where is the meat that we shall eat?" asks a voice, and all reply, "The meat will come!"

"Is it a ram?"

"It is a ram without horns and more than a ram; and we shall butcher him."

"Is it an ox?"

"It is an ox without horns. . . ."

Meanwhile, the heroes notice how the rejected woman begins to banter with Mohamed.

"Is the meat ready to be cooked?"

"It is ready, it's ready!"

"Is the pot hot to cook it?"

"It is hot, it is hot!"

"Great God," gasps Leo, "it was written on the clay fragment that there were people who put pots over the heads of foreigners."

Holly jumps up, seizes his pistol, and aims instinctively at the devilish woman who has grabbed Mohamed. The bullet hits her, and at the same time it kills Mohamed who is spared a more horrible death.

With the shot a general uproar begins. The white men defend themselves against the onslaught of the savages until finally Leo collapses. At this point, Ustane throws herself over him to save him. A terrible voice shouts, "Drive the spear through both of them; then they will be married forever!"

"Cease," a thunderous voice is heard through the hall as Billali appears.

After leaving the realm of water, the heroes have entered that of fire. The circle of fire is a place of the cannibals, of those emotions that are the more barbaric as they are rejected by our consciousness. Thus, this place represents an initial symbol of the Self's wholeness. The two rational Englishmen here run into the type of primitive, emotional nature that slumbers in each one of us and without whose richness and danger we would be but half human beings, simply surrogates without depth.

At the same time, the circle of fire is the place where marriages are contracted. Through marriage the emotional aspects of the Self are built into a culture. By declaring marriage a sacrament, the church affirms that emotions enter the human realm as something extra- or super-human, as divine power, as some formidable force that must be guarded with care and veneration. Yet, all too often the other, dangerous, destructive side of the impulsive-divine energies breaks forth. Uncontrollable, negative affects originating from within may be turned against the "woman." Day-to-day married life offers many occasions for dissatisfaction over the spouse. Thus, the wife is commonly blamed for the husband's moods and fits of anger.[77]

Ustane, the black spouse, does not solely portray the married woman. As a member of her tribe, she also represents the dark, impulse-bound emotions in the man, his unrealized emotional dependency. Leo accepted the tie to his shadow-spouse which was forced upon him in the fiery circle of emotions. Yet Job, identified in the novel with law and conventionality, is no hero but an ordinary, narrow human being, who is simply the servant and shadow of the heroes and who rejects the appeal of the feminine side. For Job, marriage is an affair of the registrar's office rather than of the emotions. The tribe, however, cannot tolerate the rejection of a "natural emotion." This infraction against the law of the land brings forth a wild reaction. As is common in the case of infractions against the inferior side, this reaction becomes manifest only after several days.

During the feast to which everyone is invited, jugs decorated with love-scenes and taken from the graves are passed around. The decorations are somewhat like the Dionysian vase with pictures alluding to regeneration and rebirth.[78] It is not unusual to encounter such ancient jugs and Dionysian scenes also in dreams, whenever the process of exploration reaches the deep levels of the ancient soul. We are astonished when we discover that past rites and beliefs have been preserved by the unconscious and are reawakening in order to complete and revitalize our consciousness that has become too one-sided. From the graves, out of the memories of the ancestors, emerge pictures of a high culture in which free love belonged to the cult of the great goddess.

The savages in the novel and their cannibalistic customs probably represent a degenerated form of this high culture. While we educate the intellect, we leave the emotions to themselves so that they succumb to our primitive, barbarous side. Love, which in this region of Africa was expressed as a natural emotion, was refused by Job and thus turned into hatred. The incandescent pot which is to be put over the selected victim's head images the strong affects that overcome him. His head burns, he turns crazy. He becomes the victim of cannibals. Psychologically, this means that one no longer deals with this one human being but with a band of enraged savages within him. "A ram without horns, an ox without horns, and more than an ox . . ." A man is the selected victim, a buck that has changed himself into a eunuch and who, therefore, also lacks will to fight and spiritual creativity. The split-off emotions will grow over the head of such a man if he gets too close to the unconscious. Whoever is unwilling to serve nature will become its victim.

As container and as cooking-pan in which the contents are transformed by heat, the pot can be viewed as analogous to two bodily organs, the stomach and the womb. In many persons, certain intense emotions are the source of burning gastric disturbances. Also the womb can be likened to a container within which warmth contributes to a creative process. As mentioned in connection with the message on the amphora fragment, the vessel is a primary symbol of the feminine. Erich Neumann states, "The feminine is experienced as the perfect vessel for good reason. Woman as a body-vessel is the natural expression of the experience that the feminine carries the child within herself, and that the male, in the sexual act, enters into her."[79]

The term *hysteria* is not accidental. The incandescent pot over the head is equivalent to the rising of hysterical affects. In fact, when a man rejects emotions because of rigid conventionality, the heat of this feminine side turns into an evil fire that consumes his brain. That which could have ripened towards creative involvement can change suddenly into hysterical rage which destructively inundates the entire person. It is Job, self-righteously defensive against the dark side of nature, who evokes this peril. Significantly, it takes several days before the tension leads to a discharge. The fury, however, does not aim at the conventional side, Job, but against the weakest point which in this case is Mohamed. As the most primitive among the four, he becomes the defenseless victim of the intense emotions. The uproar breaks forth from the collective unconscious like a mob. If the destructive rage cannot be stopped, reality will disintegrate. In such a state a man does not remember what he said or did. He will act surprised when he sees those around him responding defensively or fearfully. Most of all, he does not recognize to what extent he has bullied the feelings of his wife and children.

The unconscious responds to rejection with a sudden attack of which Mohamed is the victim. Holly's bullet hits him and the black woman simultaneously, saving him from a cruel fate. Holly acts. Reason defends itself against affect. Just as Job is Holly's shadow, so Mohamed is Leo's. While Leo is induced to become active, Mohamed becomes the passive victim of primitive impulsivity. Holly's bullet unites the black woman and Mohamed in a gruesome death-wedding. Thus, an intuitive insight demands that the resolution of, and freeing from, hysterical explosions consists in the linkage (and transformation) of hostile opposites, even if at first only the most radical methods suffice to save the endangered consciousness.

When Leo is near defeat, Ustane throws herself protectively over him. She is not only nature but also love. Therefore, this pair is less imperiled than the other. Nevertheless, the same fate hangs over Leo and Ustane as over Mohamed: the danger of a brutal death-wedding. It is as though some primitive reason were attempting to arrest any further growth by Leo. The unconscious is trying to swallow back both Leo and Ustane. If the hero does not want to forget his task, he must defend himself with the weapons of his intelligence against the onslaught of his primitive, inner world. It becomes a matter of life and death, with the likelihood of an ominous result. A higher principle from the depths of nature must arrive and intervene. She, the white queen, must save him, since her own destiny depends on the hero's life and love.

Whenever a man on his inner journey confronts the shadow and the figures of the unconscious, he risks being flooded with the primitive, barbaric sides of his being. In such moments, he must, like Leo and Holly, defend himself with his intelligence, his will, and his superior knowledge. If a man yields to his primitive reactions when he projects his Anima upon a woman, he not only becomes arrested but also degenerates and in turn becomes more primitive. The goal then, as with Leo, is the acquisition of feelings and wisdom. It is necessary to know about the barbarous potentials lurking in each human being. Conscious dealing with the abysses contained in the soul protects one against being unexpectedly overwhelmed by the internal peril. Conscious awareness renders one immune to contagion from psychoses which otherwise can lead an individual to lose track of his higher nature.

Billali, in the name of the queen, orders the uproar to cease. He explains to Holly later that it is a custom of the land to kill foreigners with the incandescent pot. It is a law of the unconscious to attack invaders suddenly. The unconscious then fills their heads with affects and passions, with everything that is suppressed, but not truly contained, by civilization and Christian veneer. Right below the surface of the gentleman is still the barbarian, not in his natural state, but degenerated towards unnatural evil. This barbarous layer—visibly in the open in the East—is right below the surface in Western cultures. There are various ways to deal with it. In Haggard's novels, the spiritual side fights against the barbarian in self-defense, because of compassion for the victims, and because of faithfulness to friends and idealism. Consciousness halts the destructive eruption of the unconscious at least until help from within rescues those who put up a courageous resistance.

The Mummy

Holly passes a restless night after the fire orgy. He dreams of a veiled, lovely woman who first turns into a skeleton, then regains her human figure and says: "That which is alive hath known death, and that which is dead yet can never die, for in the Circle of the Spirit there is neither life nor death. Yea, all things live forever, though at times they sleep and are forgotten." The following morning he learns that once the mummy of a beautiful woman had lain on the stone bench on which he slept. And Billali further tells him that, as a boy, he had felt drawn by this mummy and had loved her, and that wisdom had flowed from her into him. In her, he recognized the transitory nature of all things, the brevity of life, and the long duration of death. Billali's mother overheard him and cremated the mummy in fear that she was bewitching her son. Only a small, white foot remained untouched. Billali then brings it out from under the stone bench: "Shapely little foot! Well might it have been set upon the proud neck of a conqueror bent at last to woman's beauty, and well might the lips of nobles and of kings have been pressed upon its jeweled whiteness." This is what Holly thought as he enclosed the relic in a military pouch.

The battle against the eruption of primitive emotions has not been fruitless. Holly has had a dream which brings an insight, transmitted by a mummy who becomes a beautiful, veiled woman, who reverts to a skeleton, and who speaks of eternal life in the sphere of the spirit.

Speaking of the mummy, Paracelsus claims that it [she] is an "antidote against mortality."[80] His treatise *De Vita Longa* begins with "Truly, life is but a kind of an embalmed mummy which protects the mortal body against the mortal worms."[81] And Hippolytos speaks of the "upper human being," of the "Protanthropos" whom the Phrygians called Papa (Attis), saying: "He is a messenger of peace and calms the battle of the elements within the human body. This Papa is also named Nekys [corpse], since he is buried within the body like a mummy in a shrine."[82] In the mummy Holly encounters an Anima which remains at the stage of a chrysalis. She is the still-veiled psyche, a seemingly dead remainder from distant times, for the Anima is the man's original experience of the woman. At this point she appears only as a ghostly figure. Yet through this she can manifest her spiritual, non-material being. Both the mummy and the ghost point to the appearance or reawakening of the supra-personal, spiritual Anima.

The veiled, invisible, or spiritual woman brings peace after the battle. She symbolizes the life that enlivens the body, the integration of the soul in the body that manifests itself bodily and then disappears without perishing. She is alternately nature and spirit. She speaks of the flow of things in the periodic alternation of becoming and vanishing, and of the fact that in the sphere of the spirit there is neither life nor death. In place of the opposites and their brutal battle, there appears to Holly the presentiment of another possibility: a rhythmically flowing alternation of existence in the spiritual realm with everyday reality, so that both remain related to each other. Here the opposites relieve one another without ever extinguishing each other.

Billali, the nature-spirit-father, received his wisdom from the mummy until his mother pulled him out of his seeming madness. With good reason she had suspected that this "spiritual Anima" might lead him into an unreal world. Now, only a foot of the mummy has been left behind, and Holly imagines the nobles and kings of ancient times who submitted to the reality of the eternal feminine. Yet then he places the relic that brought this insight amongst the mundane objects of his pouch. Only a foot is left, but it suffices for reawakening the meaning of the whole.

Holly, representative of the undeveloped sensation function, is the one who receives the news concerning the mummy. This remnant of the mummy becomes a window into the past as well as into the realm of the eternally alive, creative spirit. In a matter-of-fact way, Holly takes the little foot as a keepsake, and whenever he will look at it, he will be reminded of his meaningful dream. The Englishman's dry reasoning and his belief in tangible facts render him particularly vulnerable to the compensatory attacks of the irrational side.

"In this country the women do what they please. We worship them and give them their way, because without them the world could not go on; they are the source of life. We worship them up to a point, till at last they get unbearable, which they do about every second generation." "Then," Billali adds with a faint smile, "we rise and kill the old ones as an example to the young, to show them that we are stronger." Here Billali expresses the unconscious wish of the man who would like to fight off the preponderance of the mother-complex.

Matriarchy is founded upon the biological function. Women are the fountain of life of the tribe. Now and then the man must or wishes to assert his greater strength against their biological importance, thereby maintaining a relative balance. Thus we noticed in the realm of fire the play of opposites on the biological level. The power of the biological assertion of life is seen against the strength and determination of the male.

Yet the mummy points beyond the sphere of fire, beyond biological life, towards death and towards life in the realm of the spirit, even beyond the center of fire. The little mummy foot is hidden in the realm of fire like a seed. The soul reaches all the way down to the foot, and here it touches the ground of reality. With the little white foot, the heroes gain a new standpoint which leads them on to She.

Ustane wants to accompany Leo on this journey. Yet in the presence of She, Ustane loses her rights. "The word of She," Billali states, "abrogates all other rights." "But what if Ustane will not let go of Leo?" asks Holly. Billali replies, "What if a storm asks a tree to bend and the tree refuses, what happens then?" This is the cue for the next level of the journey. The heroes are going to the place of storms. She is a storm and as awesome as lightning.

The Land of Fever

The heroes are carried in sedan chairs through the swamps. Saved from the danger of the incandescent pot, Leo and Holly are racked by fever resulting from their battle wounds. "It is our own desires that stick in our flesh like arrows," says Jung.[83] One who is struck by Cupid's arrow is tortured by ardent desires. In Wagner's opera *Parsifal*, King Amphortas is ailing, wounded by his own spear that had fallen into the hands of his adversary. Behind the fever that befell Leo and which She will heal is probably Haggard's passion which drove him to write of an immortal woman and an immortal love. The same feverish passion drove Leo, the son of lovesick Vincey, to begin this journey. Leo refused the people in the fire-sphere, but the poison of their affects proved contagious. In his fever, Leo deliriously imagines that he is divided in two halves. Being torn internally is the fever's source. Leo is in the borderland between Ustane and She, and the inner division grows intolerable. In the novel *Jess*, John feels that he must sacrifice his relationship with the spiritual beloved for the sake of the more down-to-earth Bessie. Since both women are Anima-figures, however, his soul is torn. Each of the relationships offers him the experience of one side of his being. He cannot give up either of them. Not only Leo but also Job, the body-ego, is racked by fever. The body often becomes ill when the soul finds no solution to a conflict.

The Mandala of the Heart: Kor

As they journey from the swamps to the highland, they see in the distance a volcano which is ten times larger than the first one. It is the castle of She. Across the high rocks that seem to touch the sky there are thick layers of clouds. Earlier inhabitants, in long forgotten times, had used canals to drain the lake which had formed in the crater. Inside the extinct crater is Kor, the city of the heart, circular and protected by nearly insurmountable rock walls. The Mandala[84] of the heart, almost inaccessible, is situated above the volcano of the emotions. This ground has been habitable only since the waters were drained off. This motif recalls some dreams in which the waters of the unconscious must be drained before the heart begins to function as a center of consciousness.

An American Indian tradition is that we think, not with the head, but with the heart. Europeans, however, long ago abandoned the heart in favor of the head as the center of consciousness. Yet She does not live in the head but in the heart, near abandoned temples and in old gravesites. She reigns over savages and is served by deaf and mute servants. "Mistress soul," the forgotten goddess, lives her existence dreadfully abandoned, in the midst of savage and primitive people. The realm of the heart is a realm of death. Deaf-mute servants come and go. There is nothing to hear and nothing to say, since the queen of the heart, the feeling aspect of the man, is condemned to be among the dead. Nothing can be voiced about her being, her suffering, or her wishes.

The Anima is found in a grave-city of an ancient or even prehistoric period. As the personification of the unconscious, she reaches far down into collective layers. Very much embodying these early layers, she appears in men's dreams as a medieval feudal lady, as a witch, or as a priestess, like Ayesha who represents an ancient goddess. She is yesterday's truth which has been repudiated by our one-sided consciousness. She is life as it always was, in varying garb. The queen of the heart, the mistress of emotional reality, dwells near the dead among the ruins of past civilizations. Many people live, as far as their emotions are concerned, in the past. Thus we see romantics, scientists, and ordinary human beings who live in the seventeenth century, in the Renaissance, or even in the Stone Age.

Leo seeks the city of the heart, knowing that for his father Vincey life without love was meaningless. Thus the son must find his way to complete the task passed on to him by his father. Haggard himself was compelled to undertake this journey since, like Oedipus, he is one of those mother-sons who are called upon to resolve a family conflict. During his early years in Africa, on his lonely trips where he repeatedly confronted death, his unconscious awakened from its torpidity and fostered a life which was to burst the limits of his Victorian world. Holly, however, is unable to respond spontaneously to such reactivation of the unconscious. He limits himself to recording or collecting unusual, odd things or events and leaves it to Leo to become deeply affected.

She

The travelers are housed in caves containing graves. Leo is so critically ill that Holly fears for his life. When Holly is called by Billali to meet She, he picks up the scarab which in his delirium Leo had dropped on the floor.

Through a rock tunnel, Holly is led by Billali to the antechambers of She. Billali throws himself down and approaches She on his knees and then later on his stomach. Holly decides not to lower himself to that extent, since otherwise he would be expected to repeat the performance each time. Yet he, too, is overcome by fear when he senses that the gaze of the veiled, mysterious, strange figure is directed upon him. He has the impression of standing in the presence of someone uncanny. The mummy-like figure before him is a tall, lovely woman, revealing instinct and beauty in all her parts, with serpentlike graciousness, her movements flowing like waves over her body. Her raven-black hair reaches down to her sandals. "Why are you so afraid, stranger?" asks the sweet voice, one that, like the streams of the softest music, moves the heart.

"It is your beauty that scares me, O queen" is Holly's humble answer. Yet She replies with laughter that rings like silver bells, "You were afraid because my eyes explored your heart. Yet I forgive you your lie, since it was courteous." Chivalry calms the Anima and protects against her rage. She's reply shows that she knows what goes on in a man's heart. She is the truth within it.

When she notices Billali, her voice resounds clearly and coldly against the rocks, as she promises to sit the next day in judgment of the evildoers from the sphere of fire. Then she dismisses him.

The hall is filled with fragrance that seems to flow from She's hair and her white, transparent dress. "Sit down," she commands

Holly, "since you have nothing to fear from me. However, if you have reason to be afraid, you will not have to fear me for long, because I shall slay thee."

They converse about Egyptian, Greek, and Roman history; she knows nothing of subsequent periods. She speaks Arabic, Latin, Hebrew, and Greek but not English. Holly is aghast when he realizes that she has already been alive two thousand years. Yet She responds, "Do you really believe that all things perish? I assure you that nothing perishes, that there is no death, only transformation. What once lives will return. I, Ayesha, tell you that I am expecting someone whom I love and who will be reborn." "But," inquires Holly, "if it is true that we human beings are constantly reborn, how is it that you *never* die?" She explains to him that she has become one with nature: "Nature has its own life-spirit, and whoever finds this spirit and allows himself to be filled with it will live from it. He will not live eternally, since nature itself is not eternal. Nature, too, will die one day or, more accurately, will transform itself, but not for a long time yet."

She inquires about Leo's condition and suggests it would be better to wait another day and see whether he will not overcome the illness by himself.

Holly then begs her to unveil herself, yet she warns him that she is not destined for him and that he might consume himself because of a hopeless longing for her. But his curiosity is too intense, and finally she yields to his request. Her heavenly beauty, in spite of all purity and charm, is nevertheless frightful and dangerous. She is like the gods, sublime but dark—a miracle, not from heaven, but no less glorious. Her face is that of a woman of barely thirty years, showing the first blossoming of mature beauty, but it is also marked with unutterable experiences and deep acquaintance with grief and passion. Even her lovely smile cannot hide a shadow around her mouth that speaks of sin and sorrow. It shines even in the light of her glorious eyes; it is present in the air of majesty; and it seems to say, "Behold me, lovely as no woman was or is, undying and half divine; memories haunt me from age to age and passion leads me by the hand—evil have I done, evil shall I do, and sorrow shall I know until my redemption comes." Something radiates from her eyes which confuses and blinds Holly.

At this point she notices the scarab. She rises like a serpent who is about to strike. From her eyes a flame-like light breaks forth, and

Holly draws back, terrified. This helps her regain control: "Forgive me, my superhuman spirit becomes impatient over the slowness of your finiteness, and I am tempted to use my power out of vexation. But why do you have the scarab?" At this point, Holly is so confused that he can barely explain that he has found it.

Her face is that of a woman of barely thirty years. At the time of writing *She,* Haggard, too, was thirty years old. The Anima has caught up with him. She has reached his age and has turned into a conscious problem; she mirrors his soul, his experience, his suffering, and his passion. But She is more than that; She is two thousand years old. That is how old the soul is. She was born in the times when the gods died. Before then, she was far removed and dwelled, as the Great Goddess, in the "eternal place." Then, with the decline of the cult of the Great Goddess, the highest values disappeared from consciousness. Later on, a new vessel was discovered in the person of the Virgin. Other aspects of the original feminine image reappear in medieval chivalry, in the belief in witches, and in the Romantic period. Among Protestants the lost values and dangers manifest themselves in the form of projections upon actual women, since goddesses and nature-spirits lack any sense of reality for the enlightened, liberal mind.

The renouncing of a woman, which was the occasion for writing *She,* directed Haggard's focus away from the outer object towards the inner image. The image conjured up by Haggard is endowed with all the magic of an angel and of a serpent. Thus She is wonderful, fascinating, and dangerous; tender, lovely, and evil. She can be ruthless and cold when angered. She as a primary form of feminine nature is an enhanced, overwhelming, irresistible force of passion, a contradiction in the wealth of possible emotions that it contains. She is abysmal in destructive will, unmatched in pride and capacity to suffer. She is the blind will of nature, which is stronger than consciousness. Yet she is a light in nature, full of mysterious knowledge about nature. Not only is she nature and the spirit of nature, but also Soul, *Anima animata,* full of passionate psychic energy.

The name of She-who-is-to-be-obeyed is Ayesha, "the live one";[85] She is life in itself. Ayesha was also the name of Mohammed's favorite wife and daughter of his friend Abu Bakr. Married to the Prophet at the age of six or seven, Ayesha received over a thousand communications from him. After Mohammed's death, she became "The Mother of the Faithful," and as such she was frequently consulted in questions of orthodoxy and of proper living. She involved herself in the political battles over the succession to the Prophet and was part of many intrigues. Furthermore, she was famous for the story about a necklace which provoked suspicions concerning her adultery with a young man.[86]

This Ayesha had both a niece and a sister-in-law with the same name. The latter, a younger sister of the Prophet, was a poetess. The niece, a granddaughter of Abu Bakr and daughter of Talka and Umm Kulthum, was famous for her beauty. It is said of her that she never veiled her face. When her husband Mus'ab reproached her over this, she allegedly replied, "Since God the Almighty stamped me with the seal of beauty, I want that all men may see me, so that they recognize his grace towards men; therefore I will not veil my face. There is indeed not one defect in me of whom anyone could complain." Since her husband could not master his jealousy, she refused herself to him, reconciling with him only when he returned victoriously from the battle.[87]

The three women with the name of Ayesha encompass the picture of the sister, daughter, and companion of the Prophet: the most beautiful, the most self-satisfied, the intriguing and the spiritual woman, namely, the woman who transmits spiritual values. In terms of historical tradition, this name is well-suited for the Anima. Margaret Smith mentions in her book about Rabi'a the Mystic several equally independent Arabian women who waged war on their own and concluded treaties. Such was Sajah, Harith's daughter, who proclaimed herself a prophetess and intended to attack Abu Bakr.[88]

Just such a daughter of an Arabian chieftain, untamed by patriarchy, is Haggard's Ayesha in her youth. Reared motherless, never taught to keep a household, she lives on her horse and rides into battle with the men. She is one with the active male instincts as an embodiment of the emotions that inspire masculine feats. Yet then she encounters Noot, the wise old priest, who ordains her as a priestess of Isis, as the earthly representative of the Great Goddess, of Mother Nature.

The Anima's turning towards the old wise man of whom she becomes a student reflects a change within man's soul which coincides with puberty. The Anima prepares herself for her future function: a mediator of inner, religious images. She is being withdrawn from the exterior world, in order to turn towards the inner world and its spiritual contents. As priestess of the heavenly "Great Mother," she attains spiritual heights in which, however, she is unable to remain during the next developmental phase. If a man must create himself a place in this world, he cannot spare the Anima from becoming involved in earthly wishes, though for the priestess they represent sin. Only much later, in the second half of life, can these desires be taken up again after their first appearance during the storms of puberty. Rediscovery of the spiritual Anima and her development now become an inner task. Her relationship to "the old wise man" becomes meaningful only now, inasmuch as he administrates the wisdom of the unconscious. With his assistance one reaches maturity and therewith the fulfillment of old age.

Ayesha and the old Noot are a pair like Solomon and the Queen of Sheba. From the wise old man She has received her interest in the natural sciences. She possesses an alchemical laboratory. The wisdom of the Anima reveals itself in She's comprehensive knowledge and foreknowledge, as well as in her mastery of several ancient languages. When the aged Noot died two thousand years ago, all his knowledge—even the secret of the fire of life—went over to Ayesha.

Noot's death signifies that priestly wisdom has disappeared from the realm of conscious contents, thereby being taken up by the unconscious and the Anima. The Anima creates reality, like Maya, Shakti, and the spinning women of the Chinese.[89] It is unavoidable that Ayesha, in spite of Noot's strong warning, would try out on herself the fire of life that she was charged to guard. Her bathing in this fire results in her feeling superior to the gods, even to Isis, the great mother, and in placing herself beyond good and evil. Wisdom and the power of the gods and their priests have fallen to the unconscious and the Anima. Because of this, under the cover of Christian consciousness there occurs a self-glorification of man, who, Anima-driven, sees himself as the crown of creation and in his hubris no longer recognizes a law above him but thinks there are no limits to his intelligence and power.

In Haggard's mind Ayesha is a human woman who has usurped divine attributes. Just as the Christian receives his heavenly spirit through the baptism of water, so the Anima goes through a baptism of fire in which nature enters her. This fire-spirit finds not a purified soul, but an ordinary human being tainted with original sin, a woman who, according to the story of the Garden of Eden, is far more accessible to evil than is man. The fire-spirit that takes hold of Ayesha increases in demonic proportions not only her natural beauty but also her "evil" nature. This She is not a savior figure, in spite of her baptism of fire. Rather, like Sophia who fell into Hyle, she herself is in need of deliverance from her inferior nature. She remains a sphinx, though no longer in the monstrous form of a beast, but as a soul who carries within herself the promise and peril of the potential inherent in the sphinx-animal: the deadly coldness of the serpent-body, the grabbing power of the lion-paws, the nourishing, healing fullness and warmth of the emotions, the distancing and seductiveness of the smile, as well as the wings that carry the spirit upwards.

The Anima, like the sphinx, is an iridescent figure. Depending on the man's disposition and his stage of development, she shows him a different face that compensates for or completes his consciousness. She can manifest herself on the most different levels, between animal and goddess, inasmuch as she encompasses life, impulsivity, eros, and spirit. With Haggard, the accent rests mostly on the subtler, immaterial aspects of the soul. Benoit's novel *Atlantide* shows the other aspect. In this widely read, turn-of-the-century novel, Benoit also sketches a fascinating, striking picture which in part is in startling agreement with Haggard's *She*. Benoit was unfairly accused of plagiarism. Inserted here is a brief chapter about Benoit's *Atlantide*, since this French novel completes the picture of the Anima in significant respects.

Benoit's Atlantide

Benoit offers the following etymological explanation for *Antinea*, the name of his Anima-figure. *Antinea* signifies the woman at the prow of a ship; thus she is a Nike or goddess of protection and victory. She can be a priestess, ancient; yet *Antinea* also means the blossoming-one, the striding and flowing-one, the one who spins or weaves, the one who gathers in.[90] These are all designations of the goddess of destiny. As *Nike,* the Anima incites to action; she is the goddess of victory who furthers engagement and success in undertakings. As priestess she is the link to impersonal, spiritual powers. Ancient, she encompasses all the past; blossoming, she continues to offer promise for the future. She is the striding-one, life's journey towards a goal; she is the flowing-one, the life that flows from the inexhaustible depth of the collective unconscious. Spinning and weaving, she forms the texture of fate wherein a person gets entangled in good and in evil. As the gathering-one she prepares karma, guilt, experience, curses, and blessings.

Commonly, this destiny-shaping factor remains split-off from consciousness, in the unconscious, and tends to be projected. As long as the Anima is not recognized as part of his own desires and as an aspect of his own soul but, instead, is experienced as an unfamiliar, external event, the man will blame any woman he meets for his destiny. He is not aware that he is driven by internal forces to always select those women who correspond to his unconscious prejudices and that he pushes and influences them until they fit his destiny.

Antinea is the granddaughter of the god of the sea, Neptune. Her mother was a seductress. In this combination is revealed the ambivalence of the Anima-image which shows a different expression depending on how one approaches it. As Neptune's granddaughter, she is a nixie and a goddess, half-fish and half-woman. It is said of her that her body is willing but her soul inexorable. Though she passively offers her body to the daring young men who advance through the deserts towards her, her soul rules. The first queen who does not allow herself to become a slave on account of her passion, she is the only woman who succeeds in separating the two inseparable things: love and lust.[91] Since she is passion itself, she never becomes a slave but remains the mistress of the man whom she enslaves. She takes from the man as much as he is able to give. Through her the man gains experience of the woman who corresponds to his own ability or inability to love. Lust and love are separated in Antinea, because sexuality and feelings are split in the man. If the man seeks only the body, only nature without soul, then he cannot attain the feelings and the entire range of spiritual values. A victim of his own split, he turns into a Don Juan. He only finds as much as he gives or as he is able to receive. That which he really seeks, and that which he could only find through a full connection of body and soul, eludes him. As long as his soul corresponds to that of Antinea, he cannot appreciate any other type of woman. He is compulsively enslaved by a vamp.

The men who are delivered to Antinea—namely, to this interior reality—are unrelated, incapable of committing themselves to a real woman. Once they leave behind what is for them the arid region of communal life, they begin to sense a fascination from within. They are assaulted by the interior image and irresistibly drawn into its circle. Alcohol and other drugs further this illusory dream life. Searching for a faraway ideal, these men escape reality and its responsibility; they strive for sensory satisfaction, when what they could have is an irrational spiritual experience. Such an experience could bring realization of the wholeness of their own being with its own ordering center. In *Atlantide* they find as the center of life a spring of pure water—the source of the spring of eternally self-renewing life—which flows from the depths of the desert. The center and the spring are in fact reached, but only through regression into death. In a large rock cave illuminated by copper pillars (copper being Venus's element) are already prepared the niches and caskets for 120 mummies, the corpses of the lovers, covered with orichalque.

Orichalque, according to Lippmann, is a copper-containing substance. In alchemy it is used for blanching the black "original matter" (prima materia).[92] The corpses of Antinea's lovers are mummified by being covered with a coppery substance, the metal of the love-goddess. The body as prima materia is ennobled through love and is thus transformed into an early stage of the stone of wisdom. As dead persons, the lovers put on the soul-dress.

The solution thus remains unsatisfactory and incomplete, since the body is conceived of too concretely, rather than symbolically as an image of the need to transform real life. Furthermore, transformation of the body consists only in superficial whitewashing by means of a substance. There is no transformation from within. The alchemical process terminates with the whitewashing, never attaining the goal—namely, pure gold. There is a hint that some insight is being gained into the nature of the previously black, and thus unconscious, contents, but the men remain subjected to the love-goddess Venus (copper), to the Anima, without having gained wider consciousness (gold) and without having reached the Self. The material body gains in value. The heroes, however, are returned to earth as mummies, remaining there forever in a rigid, unconscious state. They become surrogates for the goddess. Enveloped by a strange glow, but unconscious and effeminate, they are eventually lost to life. Instead of the expansion of consciousness, a regression takes place.

It is significant that not even one of the heroes is wedded to Antinea, the bride: this would mean union of the opposites and achievement of individual wholeness. Instead, there are 120 lovers congregated around one center, approaching an eternal sleep within the magnificent cave. Return to the clan, thus accomplished, replaces the wholeness of the human being with the multitudes of a population relating to one deity. Though each person is distinguished from the next by name and number, nevertheless his destiny remains always the same: a return to the goddess Ishtar from whom already Gilgamesh freed himself, reproaching her for the innumerable lovers she had corrupted.[93] Every single one of Antinea's lovers has forgotten his family, his home, his honor, and everything consciously dear to him. Each loses all because of this addiction into which he drifts, which intoxicates him, to which he submits without battle and to which he succumbs.

The only exception is Morhange who resists Antinea for ascetic, Christian, moral reasons. His scientific curiosity had driven him into the desert. Yet his inexorable attitude is just as ill-suited for bringing forth a solution as is the blind fascination of Saint-Avit, the male protagonist of the story. Morhange's one-sided scientific passion is an expression of the type of extreme masculinity which suppresses and thereby perverts the emergence of eros.

Saint-Avit, "the Anima-possessed" man, searches for the untouched, virginal nature by fleeing from the city into the desert, from his own period into the pre-Christian past. He seeks it by whitewashing the body with orichalque. Though mummification is a rite of rebirth, it is arrested here at the level of overrating the body and thus does not lead to the purification, separation, and new synthesis of the natural human being's elements. In this longing for the "untouched and virginal nature" one recognizes Rousseau's call "back to Nature," which at the turn of the twentieth century brought forth nudism and fanatic vegetarianism, all of which are incomplete and superficial understandings. What was truly intended was the return to the natural human being and the distillation of "silver" as the quintessence of this inner nature—namely, the conscious rendering of the innermost meaning of human nature.

Saint-Avit's other great longing is for a mysterious love; and he exclaims: "Shame on him who spreads the secrets of love. The Sahara desert encircles Antinea like an impassable barrier. . . . this renders her [this love] more chaste than any marriage and its inevitable publicity."[94] He searches for love as mystery, as a secretive union with the godhead, hidden like the *hierosgamos* (sacred marriage) in the ancient mysteries, segregated from any mixing with the world and its opinions, like the processes in an alchemical flask.

Yet the endeavor for nuptial union of the opposites fails because Saint-Avit murders the moral aspect of his person—portrayed by his friend Morhange, the Christian and scientific spirit—and thereby also fatally wounds himself. Antinea, the Anima, turns him into an assassin. She loves Morhange, the spiritual man, and avenges herself when she receives nothing but coldness and rejection from this ascetic, who unfeelingly remains true to his principles. This explains why Antinea appears as such a cold-blooded, man-killing monster. Benoit states: "Antinea must avenge herself. It is a very ancient struggle, a struggle that goes well beyond the present time. How many barbarous queens of antiquity were exploited by men who, driven by fate upon a foreign shore, became their lovers, only to abandon them or to return as conquerors with troops and ships!"[95] Antinea, the Anima, takes revenge for all faithlessness shown her by men. She is the compensating justice which reaches man from within himself and lets him find his ruin in a mirage, if he is unwilling to accept love as a commitment and responsibility.

Since, as Anima, Antinea has access to the wisdom of the past, she owns an immense library of rare manuscripts lost to the world. However, her wisdom, that of emotions and of the inferior functions, is of minimum interest to the man. In addition, Antinea has a predilection for languages and train schedules, knowing even the smallest details. This skill comes because she deals with time as a concrete reality and because she is so interested in France, her lovers' native land. Among Antinea's victims are the one-sided officers who only know their professional duties and scientists living solely for research. Other victims were men like Gerard de Nerval[96] or St. Exupery,[97] idealist poets unable to reconcile the wonders of their dream-world with everyday reality, whose genius blew apart the dimensions of their actual life.

With inexorable consistency Antinea murders all her lovers until the mummies, shining like gold, close the circle around her. She lies down to sleep in the center, as if Briar Rose had never obtained the awakening kiss from her knight. As a result of addiction and fanaticism, the individual drifts back into the collective psyche. Longing has reached its goal, the Anima, only to perish, being unable and unwilling to carry back into the conscious, everyday reality the acquired increase of life. The heroes who had set out for the new land do not return.

All too often encounter with the Anima ends in such a disastrous way unless, through the ego's strength, dikes are erected against the eruption of the unconscious.

The Reverse Side of the Heart

Holly is frightened when he realizes that She must be two thousand years old, for this means that he is dealing with the primordial experience of the feminine, with the other half of creation and the godhead. Ayesha is everything that stands in opposition to the consciousness of his time. She is simultaneously liveliness itself and a continuous death-threat, nature as well as mediator to the spirit embodied in the aged Noot. She moves like a serpent; like a serpent she rises in anger. Like the serpent Kundalini of the Tantra-Yoga,[98] she is the energy hidden in nature. Ayesha is the unmediated inner experience and the inner truth as revealed in anger and desire when these are not deflected or hidden by prudence or by considerations of external rules. Neither good nor evil, she represents the reactions born directly from instinct, concerned with no law or moral beyond their own nature-given, stormy will. She stretches from the roots of bestiality to the glaciers of the spirit, from Kali up to Paravati, the golden mountain-goddess. Haggard's novel *She and Allan* speaks for her as "She who veils her head like the peak of a mountain."

The encounter with Ayesha shocks Holly. Though he has been a woman-hater since his early youth, he knows he will never forget those eyes. This woman's devilishness which terrifies and repels Holly attracts him at the same time. He feels close to madness, pulled back and forth by repulsion and admiration.

Suddenly, he remembers he must look after Leo whom he has almost forgotten because of his encounter with She. Holly finds Leo even sicker than before. As much as Holly is deeply affected by She, he does not want his friend to die, even if the latter should become an obstacle to his relations with Ayesha.[99]

An inner restlessness keeps Holly awake during the night. He leaves his room and discovers a hallway and a staircase through which he reaches Kallikrates' burial chamber. In front of the Greek's mummy, Ayesha convulses with longing and despair. Holly overhears her. Filled with blind passion and dreadful vengefulness, she hurls curse after curse against the Egyptian princess, Amenartas. He feels as if he has heard a soul in hell.

Holly is witnessing the secret of the mistress soul. The reasonable English gentleman, who raised Leo in a strictly Christian tradition, Holly must look down into the soul's abyss and discover that it is haunted by passion and vengefulness. It is no wonder that, in the secure university environment, Holly was more afraid of women than of a rabid dog.

Antinea takes revenge on men and turns them into playthings for her desires. Ayesha, on the other hand, curses Amenartas, her rival and wife of Kallikrates, since she sees in her the obstacle to the realization of her wishes. Deep down, however, it is not so much the wife who stops the husband from his own growth, but it is his own justified fear of an insoluble conflict regarding the dangerous wishes and demands of his Anima. Sometimes the Gordian knot is then abruptly cut by means of a divorce, when it would be more meaningful to remain faithful in one's commitment to marriage while not evading the conflict of the feelings within.

The following morning Leo is even weaker. Billali believes that he will not survive the evening. Meanwhile, Holly is summoned to Ayesha's court where She condemns the native evildoers to be tortured. If any survives, he is to be killed with the incandescent pot. Holly tries to soften her, but she replies that she reigns not by power but by terror and that, if she were not merciless, Holly's and Leo's lives would be in daily jeopardy. She adds: "My moods resemble the small clouds which seem to drift aimlessly hither and thither; yet behind them blows the great wind of my purpose." The Anima of the heart avenges the transgressions of the primitive instincts.

Haggard was often reproached for the cruelty and bloodthirstiness of his books. He would reply that he simply presented reality as it was and as he had seen it in Africa. In the presence of savages, of a primitive tribe, where sovereignty is not based on genuine relationships or reason, one relies on cruel means to remain as ruler. Though European civilization fancied itself Christianized, its subjugation of foreign populations easily fanned and maintained the white Anima's fire of gruesomeness. Of the Boers, Haggard says they were disliked by all for their hardness and cruelty towards the natives. Yet he later recognized that in his youth he had judged them unfairly, by not taking into consideration the difficult conditions under which they had to live. In the Boers one clearly observes the effect of colonization upon the white people's soul. They lived widely scattered amongst warlike tribes without any protection from allies. Thus, they asserted themselves against the blacks only through violence.

Following the court session, She invites Holly to visit the burial caves, and in his curiosity he seems to forget Leo. It is possible to forget the present for the sake of the inner world of images, but also on account of collecting antiquities. Scientific interest can divorce itself completely from feelings.

Once they enter the city of the dead within the mountain, with its innumerable gravesites, however, Holly finally connects with his feelings. As Ayesha shows him a young couple united in death, Holly has a vision where the mummy before him is a pale young girl being escorted to wed an elderly man in purple clothes. Suddenly, a young man rushes out of the crowd and kisses her. In the same moment, guards fatally stab the youth, and the girl grabs the dagger and takes her own life. Although this is a fantasy image, Haggard asks himself at this point, "What is fantasy? Maybe fantasy is but the shadow of a truth that cannot be grasped; maybe it is a thought of the soul!"

Perhaps this vision mirrors Holly's own repressed wishes. Or it may cast Holly as a representative of tradition, where he sees himself as the old king. The young bride was to be given in marriage to the old man. The ancient ruler—the traditional, established principle—demands that the soul, the feelings, unite with him. Yet the bride has grown up loving a youth who embodies the new truth, a not-yet-recognized form of consciousness. The new principle breaks through at the very moment the old principle wants to propagate itself unchanged. Since the times are not yet ripe for the new truth, the young couple's only possibility is union in death. This is indeed the bitter shadow of Rider Haggard's problem: a new order of things, a new orientation, seeks to assert itself within him, but the old principles and conventions are still too strong. His feelings have only the options of either bending before the predominant lifestyle or, as the inner, new truth breaks forth, showing allegiance to the new principle through self-sacrifice.

She is not ready to dismiss Holly so that he can attend to Leo. Holly has seen her torn by emotions during the night, yet ice-cold while in court and magnificently somber near the dead. Now she appears to him as radiant Aphrodite, as ecstatic life, as the quintessence of seductive femininity, and more perfect and spiritual than any other woman. Holly thus falls to her feet, stating he would risk his immortal soul to be allowed to marry her, for "who could ever resist her when she emanates her force."[100] Yet Ayesha laughs at him, saying that she is not destined for him but only wanted to demonstrate to an old bachelor her power. She is rich in changeable moods, like a mirror which reflects everything without changing itself. Later, She and Holly philosophize about religion. Here, too, She is a mirror of opinions that seem familiar to Holly, but he never finds out what She thinks, nor is he capable of convincing her of his position—for, in fact, She represents the possibilities that oppose consciousness. Just like Shakti mirrors the thoughts of Shiva, so Ayesha mirrors every imaginable concept. Like Maya, She is the variegated veil of wishes and illusions; if one follows her, one gets caught in the net of desires.

Finally, She and Holly visit Leo and find him drawing his last breaths. Caught up in the changing play of moods and discussions, the Anima has nearly forgotten the present moment: namely Leo, the beloved, for whom she has waited such a long time. Now she recognizes in him the reborn Kallikrates who again is at death's edge. Her mixed potion pulls him back to life. Like Isis, She has healing powers.

Then She sees Ustane at Leo's bedside and tries to turn her away, but Ustane refuses to obey. Thereupon She presses three fingers upon Ustane's hair, marking her like Cain with a white sign. To this magic superiority, Ustane must yield. Leo's first question upon awakening is about Ustane, and Ayesha lies: "She wanted to leave!" The Anima may resort to lying to achieve her purpose. She suggests to the man what to believe, since she pleads her own truth and pursues her own goals which are often opposite to conscious intentions.

The Feast of the Animal Masks and Epiphany

A feast is celebrated to honor Leo's recovery. Mummies are piled upon a pyre and lighted; others burn as upright torches. In this awesome setting the savages play a game of murder and of being buried alive. Suddenly a woman is possessed by a demon. He asks for a black buck's blood and leaves her in peace only after he has obtained it. Thereupon begins a dance with animal-masks: lions, leopards, bucks, and even a serpent's skin which a woman drags far behind her. A leopard succeeds in gaining Leo's attention, enticing him into the dark. It is Ustane who wants to escape with him. But She discovers them immediately. Facing certain death, Ustane shouts to her enemy that even She will not obtain Leo as her husband in this life. With that she collapses, killed by the queen's will.

Leo attacks the murderous She with a curse. Ayesha cannot see any evil in the execution of her sentence; she has simply removed an obstacle to her love. And now, beside Ustane's corpse, she unveils herself for the first time in front of Leo, "like Venus who emerges from the waves, like Galatea who emerges from stone, and like a blessed spirit from the grave." In spite of his inner reluctance, Leo cannot escape this sorcery. Seemingly, all manliness is taken from him. Holly has already observed in himself how this woman destroys all his moral sense. Similarly, Leo senses that he pays with his honor in succumbing so rapidly to Ustane's murderess. He despairs and thinks of escaping, but he cannot sacrifice what he has finally achieved, since it has already taken possession of him. Stunned to see how quickly Leo becomes the

´prey of this sorcery, Holly tells him that his sin will eventually return to haunt him. "Yet the temptress who seduces him towards evil is more beautiful than the daughters of human beings."

At the feast that She prepares for Leo and Holly, mountains of mummies burn in a large fire. Fire festivals, known in all cultures, expel evil and encourage the rebirth of light and the increase of fertility.[101] Such rites of spring we see preserved, for example, in the Zürich *Sechselaeuten*-festival. Closely linked to winter's death is the epiphany of the spring-godhead and her holy wedding. The old, rigid forms dissolve in the fire, transformed into new life. Masked festivals also belong to the winter and spring rites in Ur and Sumer where animal masks accompany the gods to the holy wedding.[102] In Egypt the gods themselves wear animal heads.

Even now animal and ghost masks are common in winter festivals and carnivals. The animal-mask festival, a primitive rite, reconnects us with the animal soul, thereby assisting life's renewal. Thus, the Anima brings to light the psyche's dark background. As the Great Goddess, she is also mistress of the animals.[103] The possessed woman's desire for the black-buck blood reminds one of the blood-intoxication which seized the Greek women honoring Dionysus. The god, in the guise of a kid, was dismembered, and the maenads (his female followers) tore apart young roebucks and drank their blood. Here the primordial, wild, ecstatic nature, repressed by patriarchal society, broke through. Worthy Athenian matrons, seized by blood-intoxication, streaked through the forest until, exhausted and then renewed, they returned to the narrowness of their homes.

In the animal-mask dance the unconscious's beastly aspect shows itself once again. As a game of the savages, however, it does not touch the heroes but ends without being interpreted. Nevertheless, it is a force that cannot be ignored, to which one must find a relationship if the quest is to succeed. Just as in fairy tales, it is the animals who often assist the struggling humans to solve a seemingly impossible task. The shaman must learn the language of animals to execute his journey into heaven and into the netherworld. In this quest, he must change himself into an animal by imitating animal voices and by wearing animal masks, feathers, and skins.[104]

When Ustane, in the shape of a leopardess, a fighting cat-mother, undertakes to reach her lover again, she runs into She's jealous wakefulness. Ayesha had already marked Ustane with a sign on her forehead, thereby signaling her fate. Thus Ustane becomes the scapegoat and sacrificial animal. Unwilling to relinquish Leo voluntarily, she is simply destroyed by her rival. In the cases of Amenartas and Jess, faithfulness to the spouse and respect for universal moral laws led to the sacrifice of the beloved object and of inner truth. Now She strikes back and murders Ustane. In so doing, Ayesha obstructs the realization of her wishes. Ustane has prophesied that She will not reach, in this life, her goal of union with the beloved. Ustane represents the other, darker, earthier manifestation of the Great Goddess. Ayesha must also eventually reach the ground, the blood, the emotions, the earthly reality. By killing Ustane she separates herself, through guilt, from this ground. As goddess and Anima she denies her own dark, instinct-bound side. In other words, the Anima must not eliminate the wife.

Yet, "the seductress was more beautiful than the daughters of human beings!" The compelling force that flows from her destroys not only the man's persona but also his moral stance and thus his self-respect. If a certain woman provokes such moral danger, she does so only because the man's Anima is projected upon her. "More beautiful than the daughters of human beings": in these words we are reminded of the sons of god who descended from heaven to the daughters of human beings.[105]

Ayesha is her own law. Her natural will is so powerful that it challenges the entire human being to commit himself to the realization of her goal. Her will is also so ruthless that it recognizes no crime. The Great Goddess does not acknowledge morality in the male-patriarchal sense. The man, therefore, is justifiably afraid of Anima-possession. Her enticements must blind him to her ruthlessness. The greatest moral efforts are required to assert oneself against the Anima's unreasonable demands. A man must persevere in fulfilling his duties when he feels overwhelmed by his desires for love and life. The hunger for life that breaks forth from his unconscious must be confronted continually with conscious values and standards. He must attempt to find a balance—tolerable to the entirety of his person—between unconscious impulses and conscious morality. It is a matter of broadening the personality and accepting conscious responsibility, a deliberate change from the previous tendency to let oneself drift or to shut one's eyes so as not to see what one is really doing.

Standing beside Ustane's corpse, Ayesha intones:

"There is only one perfect flower in the wilderness of Life.
That flower is Love!
There is only one fixed star in the mists of our wanderings.
That star is Love!
There is only one hope in our despairing night.
That hope is Love!
All else is false. All else is shadow moving upon water.
All else is wind and vanity."

And She concludes:

"Crowned shall we be with the diadem of Kings.
Worshiping and wonder-struck all peoples of the world
Blinded shall fall before our beauty and our might
From time unto times shall our greatness thunder on."

Because Leo falls in love with her (in spite of the murder), her intoxication with her victory grows enormously towards a fantasy of world-domination. Terrified, Holly and Leo try to enlighten her about the facts of external reality and to make it clear that her "blasting methods" would be unacceptable in England. Yet She simply laughs, claiming to be above any human law.

In an overwhelming and repugnant way, She is extremely possessive. This possessiveness has many roots which we must explore since intoxication with power is the great danger from the unconscious that assails individuals. As the feminine side, as emotion and irrational force, the Anima is suppressed by the man's consciousness, which aims for what is useful, prudent, and rational. But the Anima's natural and fundamental claim on life becomes immense and intolerable because nature, love, and emotions are disparaged.

Another root of Ayesha's greed for power lies in Haggard's own circumstances. At just nineteen years old, he became secretary to the highest authorities in Africa. Wherever he went with his superiors, they received royal honors. When twenty-one, he became a high magistrate. Through all this he retained his human, Christian disposition. On the one hand an ordinary English citizen, he nevertheless was almost a king among both blacks and whites. When he returned to England, however, he had to act as if nothing inside him had changed. The power he had exercised fell to the unconscious, the Anima.

The third root of She's superior force is her bath in the fire of life, where she became one with the creative dynamics of the unconscious. The crown she promises to her beloved is the crown of wholeness, a symbol of the Self.[106]

Now a sinister scene follows. Ayesha leads the two men to Kallikrates' mummy, in order to demonstrate to Leo, in front of this image, her two-thousand-years-old love. She then destroys the corpse. By this confrontation with Kallikrates, Leo becomes aware that the age-old drama repeats itself, that his life imitates an archetypal event. The image of Kallikrates, wounded in his side and mourned by the goddess, reminds one of the precursors of the Pietà, of the mother-goddess of Asia Minor who weeps over her son-lover whose death, as a yearly sacrifice, she must decree. It is the drama of the Great Mother who never allows her son to grow up because she wants to retain all the power. She loves him as child and youth, as her creation. When he resists her in order to grow up, she slays him in anger.

Now that the beloved son is resurrected, however, the holy marriage is to be celebrated. Leo is bound no longer to a mother-wife but to a sister-beloved. To unite himself, as an equal, with the goddess, he is to be changed into a demigod by bathing in the fire of life. Holly, on the other hand, will renounce such a prolongation of life, as he would otherwise torture himself for millennia, longing for Ayesha.

The Temple of Truth

The following morning they start out for the fire of life. They cross the city of ruins, and in the evening they reach a temple in which they pass the night. Inside the temple, in the center of a court, on top of a cubic rock on which rests a large sphere made of black rock, they find a colossal statue. This winged figure of a woman is naked except for her veiled face. Below, the inscription reads: "Is there no man who will draw my veil and look upon my face, for it is very fair? Unto him who draws my veil shall I be, and I will give him peace, and sweet children of knowledge and good works." And a voice cried, "Though all those who seek after thee desire thee, behold! Virgin are thou, and Virgin thou shalt be till Time be done. There is no man born of woman who may draw thy veil and live. By Death only can thy veil be drawn, O Truth!" These words recall the goddess of Sais[107] who, as an early Great Goddess, also held the keys to the netherworld, thus encompassing both aspects, life and death.

Here, at the beginning of the great adventure which Kallikrates could not master, we see Holly and Leo confronted with the Truth, with an image and symbol that is to prepare them to descend to the fire of life. In the sacred, enclosed court of the temple, upon a cube and sphere, stands a nude, winged figure. In the first place it is the naked truth of the body, human nature as such. However, it is not only the body but, as evidenced by the wings, also the soul. No longer does the sphinx rule here, for she has shed the animal body. Human reality points beyond itself to a spiritual realm: the Anima is an angel, a messenger from the air who barely touches the earth and who is always ready to fly to other spheres.

We may also view the dark sphere as the earth's and the figure as *Anima mundi* or "soul of the earth." Visible only in her naked body, as matter, the figure is veiled in terms of her deeper meaning. Only at death does she unveil her face, only when she carries the human being across into a world of spirit and meaning in which she participates.

The dark sphere, however, is also the great roundness, the encompassing whole made visible, the Self from its dark side resting upon the cubic rock symbolizing its realization in the world. The winged figure addressing the human being is simultaneously goddess and soul, the truth of the world and the truth of this individual human being, a mediator between the reality of the earth and the realm of the spirit. Here in the inner sanctum of the ancient temple, in the city of the heart, stands an effigy that points beyond time, beyond what has been achieved. For an instant the Anima's meaning becomes transparent. She is the inner truth, the soul's immediate reality; as mediator she shows the way to the gods, to the primordial images, and to meaning. Sister of the paradisiacal serpent, She would like to seduce the man, that he may not only know good and evil but also recognize the truth of what he himself is in terms of good and evil. Yet the price and condition of recognizing the whole truth—not only the physical reality but also meaningfulness—is, as in the Garden of Eden, death.

"She-who-is-to-be-obeyed" is the live truth as a man experiences it in the heart's mandala. She is the changing play of his contradictory, subjective emotions which may act as compulsions and among which he often gets lost. He feels seduced, fascinated, repelled by his own abysmal potentials for irrationality and yearning. Whereas in his earlier experience the man was but the passive victim of his condition, however, he now can see what is being played and can value what happens to him. What has been transmitted from the past, religion and philosophy, gains in meaningfulness, though Holly does not know what to believe. Thoughts and emotions resemble drifting clouds which keep changing and convey somewhat deceptive meanings. Good and evil become relative. Real is the external environment by which one feels unavoidably trapped, as by Kor's rocky walls. Equally real are the drives which originate in the Anima and which represent a changing, iridescent, internal, instantaneous truth, in contrast to external reality.

Whereas She is the truth as a man finds it in Kor, in his heart, She is not yet the transcendent truth as it appears in the veiled/unveiled temple figure. Dominated by subjective wishes and greed for power, She wants to gain possession, no matter at whose expense. She becomes like a tornado which eliminates every obstacle in her path.

Yet also in Ayesha signs appear which point to a higher truth. "Like Venus from the waves, like Galatea from the stone, like a blessed spirit from the grave," so she too steps out from her dark cloak, and her presence is accompanied by fragrance and the silver bells of her laughter. During the celebration of the epiphany, everyday reality and matter are changed into divine presence.

The concreteness of spiritual presence, the truth to be unveiled already exist in the form of a presentiment. The journey to its realization leads through death. Omens of death have become numerous. In a vision, Holly has seen the death of the young couple; the spirit of Job's deceased father has appeared to him to announce his early death. Most of all, Ayesha has carried evil forebodings since she murdered Ustane.

Transitus

The next morning they start out before dawn and reach the crater of the volcano which towers before them as a steep wall of rock. Here they leave behind all the servants. Only Job begs to be allowed to proceed with them. Ayesha consents and has him carry a large plank. They come to a fissure in the rocks, a natural cave through which they reach an abyss inside.

This path was not cut by human hands into the volcano's ancient rocks. It was made by nature itself, either by the earth's convulsions or lightning blasts. Eruptions either of the innermost fiery nature or of cosmic energies have been at work. The heroes enter this very old rock formation—namely, the deepest foundation of being—following a path formed by natural forces. This path is neither found nor traveled without distress, as the soul's depth is approached only through massive upheavals.

A rocky ledge, stretching across the abyss to the crater's middle, quivers in the gathering storm. The travelers must cross this rocky bridge that juts out into what appears to be a void. They seem to be hanging between sky and earth in the midst of a dark, raging storm which whirls clouds and vapors around them. A sudden gust of wind carries Ayesha's dark coat into the void. Without her dark cover, the white figure seems to be "a ghost riding upon the storm towards the depths." Reaching the ledge's beginning, they cling to the trembling rock in complete darkness. Here they must wait until a ray of the setting sun breaks through a crack in the opposite rocky wall; in this narrow light-shaft, they will be able to see the entry into the inner crater. On the crater's edge rests a flat stone, balancing like a coin precariously placed on the edge of a water glass. They lay the plank, which Job has been carrying, across to this stone. Crossing over this wavering bridge, they reach the inner crater. Job, the last one to dare to cross, slips. Holly's grip keeps him from disappearing into the depths.

This dreadful crossing leads them towards still greater depths, while storms and clouds rage around them. The experience resembles that of Goethe's Faust when he descends to the "mothers." The heroes are caught in storms of the spirit, and no one knows whether this path will lead to death or rebirth. This precarious passage across the protruding ledge between sky and earth powerfully expresses the great risks one faces when entering total insecurity, the powers of the unconscious. There can be no simple return.

Here, in the midst of the raging storm, the Anima reveals herself as spirit. Similar to a light, she is the only one who knows about the path. Only She possesses the self-assurance that knows when to wait or to act, in order to reach the goal known only to her. She only knows that there will be an instant when the path becomes visible, when a light ray will fall, like a cutting sword, into the darkness and across the abyss: a moment of intuitive insight. When facing such an abyss that separates without and within, great care and all one's masculine courage are required to risk the transitus (the passing) and the complete renunciation of the external world. When on our internal journey we meet seemingly insurmountable difficulties, when reason fails, then we are entirely dependent on the light from within, on the advice, warnings, and explanations in our dreams. The Anima who previously seemed to be sheer seduction can then prove herself as a helpful light.

The crossing is possible only because Job carries the plank the way Simon carried the cross, or Attis the fir. He is the human aspect who takes upon himself the cross and death. When a hero seeks a new path, the human ego's load becomes heavy. Yet this load, this apparently impossible situation, eventually bridges the abyss, so that the inner center, the life-secret, is reached. The insoluble problem becomes the bridge between seeming opposites.

The balancing stone hovers on the crater's edge in a fashion that seems to contradict its weight. Haggard comments that it may be a glacial stone which is dancing on the narrow crest. This stone upon which they land is a place of contradictions where opposites paradoxically touch each other.

In his book *Shamanism*, Mircea Eliade describes how the above-mentioned situation belongs to "the complex of the difficult transition": the near-invisible entrance into the rocks, the narrow passage, the dangerous, nearly impossible crossing of the abyss on a path "tread only by spirits and by the dead." He adds, however, that a few living individuals dare to make this transition: the shaman during an ecstasy, the hero through his force and courage, or the initiate through ritual dying and rebirth, or the old wise man.[108] Eliade quotes Coomaraswamy as saying that this paradoxical crossing can be accomplished only when one transcends an apparent dichotomy. The shaman who overcomes this difficulty proves he is a spirit and no longer an ordinary human being. He strives to reestablish the original condition where human and superhuman levels were not as yet separated, the original wholeness of the cosmos.[109] Eliade also describes the journey into hell, in contrast to the ascent to heaven. Descent to the netherworld, far more difficult, has rarely been described. Potanin pictures it as a long voyage south across a mountain range to the iron mountain which touches the sky and which the shaman climbs. On its other side he finds the entrance to the netherworld, the chimney of the earth, as smoke leaving from a man's abode. Across a bridge thin as a hair, passing skeletons and scenes from hell, he reaches Erlik Khan, the master of the underworld.[110]

The heroes travel the age-old, archetypal path which leads to the dead, to the ancestors, and to the gods. At this destination Leo is to unite himself with Ayesha, the spirit with the soul. The arduous path corresponds to the task's difficulty. Transition into the new condition demands a suspended balance between opposites, a balance jeopardized by Job who, through his fear, endangers the others. Holly's strength and skill save him. Job imperils the enterprise because of his rigidity and fear of anything unfamiliar; an overly narrow, Protestant, conventional attitude endangers Haggard. For a narrow-minded human being whose ego is chained to the everyday world, such a path is impassable. He requires the intervention of the transpersonal, archetypal figure, the hero or the wise man.

The travelers now descend into the crater and reach a rock hall where Noot, the wise old man, teacher of the Anima, died as a hermit two thousand years before. One of his teeth remains. This white tooth that has lasted throughout time is like the seed of Yang in the Yin of the Chinese cosmology, the seed of light in the darkness. Noot, the genuine wise-old-man, stands behind the Anima. With his intelligence, Holly represents only a small part of humanity's wisdom which is personified in Noot.

The Anima has received her knowledge from the archetype of the wise old man. Through him comes her power. He showed her the path to life's secret but he also warned her, just as God warned Eve in paradise about the fruits of knowledge. Ayesha, however, would not be Eve's daughter were she content with the knowledge. She must test it for herself. As the old man's daughter she turns his formidable knowledge into a dangerous, god-forbidden action. The renewal of life by the Anima does not stop at the head, at the accumulation of knowledge. It encompasses the entire human being, even his unconscious functions that are not subject to his will. If a man, urged by the Anima, tries to translate his thoughts into action, they become concrete and real. If he feels responsible for his thoughts, he becomes careful. If he acts with a conscious sense of responsibility, he can become wise.

Noot is dead, and She has usurped his secret. She owns "forces that act like electricity." Because these are a part of life's hidden fire, she becomes dangerous like sudden powerful flashes of lightning, impulsively driving a man to act before he is able to reflect. Whenever the Anima within him is touched, she reacts unreflectively and is therefore very convincing to him. He is in constant danger of being carried along by her moods and inhumanity. Only through great effort can he free himself of this Anima-possession, and only then is he capable of separating himself from his "compelling emotions" and from the so-called "power of the instincts."

Haggard relates that, during her two thousand years of exile, She was busy exploring the forces of nature. Though the goddess was no longer to be found in heaven nor in the temple, she could still be met in nature.

In Noot's hermit cave, She relates once more the tale of Kallikrates' death, of her guilt, and of her despair. Leo's love must become her door to redemption. She asks his forgiveness, and he forgives her to the extent that it is in his power. For the first time he is not only fascinated but also filled with love. Because he loves her, she is ready to submit herself to him. She bends her knee before him and kisses him to prove her womanly love. After this she forswears all evil and ambition, promising herself to Leo for all time to come. Her bridal gift is to be the "starry crown of her beauty," eternal life, unlimited wisdom, and boundless wealth. The mighty ones of the earth will bow before him, the beautiful women will be blinded by his looks, and the wise will seem small in comparison to him. He will lead others according to his will. Like the sphinx he is to reign over them for all time, and they will ask him to reveal the riddle of his greatness, yet he will respond with silence. With these offerings, She places the world at his feet; like a god he is to hold good and evil in his hands. She thus submits herself to him, to her master, the beloved of Ra, the master of all.

The instant Leo loves her, she becomes humble and subjects herself to him. She wishes to transfer her godly attributes to him, exalting him beyond any human measure and making him the worthy companion of the mistress of the cosmos. She promises him no less than deification. Becoming one with god is the aim of all mysteries and of all mysticism. Yet purification, sacrifice, and conscious subordination of the ego to the godhead must always precede this process. Ayesha, the consecrating priestess, however, feels superior to Isis. Since she entered the fire of life and united with it as with a god, she no longer feels responsible to anyone nor bound by any law. Only where she both loves and is loved in return can she give herself, offering to her beloved the exhilarating gifts of superhuman power, wisdom, and beauty. She intends to infuse him with her wishes and goals, thus turning him into an extension of herself. Her bridal gift is an inflation of cosmic proportions; it is the gift of her own godliness which, if misused, can lead to a boundless intoxication with power.

This scene has yet another aspect. In the last analysis She herself is the Great Goddess, and she wants Leo to become like her. Leo would have to allow himself to be reformed and deified in the fire of life so that all the earthliness would burn out of him. Leo and She are the divine couple, be it called Sol and Luna, Helios and Selene, or Isis and Osiris. Luna, who otherwise submits herself to no one, yields to the stronger light of Sol. Carrying within her all the life of nature and of the unconscious, she brings it to her beloved son.[111] Helios and Horus (both also sun symbols) are consciousness quietly hovering over the earth.

However, inasmuch as Leo is a human being and insofar as these ancient images of the god's holy wedding awaken within the human being's soul, there is not only the opportunity for renewal of life and consciousness but also the danger of hubris, of unbounded pride. A reflection of the superhuman figures falls upon the human being who experiences such events. It elevates and transports him. Thus everything depends on his not allowing himself to be blinded or inflated by these powerfully meaningful images. If he is cognizant of his shadow-aspects, they can be a healthy counterweight against the enthusiasm that flows from these images. He must not forget his social position and his daily professional duties. On the contrary, he must pursue them with increased seriousness, fulfill them with added concentration, and devote himself with additional efforts to the care of his family. The inner experiences may entice the human being away from reality. Instead, they should serve to make him into a whole person, who devotes himself more fully than before and with his entire soul to his daily tasks. The internal wedding aims for the inner reconciliation of opposites, for the amalgamation of spirit and soul, for the connection of thinking and feeling, of rationality and irrationality. The powerful experiences must render the human being more, and not less, conscious, more fit for the fulfillment of his internal as well as external tasks.

In order to complete the marriage of Sun and Moon, the group takes the lamps and descends a stone stairway into the crater's depths to the fire of life, with Ayesha, light as a mountain goat, leading the way. The travelers descend the way Faust descended to the mothers. As he was guided by Mephistopheles, by the curiosity of eternally dissatisfied reason, so Leo is guided by Ayesha, the desire for heightened life. Mephisto and Ayesha are the two aspects of Mercury, of that spirit hidden in matter and in the soul who longs for consciousness.[112] Crawling on the crater's floor, Holly, Leo, and Job reach an immense cave where, in absolute silence, like lost souls in hell, they continue to follow the white, ghostlike figure of Ayesha. Through another passage they enter a smaller cave which ends in a third passage. A dim glow emanates from within.

"It is well," She says, "to prepare to enter the very womb of the Earth, wherein she does conceive the Life that ye see brought forth in man and beast—aye, in every tree and flower."

The caves through which they walk are graves. The path leads into the "untrod, not to be treaded." Mother Earth is also Mother Death: Cybele carries Attis, her son, in the form of a fir into a cave, there to mourn him.[113] Here everything that has been reaches its end, yet from the womb of Mother Death grows ever-new life. A cave-like stable became the place of birth in Bethlehem,[114] and in Eleusis the mysteries of birth occurred in the darkness of a cave.[115]

Finally they arrive in the third cave, illuminated by a golden light. Threefold is the dark Hekate of the netherworld, three are the goddesses of destiny, mothers of what becomes and of what passes away. This threesome from the netherworld is mentioned by Mephistopheles advising Faust—"a glowing tripod will tell you that you are on the deepest, the very deepest ground." The small group has reached the place of the inferior threesome which stands over against the Trinity, the place of the earth's creative principle. Then with gnashing, thundering noise—so horrendous that everyone trembles and Job falls on his knees—there comes from the cave's distant end a dreadful, flaming fire-pillar, multicolored like the rainbow and bright like lightning. The pillar slowly turns about itself, and finally the awesome noise leaves behind only the golden light.

"Draw near," Ayesha calls to them. "Behold the very fountain and heart of life, the bright spirit of the earth without which it cannot live. Draw near and wash yourself in the living flames and take their virtue upon your poor bodies."

They follow her to the end of the cave, where the great pulse beats and where the flame dances. They are filled with such wild and wonderful intoxication, with such a great intensity of life, that whatever peak experiences they had had before seem flat in comparison. They laugh; they feel inspired. Holly speaks in verses of Shakespearian beauty, with ideas surging in him, and his spirit feels free, able to ascend to the very heights of its original potentials.

The flames come closer and closer as if all the sky's wheels of thunder were rolling behind the horses of lightning. The view is so overwhelming that all but She sink to the ground and bury their faces in the sand.

"Now, Kallikrates," She says, "when the great flame comes again you must bathe in it. Throw aside your garments, for it will burn them though thee it will not hurt. Thou must stand in the fire while thy senses endure, and when it embraces thee, suck the fire into thy very heart and let it leap and play around thy every part so that thou lose no moiety of its virtue. Hearest thou me, Kallikrates?"

"I hear thee, Ayesha," answers Leo, "but of a truth—I'm not a coward—I doubt me of that raging flame. How do I know that it will not utterly destroy me, so I will lose myself and lose thee also? Nevertheless I will do it."

Ayesha reflects for an instant, then she says, "It is no surprise that you hesitate; but tell me, will you also enter the flame if you see me unharmed inside it?"

"Yes," he answers, "I will enter, even if it slays me. I have said that I will enter now."

"See now, I will for the second time bathe me in this living bath. Fain would I add to my beauty and my length of days if that be possible. If it be not possible, at least it cannot harm me."

Yet She has a deeper reason for this decision. She would like to cleanse herself of the passion and hatred that is burned into her soul. Thus it is as if "Kallikrates" or Leo is to ready himself for death; for from the seed of this moment will spring forth the fruit of what he will be for endless time.

Now the rotating pillar of fire comes again, from far, far away. She drops her garments and stands there the way Eve stood before Adam. "Oh, my beloved," she murmurs, "will you ever know how much I loved you?"

With that she places herself in the column's path. The fire approaches slowly and surrounds her with its flames. The fire runs up her figure, and she lifts it like water and pours it over herself. She draws it in with her lungs. It plays like golden threads in her hair and shines from her eyes which are still brighter than the pillar. Suddenly there is a change. The smile disappears; the face becomes pointed; she turns old and shrivels. As she touches her hair, it falls to the ground. Now she looks like a poorly preserved, unspeakable old mummy with thousands of wrinkles.

She still asks, "How can the principle of life change?" and dying, she says, "Kallikrates, do not forget me, have pity on my shame—I shall come again and shall once more be beautiful."

Job falls down dead from the frightful shock. Leo and Holly, after having been dazed for a long time, shaken and exhausted, begin their way back. Leo's golden curls have turned gray. While they are waiting on the balancing stone for the sun ray which is to illuminate their passage to the external crater, a gust of wind brings back Ayesha's lost coat and covers Leo with it. Since the plank is gone, they must now jump across the abyss. As the last one crosses, the balancing boulder crashes into the internal crater and forever closes off the path into the depths.

Eventually, they find Billali who guides them through the swamps. After many more adventures they return to their college in Cambridge.

The "pillar of fire" has such horrendous, frightful power that the heroes throw themselves to the ground. To explore its various aspects, we must first deal with the meaning of ordinary fire. Fire burns, destroys, and shines. In the hearth it warms and glows, and when used for cooking, it modifies foods. Fire is one of the foundations of human culture; its taming is an important but dangerous step which brings human beings closer to the gods. In Ustane's land we encountered hearth fire. From the viewpoint of psychological experience, this was the place of burning passions, of love, which all too easily can turn into burning hatred. When passion mounts to the head, "the brain is burned," consciousness is extinguished. This is the libido, the instinctual energy hidden within the body, which can either express itself in blind rage or transmute itself into purposeful will, thereby creating culture.

Yet the fire of life is more supernatural than natural. It lights up like lightning and roars like thunder. It burns dead matter, yet heightens life. The creative spirit inside earth's womb, it creates all life. It is both a cosmic fire and a spiritual essence with a hidden, creative mystery. Dwelling in the continually rotating motion at the center of the earth, at the innermost place, it becomes the fountain of inexhaustible energies.

If we look for parallels of this magic fire, we encounter them in Heraclitus and Simon Magus. For Heraclitus "fire metamorphoses itself into the All, and the All metamorphoses itself back into fire, just as gold changes itself into coins and coins change into gold." "This world, the same for everyone, was created by neither god nor human being, but it was, is, and will be forever a live fire which periodically lights up."[116] This same periodicity we see in the Indian myths of creation, where the world alternatively becomes visible and then vanishes, shaped by Shiva the destroyer and creator who dances in the circle of fire. Heraclitus states, "fire is want and satiety. It is desire, greed and fulfillment, it is glowing spirit which out of its want and desire creates the images of its greed as a reality." Simon Magus says, "And now the created cosmos came forth from the uncreated fire."[117] The presence of God in the human being is fiery fulfillment; being seized with spirit manifests itself by a flame upon the head.

But also the devil deals with this power, tormenting souls in the fire of hell. In the book of Enoch, Enoch views God's house made of crystal and surrounded by fire; yet behind the mountains, where sky and earth end, "I saw an abyss with high pillars of fire, and I saw the pillars of fire fall down again. Behind this abyss I saw a place that had no heavenly vault over it, nor earthly ground below it; it was an evil, dreadful place. There I saw seven stars, like large, burning mountains. . . . Then Uriel spoke to me and said, 'Here remain the angels who became involved with women, and also their spirits which take on many forms and defile the human beings.[118] Here the fire is the place of punishment, the place of the fallen angels and of the unclean demons. The fallen sons of God burn in their own greed.'"

Fire, therefore, is the common element, belonging to the Trinity as the highest good, as well as to the devil as the epitome of evil; therefore, fire is a unifying symbol. It is the luminous form of divine persons as well as of the abyss; common to all of these is dynamic power, loveliness, energy, and captivating force. Impure greed devours the soul in hell for all eternity, and the purifying pain of remorse removes earthly remnants in purgatory. In the uppermost circle of purgatory, Dante must cross a circle of fire, so that his senses will be opened up for the song of the blessed in paradise.[119] After this crossing no more is said of fire in the *Divine Comedy*. Instead there is only talk about light. Under Beatrice's guidance, all passion and remorse have changed to longing and fulfillment, vision and knowledge.

The paradoxical aspects of these graded steps are well recognized in alchemy. Fire is simultaneously infernal and divine; "it is the secret fire of hell, the miracle of the world, the aggregate of the forces from above within the inferior."[120] "God has created this fire within the earth like the purgatory fire in hell. In this fire God himself glows in divine love."[121] "This Fire is the Holy Spirit and unites Father and Son."[122] The alchemical fire is identical with Mercury, for it is an "elementary fire," invisible, secretly acting, divine, and the universal and sparkling fire of the natural light that carries within itself the heavenly spirit.[123] Concerning the fiery center of the earth, Jung quotes from alchemy: "Indeed all things come from this source, and nothing in the whole world is born if not by this source."[124]

Since Leo sees the fire of life in the shape of a column or pillar, we must investigate the meaning of this shape. In *The Faith of Ancient Egypt* Kees writes:

> Amongst the monuments best known for their symbolic importance in Egyptian culture there are three of particular importance: (1) the Obelisk in Heliopolis, (2) the Junu-pillar in Anan, and (3) the pillar of Djed in Busiris. At one time these monuments were independent deities, and because the idea that the origin of the world is linked to the obelisk in Heliopolis, such locations were called by the Egyptians "the place of the first time." Yet a pillar could also signify the bearer of the world, or the center of the world-edifice. In the Egyptian language, pillar also means support or poise.[125]

So it follows that the word *Djed* means "durable." The image of the Djed-pillar is a popular, protective symbol and a sign for enduring good-luck, which one wishes, along with life and power, to the divine king.[126] Later, the Djed-pillar was identified with Osiris and interpreted as his backbone.[127] In the region of Memphis it was taken over as symbol by the god Ptah, while in other places it symbolized the god Seth.[128]

We can consider the pillars, which Kees describes, ancient local gods endowed with supreme power—as original expressions of the godhead in his phallic or creative aspect. At a cultural level where natural and spiritual fertility are not yet separated, the pillar is symbolically imbued with divine power.

In his book *Shamanism,* Mircea Eliade carefully pursued the function of the *post* and of the *column* in the thinking of the earliest shepherds and hunters. Important evidence links them with the *tree* and suggests they symbolize the center of the cosmos. He notes that the cosmos is commonly viewed as three levels linked by a central axis. This world-axis was pictured concretely as a pillar holding up the hut, or as a post or tree standing alone, and was called "the pillar of the world." The post indicating the world's center is simultaneously the door into other worlds, the place where the world of ghosts touches upon this concrete world. Prayers are offered and sacrifices performed at the pillar's foot.

The Ostyaks from Tsingala call their pillars "human being" or "father" and offer them bloody sacrifices.

As the pillar or post is the middle of the hut, so is it also the center of the cosmos. For this reason the Mongols designated the polar star as the "golden pillar." The Kirgises call it the "iron pillar" and the Teleutes "sun-pillar." It is the cosmic axis around which the sky turns.[129]

The world-tree, too, links the three regions. The Vasyuagan-Ostyaks believe that its branches touch the heavens and its roots reach into hell. Other tribes speak of three cosmic trees: the first is in heaven, and human souls sit on its branches like birds, waiting to be born as children on earth; another tree is on earth; and a third one in hell. Speaking of the world-tree, Eliade states,

> The symbolism of the world-tree encompasses different religious conceptions. On the one hand, it portrays the universe in a process of continual renewal. It is the inexhaustible spring of cosmic life, and the true place of the saints. On the other hand, the tree symbolizes the sky and the planetary spheres. . . . In many old traditional beliefs the world-tree is linked with the ideas concerning creation, fertility, initiation and immortality. Enriched by numerous additional mythologic symbols (Woman, Spring, Milk, Animals, Fruits), the World-Tree appears as source of all life and as master of destiny.[130]

In his book *The Great Mother,* Erich Neumann asserts that *pillar* and *fire* were subsumed in the matriarchal layer of the mother-goddess.[131] Pillar and midpoint around which everything turns is the world-mother, from whom all life is born and to whom all created things return in death. In her womb is hidden the fire, the dynamic forces of life. In all times this fire was experienced both as devouring and destructive, and as the fire of transformation.[132] The Great Goddess is one with the tree of life which is rooted in the earth and from which the sun is born. She is the cosmic world and sky-tree, the light-tree of the night sky, the soul-tree of resurrection, on which every creature who dies enters the eternity of the great sphere in the form of a star.[133]

According to Hegemonius, the moon ferries the souls of the dead to the *Columna Gloriae* (The Column of Glory) which is called *vir perfectus* (perfect man). This man is the pillar of the light, for the pillar is filled with pure souls and is the source of the souls' salvation.[134]

In Haggard's book we find that rotation around itself is added to the flaming and flowing movements of the pillar of fire. An expression of the collection of all energies, desires, and impulses flowing from one creative will, this tightly fashioned column rotates around an invisible center.

In nature, time is seen as circular motion, as eternal return,[135] as unchangeable, rhythmic alternation of becoming and fading. It is the unperturbed course of nature, where a new beginning follows upon each end. Circular motion aims at drawing the human being back into his rhythmic course of natural events.

From all this evidence it becomes clear that the pillar of fire is a primary symbol arising at a deep transpersonal level. It is mother and father, creative and destructive; like the great, all-encompassing goddess, it is the source of birth into the world, as well as the source for birth as a star in the sky—the higher, divine rebirth.

Let us now try to interpret the complex and paradoxical facts concerning Haggard's pillar of fire. "She," the Anima in Kor, the realm of the dead, represents the immortal aspect of the sacrificed emotions. In the guise of his soul, she leads the hero into his own depths and confronts him, not with the moral law, but with the fire of life. The latter is the innermost, destiny-shaping, fiery will of life which, from the very depth of nature, presses for ever new expressions. The pillar of fire manifests a frightful and wonderful god who glows in anger and love, a spirit who seizes us, gives us direction, and destroys old structures. In the end, it burns everything in order to let emerge anew the spiritual being, the essence. The pillar of fire is the time before time; it is the eternity of becoming and passing away; it is—like Shiva—creator and destroyer. This pillar stands for the *Anthropos* who carries within itself the souls of all the ancestors, as well as for the unconscious that releases all the new potentials. The fire of life, no ordinary fire dependent on matter, is rather a pure flame, a spiritual force, passionate manifestation, which goes along its path like "the thundering horses of lightning." The enthusiasm awakened by this flame finds expression in poetic inspiration and spiritual knowledge. For the human being this flame implies death and rebirth as well as the highest intensity of the creative instant.

Yet if one identifies too closely with it, it can bring hubris and unrestricted greed. Leo experiences the rotating pillar as an archaic experience of the world's center, where heaven, earth, and netherworld meet. This world and the world beyond, inside and outside, intersect at this point. The world's center is also the soul's. It is the kernel of the personality where nature and spirit flow together, where god and human being become one. Consciousness is meant to penetrate to this center where the godhead becomes present. It is supposed to bathe in this spring from which flows all life, and it is intended to burn in the spiritual fire, to become one with the cosmos's will to life. Then it becomes wise through the elucidation of the unconscious and is seized by the kind of life in which experience and feeling, knowledge and action become one.

The Death in the Fire

Leo and Holly have reached their goal. The ancestral mother (Amenartas) has sent the son to avenge her on her rival (She), to bathe in the fire of life, and to place himself on the throne of the Pharaohs. Yet this revenge has turned into fascination by the ancestral mother's rival, into love for the Anima. Since She, as the internal goddess, guards the creative forces of nature and encompasses the entire range of emotions, She represents an experience that reaches far beyond one's individual life. As *anima mundi* she symbolizes transpersonal life that ruptures the limits of personal relationships.

She urges Leo to step into the fire to unite with the godhead, just as the Pharaoh unites with the divine Ka, with the transpersonal creative spirit who grants fertility. He is to become a "god-man," equal to the godlike Anima and capable of withstanding her lightning-like tension. Yet, should he, like the Anima, become a victim of this fire spewing out of the unconscious, there arises the danger of his feeling so superior that he would scorn all human considerations and become enthralled with suprahuman possibilities. If on account of this increased willfulness he no longer respects people, he becomes a totalitarian representative of the unconscious's passions. This great danger still threatens even well-meaning persons when they get in touch with archetypal images and the hidden fire-quality of their passions. The only way to protect oneself against such a danger is to enter into dialogue with the internal powers, seeking a new midpoint between the views of the conscious and the unconscious, between conformist morality and the life-impulses originating in the depths. Once one reaches the realm of the ancient gods, one must repeatedly keep in mind one's human limitations, one's weaknesses and defects, as well as the social situation in which one lives and which must not be destroyed. We must bring sacrifices to the inner gods, we must assist them within our power, but we cannot permit ourselves to identify with them or, like She did, to disregard external rights and laws.

Though Leo is drawn to enter the fire of life, an all-too-justified doubt causes him to hesitate. He fears burning up and losing himself as well as his beloved. Then Ayesha shows him: She bathes in the fire as if it were water, she breathes it as if it were the life-giving air. As a consequence she dies, but first she becomes an ancient mummy, a shriveled-up, pitiful remnant of herself. She turns into what she would have become, after two thousand years, had she not once before bathed in the fire of life and attained infinite life. Dying, she speaks to Leo: "Do not forget me; have pity on my shame. I shall come again and shall once more be beautiful."

From the most beautiful, Ayesha becomes the ugliest. She is transformed from intense life to death and dust, from tangible, immediate reality to a vanishing ghost. The pendulum of nature of which she possesses the secret has swung to the other side. Nature is not only life and beauty, but just as much decay, decomposition, horror and death. It is for this reason that Leo, in a later novel, must recognize She in the guise of a death-mask. Kissing her, he must accept her reverse side. He can regain her blossoming life only if he accepts her antithetical nature.

Is She's ending in the fire a misfortune? Probably yes, inasmuch as the union (coniunctio) has been hindered and inasmuch as the development of the Self has been delayed for an indeterminate amount of time. There is no wedding; no child is born;[136] the new time will not come.

This event recalls a man's dream, in which the Anima went up in smoke after an explosion. The only thing left, a piece of silver ore, represented the end of an Anima projection and the return to his previous state. The woman upon whom the man had projected the

Anima had, in his eyes, prematurely reverted into an ordinary human being. What remained was but the projected feeling in a material form that could not be integrated by him.

Haggard himself said of *She:*

> It represents an attempt to show the effect of immortality on the inadequately cleansed, mortal human being. . . . The horrible end of She is also a type of parable; for what is science, knowledge, or the awareness of power and wisdom in the face of the Almighty? They all suffer the fate She suffered in her solitude; scorned and ridiculed they disintegrate and reveal what they truly are. At least, this is what I tried to communicate.[137]

She is a parable of the human being who becomes presumptuous. When consciousness behaves rationally and totally identifies with the powers of light, then the Anima allies herself with the godhead of the unconscious, with the creative fire, in order to misuse the soul's powers for her own egotistic purposes. She is filled, carried, and enhanced by the fire in which she consumes herself. She experiences a superabundance of passions which the man's feminine eros-aspect, his human relatedness, and eventually even his body cannot endure. Such an Anima becomes a man's downfall. She turns him into an inhuman super-being, since the unsolved Anima-problem stirs his ambition, driving him ever deeper into the excesses of his one-sided consciousness.

But *She* is more than an allegory. Ayesha is an ever-present reality which longs to be accepted, understood, and freed from her inhuman condition. In this regard She is different from Antinea, who acts only as a vengeful, ruthless vamp and drags the men into death. Benoit's Antinea is the kind of unconscious Anima of whom Jung says: "She is an autocratic being without genuine relationships. She seeks nothing but total possession of the individual, whereby a man becomes effeminate in odd and unfavorable ways. This shows itself in his moody and uncontrolled disposition which gradually spoils even his heretofore dependable and sensible functions, such as the intellect. . . ."[138]

The Anima is inclined to assume absolute power and to destroy man's judgments and morals, as long as the unconscious, feminine side is suppressed by consciousness. She is overly powerful and dangerous, probably because Haggard himself turned away from a relationship with a spiritual woman of Jess's type. Since he lacked a relationship with a woman who could mirror and exemplify for him the world of eros, the inner factor gained control of him. Since he renounced love, love (or the Anima) changed into power; but in the hermitage of the old Noot, Leo is moved by love for the first time. As a result, the Anima becomes humble and ready to subordinate herself. In *She and Allan,* a later novel by Haggard, She says: "You should have worshipped me like a shrine, but since you failed to do this, the waters of salvation cannot flow for you."

The Anima expects of the man that he recognize her as a divine power inside himself. Haggard, as a matter of fact, knows that She has something to do with his own soul. But how could he ever reconcile her primitive and overwhelming emotional reality with his English consciousness? How could he ever conceive of integrating this dreadful world of emotions, when She murders Leo's wife, whereas he himself holds his wife in such high esteem? How could he ever accept his Anima who, in no way resembling his Christian conception of the soul, is a heathen goddess and *anima mundi* that tries to seduce him into seeking tyrannical power? She is both the mirror and the reverse of his one-sided consciousness, of his gentleman-ideal, which forces him to suppress feelings and nature and to tyrannize his surroundings. Yet, what would have happened had he accepted the Anima such as she was? What moral and religious conflicts would have overcome him had the goddess managed to seduce him to feel that he was beyond human morality? An insoluble conflict persists between his consciousness and the Anima.

The Anima is consumed by her own intensity, since she cannot yet be accepted in the guise in which Haggard meets her. She loses her shape and becomes a ghost, namely, unconscious. For Leo, transformation in the fire and communion with the godhead do not take place. The hero cannot renew himself. He loses the golden curls and becomes old and gray. Perhaps one reason for the undertaking's failure is that the attempted union was not preceded by sufficient purification and developing insight. In the vision of Zosimos, for example, Zosimos himself, as well as a dragon, is dismembered. This symbolizes the required analytic clarification of the contents of consciousness as well as of the unconscious. "In the later periods of alchemy one finds the 'slaying of the lion' along with the 'slaying of the dragon,' at least in the image of cutting off the lion's paws."[139] Yet, in the beginning of the novel, the heroes were unable to dissect the lion and the crocodile on the river shore since—so it said—they were lacking the necessary tools. This means that they did not have the required prerequisites for a profound exploration of the unconscious. They stopped their self-examination at a safer and more superficial level, at that of the goose and the buck.

Thus the more primitive and powerful natural force manifests itself in its projection upon the Anima and renders her egotistical, power-hungry, greedy for possession, and vengeful. Contact with the fire would indeed have been dangerous to Leo's insufficiently purified nature. Haggard was justifiably afraid of his ancestors' passionate nature. Inasmuch as he was only partly successful in separating and identifying the contents of the unconscious, he was in danger of becoming a tool of a diabolically negative force, hidden in his body, which would be the reverse aspect of the godhead.

Nevertheless, the heroes brought back something from their long journey: the mummy's small foot and the Anima's dark coat. For Holly, for the reality-function, the small foot indicates a new, spiritualized vantage point. The coat is a symbol of being in the service of love to which Leo will consecrate himself henceforth. Reporting about the mysteries in Eleusis, Kerényi tells how the initiate was wrapped in the goddess's coat and was addressed with her name:

> The men also entered the form of the goddess and became identical with her. In Syracuse, in the shrine of Demeter and Persephone, the men also took the great oath, dressed themselves with the purple coat of the goddess and carried her burning torch. . . . In Pheneos there were the same mysteries as in Eleusis, and here the priests wore the mask of Demeter-Kidaria during the highest mystery. It was not a friendly face but rather a frightful, Medusa-like image.[140]

Thus some union with the Anima is accomplished nonetheless by means of She's dark coat. Leo is being consecrated to the goddess. The coat falls over him like a shadow and quells his youthful splendor. It brings him the presentiment that the Anima's shadow-aspect shades him too. At one time in his old age, Haggard said of himself that, like Ayesha, he was filled with changing moods. At times he tormented himself with guilt feelings. Yet he was never completely free from his service to the goddess and from his efforts to redeem her priestess. Many of his books focus upon the same theme. In one, a captive white woman must serve a crocodile-deity. In another book, an elegant English lady is abducted by priests whose idol is a wild hermit-elephant. The Anima remains a prisoner of the unredeemed instinctual power of the chthonic godhead.

In *She and Allan,* Haggard continues the dialogue with She and his debate with the unconscious. She tells Allan, who embodies the Englishman:

> Had you been someone else, I would have revealed secrets to you and explained the meaning of much that I told you in pictures and various fables. Two things, Allan, are expected of a person who visits a shrine, reverence and faith. Without these, the oracles remain silent and the holy waters will not flow. I, Ayesha, am a shrine, but you offered me no reverence before I forced it from you by means of a feminine ruse. You had no faith in me, wherefore the oracle does not speak to you, and the redeeming waters do not flow.[141]

It depends upon the attitudes of one's consciousness whether and how the unconscious releases its secrets. Though Allan shuts himself off, by means of his common sense and skepticism, from a deeper understanding of the irrational nature of the Anima, she nevertheless offers him counsel for the future. "Therefore the wise will seek to turn those with whom Fate mates them into friends, since otherwise soon they will be lost for aye. More, if they are wiser still, having made them friends, they will suffer them to find lovers where they will. Good maxims, are they not? Yet hard to follow. . . ."[142]

Later Continuations of She

In the novel *Ayesha,* written twenty years later as a sequel to *She,* the actions take place in Central Asia. Here the rivalry between Amenartas, now called Athene, and the rediscovered She continues. Athene is no longer Leo's wife but has turned exclusively into an embodiment of external might. Her husband is an Asian ruler gone mad who, haunted by distrust and jealousy, throws his enemies to the bloodhounds. Leo escapes from the insane ruler and takes refuge with a priestess who has her sanctuary on a nearby volcano. When he reaches her territory, a mummy on a pile of bones waits for him. Later on he must kiss this ghost-like being in order to awaken She to her former figure and beauty.

Her temple, hewn into the rocks, is at least three times larger than the largest cathedral, with equally enormous altars and halls. He is edified at the sight of the temple's Ankh-cross design, symbol of the life-giving Isis. The mighty halls are illuminated by tortuous columns of fire that arise from openings in the volcano. In the area of the altar, there is once again an image that anticipates the new inner condition which is to be attained: a mature, winged woman with a boy whom she consoles by promising him immortality. "All the love and all the tenderness have entered her picture, and it seems as if heaven was opening a path before her for her wings." Ayesha sits below this altar-picture with her priests and priestesses.

Now Leo is engaged to her. Yet the wedding cannot take place until Leo once more finds the fiery pillar and through it gains eternal life. Before the wedding She wants to punish Athene. As she takes off with her armies, Leo is ambushed. Ayesha and her troops, accompanied by storms and hail, lightning and thunder, overrun Athene's city and free her beloved. Leo refuses to wait any longer with the wedding, but new obstacles arise between him and his bride. Next to the corpse of Athene, who has taken poison during Ayesha's assault, She once again offers Leo power, success, and triumph over the entire world. Yet he does not want any power that is born of the murder. He wants only his bride's love, even if it should bring him death.

Ayesha senses that Leo is about to die, but she prophesies that death will no longer be able to separate them. She had previously spoken of love but had always remained unapproachable, like an icy mountain peak. Yet at this moment, a new transformation occurs in her: she becomes human. No longer is she the oracle of the shrine, no longer the Valkyrie of the battlefield. She is the happy bride. She would like to be nothing but woman. Up to this point she had not dared to yield to her longing, knowing well that Leo would be consumed by it. Yet now she wants to dare it, no matter what might result. Holly is to give the couple to each other. In his hands, Holly feels the powerful, intense stream of life and heavenly happiness flowing from She to Leo in rapid, burning waves, and he has a sense of bursting. In passionate devotion She embraces her groom and kisses his mouth. She then sings him a love song, which stops abruptly, because Leo staggers and falls down dead.

Grieving, She takes leave of her priests and priestesses. She forgives the dead Athene, praising her for having played her role with greatness. She turns herself over to the benevolent, heavenly mother, from whom all were born and who faithfully accepts all back again. No longer is She the being filled with sin and pride which she had been. She is no longer the "fallen star," but, like long ago, "the star which is victorious over the night." Her soul is again one with her beloved, as it was in the beginning. In the evening she has Leo's casket brought to the crater and kneels beside him near the abyss. Then a flame twists upwards as if it had wings, and in the early dawn Ayesha and the casket disappear. As it becomes light, Holly recognizes two glorified figures rising upwards.

New in this second volume are the multitude of tortuous columns of fire which have turned into sources of light for the sanctuary. Especially new is the image in the cathedral inside the rock, the winged mother-goddess with her son: Isis with the Horus-child. No longer is the Anima exclusively woman and beloved, nor is she simply the self-satisfied soul; she is a mother filled with love and tenderness, caring and unselfish. Leo's love changes his Anima from a sterile virgin and bellicose goddess into a loving, mature woman. Only now does she experience herself again in harmony with the great heavenly mother, Isis. The feminine principle, mother and daughter, is reintroduced beside god-father and god-son. She becomes aware that her involvement in earthly possessions and earthly power was an error, since both Leo and Ayesha are spiritual beings, spirit and soul, which, cleansed and changed by means of the flame, strive towards heaven. She fought her own other aspect, her will to power, her involvement in the world, by fighting Amenartas-Athene.

Shortly before his death, Haggard wrote *Wisdom's Daughter,* dealing with She's early life. Here, in a "prologue in heaven," the conflict between the two women is traced back to the strife between two goddesses. Isis is angry with humanity, because it has abandoned her altars in order to serve Aphrodite. Thus she orders her unborn daughter, Ayesha, to avenge her on earth and to depend only on her, the spiritual, heavenly mother. After this, Isis calls Aphrodite, who appears in her naked beauty and, laughing, alludes to the fact that she, too, is part of the great mother, Isis, and that life on earth would soon cease without her. Isis, however, seems to have forgotten this aspect of herself. She does not realize that her own increasing one-sidedness has brought forth Aphrodite, her antagonist. Enraged over the goddess of love, she leaves the field and thus delivers the unborn soul of Ayesha to her rival. Aphrodite brings her the consolation of love, with the lover in whose arms she is to forget the angry Great Goddess.

From birth on, the soul is weighed down by the striving of the two goddesses. The soul is forged by the split in the consciousness of the heavenly goddess, who has forgotten her own opposite side. Here Aphrodite takes on a role analogous to Satan. She is Lucifer's feminine aspect, the godhead's nature-side which makes creation possible. At first, She is the obedient instrument of the great mother. She grows up to be a priestess in search of wisdom. Then, however, she is overcome by love for Kallikrates, the beautiful young man. This interferes with her calling as priestess and awakens her calling as woman. Her love for Kallikrates first evokes the platonic love for the beautiful body, which widens itself to encompass the beautiful souls and eventually the eternal ideas.[143]

First, however, She gets involved in conflict and sin through her love. At the beginning of the Christian era, she stepped into the fire of life, in order to become one with that part of the spirit which, according to the Gnostics' teaching, had descended all the way down into matter. For the sake of the development of consciousness, the Christian orientation excluded this part of the spirit from salvation, viewing it as diabolical. Therefore, the Anima's ruthlessness grew larger and larger during the Christian era. Just as human consciousness identified itself with the Christian ideals, so our unconscious, natural side became one with the "lower deity." Like the Indian Shakti and Maya, She also weaves the texture of destiny. Now the time of this split-off, and therefore unrestrained, *anima mundi* seems to come to an end. She has taken whatever she desired, under the motto "where there's a will, there's a way!" Under the name and the cover of Christendom, she violently converted, conquered, and colonized. Her mounting desires consume herself, and entire nations under her banner burn up by their own greed. The world-creating *anima mundi* turns to ashes and dust. Yet, if an individual struggles for the redemption of the Anima, she doesn't have to burn up, but can transform herself in the flames. The picture in the temple, the mother-goddess with her son, anticipates the birth of a transformed consciousness and of a new era.

We have repeatedly shown that "She" recalls the myth of Isis and Osiris. The column of fire with which She weds almost as a groom[144] in *Wisdom's Daughter* largely corresponds in mythological terms to Seth, the fiery, passion-driven, twin brother of Osiris. Through his literary work, as well as through his own inner conflict, Haggard became connected with the unconscious, and these archetypes were revived—the myth of the hostile brothers, of the evening- and the morning-star as the antithetical sisters, of their joint union, and of the dying and resurrecting son or brother lover. The story of *She* is linked to what has been valid at all times, but has been lost during a relatively brief period of our modern consciousness. Haggard reshaped in a more individual form the old myths, thus completing the first part of his task. His novel *She* was a world-wide success, since it satisfied a vague longing for the lost goddess.

We, too, should find anew the lost myth, when we arrive at a boundary from which we look for a new path. Yet, just like Rider Haggard, we cannot simply take the myth in its existing form and translate it into our life. We must wrestle with the old gods, like Jacob with the angel, in order not to become "possessed" by them. Our life must become changed through the inner experience, and our being must be completed by means of the contents of the unconscious. Yet this must occur without our drowning in the myth or our over-identifying with these internal, divine figures. What Haggard accomplished in the play of his fantasy and in his literary work should be carried a step further: namely, to the point where the two spirits united in the holy marriage of death return from heaven to revitalize the body they left behind.[145] This turn of events is lacking in Haggard. He was capable of seeing the images, but remained unable to sufficiently understand them in terms of his own personal situation. He was not able to cope with the Anima-problem, with his emotions in everyday reality. As a consequence of this, we do not find a true solution of the problem even in his later works.

III. Summary of the Symbolism and of its Explanation

A pair of "Twin-Heroes" starts out to find the lost treasure: Leo, the sun-hero, beautiful as a Greek god, and Holly, the mercurial-saturnic satellite, capable of logical judgments, spiritual father and companion of the sun-child. Their servant Job is the narrow-minded human being with predominantly Old Testament views characteristic for a certain kind of rigid puritanism. Later on they are joined by a second shadow-figure, Mohamed, the Arabian steersman. We thus have a male quaternity, a preliminary male wholeness and self-sufficiency which, however, requires completion by means of the feminine principle that is suppressed by consciousness.

This feminine principle announces itself by a message in the trunk which Leo inherits from his ancestors, especially from his "primeval mother." Within a black cover, the trunk contains a silver-trunk with five sphinxes. They are the feminine symbol of wholeness, composed of a quaternity of silver and a fifth essential thing, a *quinta essentia,* in the middle. The sphinx, guardian of the tomb of the lost feminine side, symbolizes the riddle of life, which may confront us from within or from without, as a danger or challenge. She is the feminine-natural soul, still heavily contaminated by animal instinct, which must be redeemed from the unconscious. The inscription on the fragment of an amphora summons the heroes to a journey into the dark continent, where Leo is to find the white queen. Here he is to discover her secret, the pillar of fire, to take vengeance upon her, and to become Pharaoh himself.

Crossing the sea, Leo and Holly are surprised by a storm just when they approach the rock—described in the trunk—from which the path leads into the interior. In his imagination, Haggard envisions in the stormy sea the suffering, great, original mother whose suffering diminishes only when Leo, the young god, sleeping in the small boat, approaches the coast. In their "night sea-journey," the heroes transcend the abyss which separated them, the representatives of the collective consciousness, from the deep layers of the collective unconscious. The moon crescent appears before them as a vision of the bride who prepares herself for the *hierosgamos,* the sacred wedding. Dawn's pink colors bring forth a radiant new day as promise of a new "world-day" that is about to be born. In the light of the new day, they discover the expected sign, the stony head of the Ethiopian, which looks so frightful that Job compares it with the devil. The initial encounter with the inner, hidden continent is thus an encounter with evil. The latter is an inner reality, repressed by consciousness, and therefore projected upon the blacks. The heroes then find a canal and tie their boat to a blossoming magnolia, symbol of the feelings that were also repressed by narrow, puritanical morality.

The animals they kill, unicorn-goose and buck, represent spirit and soul which had been projected upon nature as transient, instinctual energies. The killed lioness is the instinctual reality which was first experienced in relation with the mother, a relationship which is now to be transferred to the royal bride. Lion and the crocodile, which the heroes cannot kill as they lack the necessary tools, represent the original antitheses of the unconscious, the "yes" and "no" to life. Simultaneously, they are symbols for those instinctual layers which are farthest from consciousness and harder to recognize. Thus the heroes cannot accept them as expressions of their own unconscious.

The travelers are led into the interior by Billali, an old man with natural wisdom, and by his tribe of leopard-people who live in caves within the crater of an extinct volcano. A black woman, Ustane, chooses Leo as her husband. In this location, marriage is experienced as a matriarchal institution maintained by emotion and general consensus. The tribe of savages embodies a primitive level of consciousness where instinct can regress repeatedly towards blind impulse. It is a level that everyone passes through, that everyone carries within him/herself, and towards which everyone can regress if he does not try to become increasingly conscious of emotions and instinctual impulses. The danger that uncontrollable passions may gain the upper hand is portrayed by the incandescent pot which is put over the head of the victim. The pot here is a symbol for male "hysteria," occurring when he "sees red" as a result of being run over by the negative Anima. Such a condition can occur as the result of regression, when a positive but seemingly inappropriate emotion is turned away because of pride, rigidity or simply because of ignorance. The reaction to the suppression of the emotion is often delayed and can then be quite excessive, such as a sudden, violent explosion with little external occasion. Such an eruption of the unconscious is portrayed by the rebellion of the primitive tribe against the whites.

The white queen She, as the higher court of the soul in this region of the incandescent pots, stops this dangerous outbreak of primitive raging. She orders the foreign intruders to be brought to her, as she has already been waiting for them a long time. On the way, Leo develops a high fever and feels that he is being torn in two. He is plagued by an inner discord. On one side stands Ustane who, as wife, is sanctioned by the external world and upon whom, as a black woman, his primitive anima is projected. On the other side is She, the interior queen by whom he feels magically drawn, who encompasses all the dangers and fulfillments of the soul, and who surpasses the external world by being a compelling, inner force.

The fever which almost killed Leo is healed by She. Yet through ruthlessly murdering Ustane, She destroys the rights of marriage and all external responsibilities. In this she not only injures the man's morality, but she also undermines her own aims, because she destroys both the trust as well as the character of the man. It is a vicious circle, since the stern, Victorian world view only tolerates a rigid "either/or" and not the free development of feelings which are independent of rules. Thus this world view exiles Ayesha, "the live one," the queen of the heart, to the dead.

She seeks for a marriage with her beloved. Yet because she is not a human being but rather an inner archetype, a divine figure, the *anima mundi,* no earthly marriage can take place. What is intended is a *hierosgamos,* an ancient, solemn rite performed as a mystery in the temple between priestess and priest, the representatives of the godhead. This union must not be confused with an ordinary, mundane marriage. In order to separate the mystical sphere from the mundane sphere and to prevent any degradation of the rite, there was the strictest rule of silence towards any uninitiated person, the disregard of which was punishable by death. The mundane marriage was an earthly reflection of this holy ritual performed in the most sublime place by the gods. This ritual conferring fertility and immortality was re-evoked in mythical tales, in order that human beings could experience and share in the fertility and immortality of the divine powers.

It is the superhuman quality of She, as well as of Antinea, that makes these two figures into archetypes in the novels. This archetypal quality reveals that we deal with compelling powers, belonging to the collective, rather than to the personal, psyche. They are powers that rule over life and death, for She guards the secret of the fire of life, and Antinea is near the spring of life. Both kill if they are offended. The Great Goddess of the Orient and of the Celts is revived in them, but in an altered form, half god, half human. Thus She is closer to us.

Originally the Great Goddess is Mother Nature, mistress of the animals, sublime mountain goddess, changing moon, Aphrodite born by the foam of the sea, love and fruitfulness of any kind, exuberant, and filled with intensity. Yet she is also mother death. In the form of her own daughter, she is simultaneously the promise of eternal life, since she is an inward psychological experience.

In her external appearances, She is subject to the creation and fading of matter, but not in her essential quality. Living in Kor, in the innermost heart, inaccessible to the world, hard to find and harder to attain, the goddess soul guards, as her most profound secret, the column of fire. This miracle rotates in the womb of the earth and is therefore designated as the secret of the Great Goddess or Gaia. Parallels from the Hebrews, from Greek sources, and from Christian and non-Christian literature show that it is a divine power. Whereas this power is seen from a Christian viewpoint as a predominantly angry and dangerous, as well as fascinating, aspect of God, it is revealed by sources originating or influenced by Greece as the divine logos, as the creative, spiritual fire.

Alchemy as well knows of this deity, incandescent with fire, abiding in the interior of the earth. It knows of her creative significance, her danger and her transforming power. Primitive parallels, such as those of the tree of life and of the world-pillar, refer to the center of the world and of life, to the orientation according to an inner center and the re-establishment of the relationship with the gods.

Man's Anima guards the secret of the fire, of warmth, of light, of fertility and creation. She seeks a link with his spirit in order to become integrated into his life. What is initially but vaguely sensed in a man's mind—as an indefinite, instinctual urge, as a fleeting thought, or as a fantasy becomes a concrete form—can be realized when he finds the access to his soul and to this fire. His spirit is born into reality by his feminine soul in the fire of deep emotion.

Leo has found the access to the secret of life, but the path gets blocked by Job's clumsiness and Holly's and his own inadequate knowledge and understanding. In his own life, Haggard was able to accept the Anima only within narrow limits, because of her irrationality, her differing wisdom, and her need to love. Her heathen nature conflicted irreconcilably with the fading Victorian world view. Because of this, She was immoderate, power-hungry, and jealous. By her death in the fire, she demonstrates to Leo (the male consciousness) that he, too, must allow himself to be transformed by love or a sacrificial death. In a later novel he awakens the goddess, who had shriveled up into a mummy, with a kiss, and this time he does not hesitate to unite himself with her and her fiery fervor. By means of his love and sacrificial death, by means of the transformation of consciousness and of the spiritual attitude, the Anima is freed of her greed for power, of sin and pride, and of her entanglement in earthly desires.

His preoccupation with the Anima brought Haggard insights that were considerably ahead of his time. But Leo and She remain blessed spirits. After their transformation they do not return to earth. Haggard could not complete the task of realizing in his own life what he envisioned. The times were not yet ripe for the necessary consequences of his inward experience. This may well be the reason why, in spite of his outstanding personality, he did not always attain the outward results one might have expected from him. His plans for reforms, which were so close to his heart and which could have had a far-reaching significance for England, were thwarted. Even his continued mourning over the death of his only son may have had its deepest root in the fact that "the union of the gods" did not bring forth a "divine son." The new birth arising from a more profound internal vision remained but a hope for the future, a hope which might then be realized by a new generation in a new time.

SECOND PART
The Development of the Anima Portrayed in a Series of Dreams

I. Introduction to the Series of Dreams

It is the task of the first half of life to grow into life, to learn and exercise one's profession, to found a family and to care for the growing children. Viewed psychologically, this is the period in which the individual integrates him/herself in his environment by unfolding his talents and by developing his skills based mostly on his/her primary functions.[146]

A new task presents itself in the second half of life: the challenge is then to discover the "inner world" and to focus upon the deeper layers of the psyche, upon the unconscious which, in favorable situations, is complementary to the conscious mind. If the laws of the psyche are insufficiently respected, then the unconscious becomes an inner antagonist that thwarts our intentions and destroys our efforts. This inner antagonist announces him/herself in dreams. If one ignores dreams, then the unconscious appears in anxieties and neurotic symptoms. Usually, the impulse for a serious dialogue with the unconscious is provided by an inner distress-situation. The appearance of neurotic symptoms occurs if one does not follow either instinctively or consciously the laws of the psyche and its manifold demands.

At times, however, it is after a particular success that the unconscious announces itself. Once everything has been achieved that could be achieved, one's path does not continue in the same direction. The former purposes are outgrown and life seems to lose its meaning until a new goal can be found. Dreams become frequent during such periods of transition, because a transformation is occurring in the unconscious. In the middle of our life, an inner restoration and transformation can begin which is no longer focused primarily on instinctual forces but rather on insight. The emphasis shifts from external expansion of power to maturation, away from one-sidedness towards wholeness and towards becoming the Self. It is difficult to relinquish one's old, habitual, and accepted ways of life and to find new goals on a different plane. Given our current extroverted environment which is so exclusively oriented towards external successes, it is usually only during periods of suffering that we are pushed to listen to our dreams and the call from our soul.

Yet, if we do turn our attention inward, we meet a new difficulty. In view of the good opinion we usually have of ourselves, our unconscious side, due to its compensatory function, will first show us our shadow[147] with all our limitations and contradictions. As one encounters one's shadow, one begins to doubt oneself and sees how questionable and selfish one's motives are, and how far they are from one's conscious ideals. In this confrontation with the shadow, dreams become most helpful, once it is seen that all dream-figures are actors on the inward stage of our being, actors who portray our various potentials.

If, with the beginning of the second half of life, a man begins to examine himself, he may possibly discover that he has become self-sufficient in his profession, with his knowledge and his skills, but much less so in his relationships to other people and to himself. He will dread acknowledging that he is subjected to unconscious motivations, childish dependencies, compelling emotions, pride and hypersensitivity. As he focuses on his dreams, many of the pressing external entanglements and inner problems can be clarified to the point where his everyday concerns are less predominant. Once the individual becomes aware to some degree of the shadow, deeper levels of the unconscious can begin to manifest themselves. Then a man may encounter in his dreams an unfamiliar woman. That aspect of his psyche which is foreign, distant, incomprehensible or unconscious reveals itself in this feminine figure. A woman discovers in her dreams of this period an unknown male partner who symbolizes her as yet incompletely developed spirit, whereas the unknown woman in the man's dreams embodies his yet unconscious soul and his potentials for genuine relationships.

The mother awakens the feminine soul-image, the Anima, early in man, while he is still a boy. Yet the Anima encompasses more than the mother's being; it is, as a psychological, archetypal image, a condensation of all of man's experiences with women. For this reason the female figure in dreams can, in the course of development, reflect all the stages and aspects of woman, as the Anima corresponds to the image of the feminine godhead. Like the goddess, and like life itself, she has a kind as well as a frightful face. Which aspects of the image become operative in the boy's psyche depends in part on the constitution of the son and in part on the nature of the mother. The way the mother is, and the way she relates to her son, influences his feelings and judgments. He will form his own relationships by her example, and from her he receives his sense of religious devotion and faith.

Even if at a later time the boy runs away from her out of rebelliousness, he will have a hard time freeing himself from her standards and from her attitudes towards life which he had already incorporated. Liberation is seemingly achieved by denying her essence and by fighting her demands. In order to become a man and to dare to go out into the world, the youth will at times have to disregard the nurturance of an overprotective mother. Yet, if he becomes subjected to the inner, idealized feminine image, because of excessive ties to his mother (often coupled with a negative relationship with his father), he can end up a dreamer, inept and effeminate. The young man must therefore consciously separate himself, not only from the mother, but also from this idealized feminine image, just as Kallikrates had to leave the priestess in order to marry the "external" queen and become the father of a son. There are men who know exactly how the Anima, as the femme fatale, looks. They know that they must flee from this type of Anima, since they sense that they were not equal to the excessive power of this inner image projected onto an external woman. It is wiser for them to marry a woman who does not evoke this powerful inner image.

Growing into a marriage and into one's own family is one of the most important tasks of the first half of life. Marriage is a high value, shaped during thousands of years by means of strict rules and taboos. There are good psychological reasons that marriage was made an indissoluble sacrament in the Catholic church. Through this trustworthy base, the family and children, in the context of a home, find the necessary support. Grounded in the family, trust grows in the child's soul as a natural fruit of feeling sheltered, and it unfolds into affirmation of life and self-confidence. Subsequent trusting relationships in one's community and country, and especially in close human situations, are founded upon this childlike trust that is gained within the family. Wherever the family—and thus the earliest reassurance and protection—fails, we find all too often that a person's ability to adjust to inward or external conditions also fails. We can now see that some of the early nervous disorders of childhood, and of later neuroses and psychoses, have a contributory cause in lack of love, insufficient security, and various tensions in the child's environment.

In marriage and in the family one feels accepted; and, during times of weakness, need, and illness, one feels supported. It is here that one learns to help and to care for someone else. The future of the generations depends upon each single, small family. Marriage is a test of endurance for both the husband and the wife, in terms of household management as well as human relations. Just as the church recognizes, not only the outward responsibilities of the parents for each other and for the children, but also a mutual responsibility for their souls and their salvation, so we too expect a marriage to be more than an economic union. Yet to be more requires the ongoing spiritual and psychological efforts of both partners, to insure that a marriage becomes a genuine relationship and friendship, as well as an inner, developmental journey. Marital bliss doesn't come by itself any more than does outward success. One must fight and suffer for it. Most of all one must not expect a marriage to flourish through the efforts of his or her spouse but rather through one's own effort.

The significance of marriage also consists in the fact that it forces upon young people choices and decisions, thereby making difficult any continued, indecisive rambling through life. When difficulties arise, the partners must solve them within the sanctioned institution of marriage. They must prove themselves in meeting unavoidable conflicts, adjustments and the needs of their children, which oblige them to educate themselves and thus to achieve another step in self-development. Marriage thereby provides the ground for individuation,[148] inasmuch as individuation cannot be attained without education, self-education and adjustment to one's environment. In his own life, Haggard achieved some degree of adjustment to his family. Where marriage is affirmed, and where it is held as a paramount value and continued obligation, as was the case with Haggard, it is likely that the second half of life will bring up questions from the yet unconscious soul. These questions can only be followed successfully on the basis of holding true to one's previous commitments. However, if the projection of the still unconscious aspects of the Anima is misused in order to find grounds for divorce and remarriage, only calamities and guilts are sown, and nothing is gained. Anyone who gets a divorce in order to marry the "Anima" loses the inner value he seeks, as well as his wife, and gains another projected image. All who blindly chase after a new projection, believing that they can possess and tie to themselves their beloved, should listen to the words of Angelus Silesius: "Do stop! Where runnest thou, the heaven is in you, / If elsewhere you seek God, you miss him more and more."

The child's unconscious image of God is lost by the adult along with the feeling of parental protectiveness. Yet being of the highest internal value, it leads to such compelling longing that it is easily projected upon any halfway-suited partner. The man, as well as the woman, seeks in the other, without suspecting it, the lost image of God. The man looks for a wonderful partner who not only understands, like a mother, his innermost being but who also awakens his creative potentials; the woman looks for a spiritual example, a paternal guide and companion, capable of awakening her activity and her sleeping spirit. Inasmuch as the marriage-partner satisfies this deepest expectation only to a small extent—if at all (doesn't she suffer also from a similar longing?), a certain degree of disillusion in marriage is almost unavoidable. Yet all unfulfilled longing continues to live in hiding. The value one sees in one's partner and which makes the partner so desirable is, in the last analysis, a religious content which cannot be appropriated by tying a person to oneself. On the contrary, this approach would lead to the loss of this value, since the illusion of having appropriated it through the possession of the partner would interfere with becoming conscious of the projected content.

In the first half of life, the fascination emanating from the Anima easily becomes a peril for a man's masculinity; yet, if properly understood, it can become the agent for achieving wholeness in the second half. Encountering "the unknown woman" in his dreams, the man discovers in later years his yet undeveloped soul, his eros projected into nature and—sooner or later—upon a woman. In his dreams he discovers the creative depths that he must explore. The development of this largely unconscious, feminine soul, of eros, of the potential for relatedness requires a great deal of the man. In all, it requires attentiveness and patience, readiness to look at things symbolically, chivalry, the commitment of his best forces. Slowly he will understand that it is not only a relationship to a woman that is called for (by the encounter in the dream), but mainly the establishment of a relationship with the inner, feminine side of his psyche, and thus to the feminine principle. The deep fascination produced by the Anima-projection resides in its religious origin. The religious images at its base are suited to compensate for the one-sidedness of the masculine world view. This will be illustrated in the subsequent dream-series, especially its second part. The gradual differentiation of the Anima makes possible a deepened, sensitive, and ethical—rather than only intellectual—appreciation of various human situations, and a more careful weighing of the pros and cons of one's own actions.

The forthcoming dream-series is meant to illustrate the development of the Anima. We deal with the experience of one person which, nevertheless, shows some generally valid patterns. Yet we must also be aware that Anima-development will show individual differences in each case. The dreamer was in his forties. The oldest of several children, he had lost his father early. Thus he became the hope and support of his mother and siblings. Raised Catholic, he married and had several children. He is an extroverted-intuitive type,[149] his feeling being his secondary function.

Let me, however, make a few preliminary remarks about this particular type. The extroverted-intuitive type puts his best efforts into his outward plans and tasks. With a fast eye, he catches new concrete and organizational possibilities which another type would notice only much later or not at all. Yet, on account of all these attractive goals, he easily forgets to tend his own field with sufficient thoroughness. Rarely has he the patience to wait for the harvest and to collect the fruits of his labor. Being full of ideas and vague presentiments, he has all too many irons in the fire. To use sensation, his inferior function, is difficult for him. In the case of our dreamer, thinking also belonged to the less developed functions, wherefore he is somewhat deficient in logical and systematic thoroughness. He is able to envision the overall, important connections, but he finds it very hard to work things out in detail. He grasps new possibilities with great enthusiasm; yet once he has worked on them for awhile, he feels trapped by what he has achieved. He is an adventurer and initiator who spreads about him life, wit, and potentials. Yet often he finds himself empty-handed and feels, rightly or wrongly, passed over. People belonging to this type think they have wings which must carry them to the goal of their wishes. Just because he is always ahead of himself with his new ideas and wishes, he does not realize how another side of his being limps behind. For the sake of a faraway goal, he ignores himself and his environment. He constantly lives under high tension until his body rebels against this ruthless exploitation with depression and physical disease.

The intuitive disposition contributed to the fact that this man, whose dreams we are about to discuss, suffered twice as hard from the narrowness and poverty of the post-war situation. In this dilemma he obtained little support from his childhood faith that had been pushed into the background by the war. Like others, he had lost several times all his financial means. The lack of housing in the post-war years made it impossible, for a long time, to reunite his family. Trapped professionally and financially, his longings were for the faraway places, for the wide world, the large metropolis. Any idea of relationship and restriction filled him with fear.

Yet he recognized after a few psychotherapeutic meetings that limits were particularly necessary for an intuitive person like himself, and that it was important that he prove himself in a restricted situation. He understood that restrictions and limitations were an essential aspect of human existence. This insight offered a basis for accepting his reality as it was at that moment. Once he recognized that he didn't need to flee the narrowness that seemed to surround him, and once he saw that everything was the way it had to be, he accepted the work with his dreams as a novel form of widening his world by which the path towards his inner world would be opened up.

We may stress at this point that he had fulfilled the tasks of the first half of life. Efficient, talented and conscientious in his profession, he had little to improve in this area. During the war, he had great responsibilities which he carried out faithfully and in a humane way. He received no outward wounds, but, as will be evidenced by his dreams, he was left with psychological injuries. He suffered from nervous tension, and his life seemed endangered by the predominance of the instinctual sphere that turned against him. After the war he had, at first, found a good position. Yet he soon realized that it would not further him in his profession. He gave it up for a new career where he had to start at the bottom. His precarious financial position required great sacrifices of him and of his wife in order to patiently hold to the goal he had set for himself. The series of dreams covers these eight long years of external restraint. Yet, shortly after the end of the dream-series, the dreamer attained his longed-for liberation, as he reached an independent and far better position.

Focusing largely on the dreams, the discussion initially dealt with his current life-situation. During the first period of elucidation of his history, he related the dreams without writing them down beforehand, and thus only a couple are included in this work. Dream One of the bugs portrays his difficult starting situation. The subsequent water-dreams, which referred to "catharsis," to self-knowledge and to the first insights into the personal shadow, are missing. Dream Two already brings to an end this first phase: a preliminary, symbolic death followed in the next dream by a rebirth experience. The plunge and death in a mountain stream portray not only a catastrophe, but also a kind of baptism, followed in the next dream by the birth of a new, inner person. The latter is confronted in Dream Four with the picture of "the royal couple" which is the new goal he must strive for.

The series contains sixty-nine dreams, starting with the dreamer's thirty-ninth year and stretching over a period of eight years. These are only the most important dreams pertaining directly to the theme; many others which did not refer to the Anima's development were left out. Even so, the series turned out quite long. However, if it were further shortened, it might give the impression that the inner path is a simple and straight affair. The reader must be able to participate in the stepwise development, rather than be confronted only with given facts. If one begins the adventurous inward journey, one must be prepared for detours, unpredictable difficulties, and reverses. One may benefit from orienting oneself with the markers left by predecessors, with the story of the journey to the Holy Grail, and with various myths and fairy tales. Yet, it is unavoidable that each person must make the journey by himself, that each must fight his own, specific dangers, and find his own solution to his life's problems.

Considering the size of the series, it was impossible to interpret the dreams following all the rules of the art, since this would have strained the reader's patience. I was primarily interested in demonstrating the main line of development which, starting with an inner split, leads to a novel experience of nature and spirit, and eventually to a gradual synthesis and integration. Some dreams were easily explained; others at first seemed unintelligible. Yet looking back periodically and comparing the dreams helped solve many of the riddles. At times it was necessary to fall back on seemingly farfetched parallels. In fact, at all times it is possible to do only limited justice to the depth of the soul and to the many layers of its pronouncements. This multiplicity of the soul's layers is mirrored by juxtaposing dreams, dream-amplifications, subjective and objective interpretations. It renders a comprehensive presentation difficult, and it requires considerable integration by the reader. Still, I have dared to present the development of Anima as it unfolded in therapy, hoping the immediacy of the dream-language will be able to communicate part of the inner experience.

I shall not enumerate spectacular external successes. Instead, I will focus much more upon inward rather than outward events; yet I would like to avoid the misconception that the path of individuation, namely the journey to one's Self, is an exclusively internal affair. First, to be sure, the concern is with inner images and their meaning, followed by a stepwise change of attitudes, by fine nuances of differentiation of feelings, and by processes of transformation that require a great deal of time. Yet development would stop at any time that the new attitudes were not applied to the concrete, outward life. Only when a new level has been fully experienced and translated into living can it be sacrificed for the sake of transition to the next level.

Professional discretion prevents me from entering into the details of the external events that accompanied the inner development. May it suffice to repeat that the dreamer was an extroverted, intuitive person whose entire energy was by nature outer-directed and who quite independently did everything in his power to succeed and progress in his everyday life. Thus it soon was possible to focus in therapy all the attention on the Anima, on rendering it conscious, and on differentiating the relationship-function. As stated previously, the dreams rarely deal with the outward life-situation or with deviant, pathological aspects of the psyche. They reflect primarily concern with the unconscious, the integration of which leads to individuation, to the wholeness of the personality.

In evaluating psychological development, one must keep in mind that, during the first half of life, progress can be measured by the degree of adjustment and—especially in men—by the amount of outward success. In the second half, this measuring by outward success is only of relative value. By discovering the unconscious soul and its existential as well as religious needs, one aims for an expansion as well as for a qualitative change of consciousness. This qualitative change cannot be measured or be described by means of rational concepts. Yet it manifests itself immediately in subsequent dreams in the guise of changed attitudes of the dreamer towards himself, towards religious problems, and towards his fellow human beings.

II. *The Dreams and Their Interpretation*

When this nearly forty-year-old man decided to discuss with a therapist his life situation and his dreams, he brought with him a dream which he had experienced some time earlier and which had both impressed and scared him deeply.

Dream One: Bugs

"A whitish-yellow gigantic head-louse comes towards me from a sand-cave on the slope of a mountain and tries to attack me. I'm smaller than the louse. With a long, thin lance I'm trying to parry 'her.' At that moment a beetle-like animal, of the same size as the louse, approaches the louse. They bite into each other doggedly and both fall down dead."

The dreamer is reminded by the louse of most unpleasant war experiences, of a life of filth and lice. The trauma of war was a contributory cause to his nervous tension. The louse (in German) is characterized as feminine through the article (*die Laus*) in opposition to the beetle *(der Kaefer)*. Thus we may surmise in "her" a first clue of a feminine aspect of the unconscious, of the feminine, instinctual soul. The latter has become negative, overpowering and dangerous, a gigantic, bloodsucking vampire. The small, thin lance of the dreamer, his limited human reasoning, his conscious will to defend himself are inadequate against such an internal threat.

Were it not for an equally gigantic adversary also arising from the unconscious against the louse, he would have fallen prey to the superior power of the negative "Anima." The beetle—or scarab—rolling its black ball through the sand became in Egypt a symbol of the sun and of its voyage across the sea of the night, an image of the spirit's rebirth. At the time of embalming, a scarab was placed in the heart's space of the dead Pharaoh.[150] In this dream we may look at the beetle as an expression of the male aspect of instincts, as a yet preconscious impulse from which the individual spirit later emerges.

The two animals which doggedly bite into each other represent the unconsciously evolving battle of the opposites. Yet this eternal battle of nature no longer occurs undisturbed within itself. The louse comes at the dreamer and tries to attack *him*. The louse (she) is an autonomous, internal agent or factor which crosses and disturbs the ego's conscious efforts. The louse and beetle have no brain or spinal cord. They portray deep-seated, inarticulate instincts which become conscious only as vague irritability. For the time being, it remains unclear what the inner conflict consists of. The only thing we can know for sure is that the dreamer has become profoundly discordant with his nature and that he is being assailed by ugly, disgusting, anxiety-producing instincts. He therefore is not only irritable with himself and others, but even his life itself seems threatened by the predominance of the instinctual sphere that has turned against him.

This first dream was followed by others of similar nature, with attacking hornets and wasps which in the end, however, do not sting. These are again "insects," no longer larger than life-size, yet still potentially capable of killing a person if they attack as a swarm.

Unfortunately, the water-dreams that come next were not written down. Dreams that deal with water, especially with the sea, are indications of an approach between consciousness and the unconscious. Water itself symbolizes the phase of purification—alchemically speaking, of the *ablutio;* in psychoanalytic terms, of catharsis. In psychotherapy this is the phase of confrontation with one's own life, one's past, one's character, and one's shadow.

Dream Two: The Crash

"There is an airplane crash into a mountain stream. I'm dead, but I still become aware of the newspaper account about the accident."

When one habitually observes one's dreams, the inner process begins to flow. The "death" of the "death and rebirth" is being prepared. As an extroverted, intuitive person, the dreamer was used to passing lightly, as if flying, over situations. Inwardly he was always ahead of himself and lived in wishes and plans for the future. It was the discussion of his current situation that occasioned the crash into the hard reality of his *present* way of being, of his existence. With a plane he falls into a mountain stream, close to the source of his stream of life, where it all began and where in his youth the direction of his life was determined by his father's early death. The dreamer dies but is aware of the accident's announcement in the papers. Things cannot continue as before. Yet, fortunately the catastrophe takes place only in the dream. Part of himself is able to acknowledge the crashed ego, able to hear the news of the accident. Through this process comes the possibility of self-reflection.

This dream is followed by others contending with sharks. This points to the danger of being swallowed up again by the original, perilous lack of consciousness. Then, after additional discussions and other dreams, a dream occurred which, following the old ego's death, announces a new or reborn consciousness.

Dream Three: Sunrise

"I'm flying slowly with outstretched, unmoving arms, high above fields, forests and meadows. Wherever I fly, the shadow below me turns to sunlight. Though I do not have the sensation of being the sun, it is in effect as if I am. I see small trees and their shadows; I see how the sun penetrates into valleys in the morning. My light awakens cows sleeping on pastures and startles a pair of lovers at the edge of a forest."

Slowly, without even moving his wings, the dreamer drifts across the awakening world far below him. He doesn't have the impression that he is the sun, but rather that all the light comes from him. A light awakens in him which illuminates the world in a new way. It is the birth of a new consciousness. Having become quiet inside himself, he can again feel one with the awakening world. He becomes aware of awakening cows, feminine-maternal arch-symbols. At the edge of a forest a pair of lovers is startled. They reflect an awakening emotional relatedness at the very edge of consciousness. The dreamer is capable of a wide overview, as he is flying high above the earth.

"Deification always follows the baptism with water," said Jung. "The new person who has a new name is born at this point. We can observe this quite well in the Catholic sacrament, where the priest holds a candle during the baptism, saying: *Dono tibi lucem aeternam*—I give you the eternal light. The candle light represents the sunlight, for after the baptism we are related to the sun. We obtain an immortal soul; we are 'twice born.'"[151]

After the enthusiasm of his flight and the strengthening of his consciousness, the dreamer is again confronted, in the next dream, by his inner conflict.

Dream Four: The Image of the Royal Couple

"I'm walking between two fronts of a war-torn country, fleeing the enemy. I reach the gate of a park. A servant lets me in and guides me to a house where everything is peaceful, as if there were no war. But then I observe in the adjacent rooms people packing, getting ready for flight. I'm disappointed, as I'd hoped to have found a refuge. In a magnificent hall I notice a tiny picture of a married couple amongst precious Dutch paintings. The master of the house, a dignified, older gentleman, possibly an ambassador, explains to me that the couple was the king and queen. He tells me he has to leave; that I could stay but that he could not guarantee my safety. I renew my flight and reach a crossroad along with other refugees. I decide which way I will go."

In the first dream the dreamer found himself between a bug and a louse. In this dream he is between people at war, fighting each other. However, a war concerns many people. This shows him that his conflict is universal, that he is not alone. In the house with the paintings he hopes to find peace by looking at his inner images. A tiny picture of a king and queen, a new form of the lost parental images, represents a distant goal. In the iconography of alchemy, king and queen stand for the quintessence of masculinity and femininity and for the matrimonial union of these opposites within the psyche.[152] In *Christian Rosencreutz's Chymical Wedding* it is a great honor to be invited to such a wedding, and the path to it is hard to find.[153] Thus the tiny picture embodies vocation and program, the dream's goal and the path towards that goal. Since the dreamer chooses the right path, he is led in the next dream to the King and Queen.

Dream Five: The Royal Couple in the Country of Blacks

"In Abyssinia, or another country of blacks, I am an ambassador dressed in a magnificent uniform, arriving at a ceremony of some sort. Very tall blacks with magnificent bodies, dressed in furs, golden necklaces, and white feather-tufts, stand in ranks and lower their weapons as a sign of greeting. Accompanied by dignitaries, I'm walking up wide stairs covered with leopard-skins. At the top of the stairs, before a throne, stand the king and queen. They, too, are most magnificent. I'm standing beside the king, turned towards the populace. It occurs to me that I have the honor of standing on the same level with the king."

As a messenger of consciousness, the dreamer penetrates into dark Africa, that is, into the unconscious. Here he is confronted by the living archetype, the original wholeness, represented by the opposites of king and queen which in the unconscious are not yet separated. Just as in Haggard's *She,* the journey to the "savages" leads across steps covered by leopard-skins.[154] These steps symbolize sacrificed bestial nature leading to the royal couple. The magnificence of this dream indicates its importance. The dreamer reviews within his unconscious that which he must later achieve on another level of consciousness. It occurs to him that he's given the honor of standing on the same level as the king. Thus he anticipates the possibility of reaching "the level of the king" in his inner journey. The king is his unconscious Self. The next dream will remind him of how far he still is from this natural order.

Dream Six: Old Man

"An old man's life is saved by an operation after an abscess has perforated his intestine."

The dream makes clear that a severe disease caused by conflict can be healed through energetic, conscious intervention. The old man, like the old king in some fairy tales, represents absolute spiritual principles and diseased, antiquated views, inadequate for solving conflicts. These obsolete principles, however, are to survive for now. The old authority is to retain its legitimacy until a widened consciousness allows for a new orientation. The old man's intestinal disease indicates that everyday events could no longer be "digested" by the dreamer. Thus an abscess, a form of self-poisoning, had developed. By means of therapeutic dialogue, it has been possible to avert immediate danger.

Dream Seven: The Wedding Did Not Take Place

"The dreamer has been invited to a wedding which does not take place. He thinks that it is better this way, as he'd only have gotten drunk. When he leaves town, he is grazed by a war invalid on a motorcycle."

The dream recalls the theme of the "chymical wedding."[155] In alchemy one's intent was to separate, through chemical procedures, the opposing principles of silver and gold, sun and moon, masculinity and femininity; to purify them; and to fuse them into one. C. G. Jung explained that these processes were more relevant to psychic events than to physical objects. Alchemy, which deals with unknown substances with unknown properties, encouraged meditation and psychic projection upon chemical processes.[156] The relatively late alchemistic book *Chymical Wedding* clearly describes a process of inner development similar to that found in our dream-series. In the *Chymical Wedding,* Christian Rosencreutz is invited to a royal wedding. He must purify himself in order to be worthy to attend the celebration and be sufficiently mature to understand it. The small letter inviting Rosencreutz to the wedding contains the following warning:

> Take heed!
> Observe yourself.
> If you don't cleanse yourself carefully,
> the Wedding may harm you.
> Harm to him who fails in this,
> beware who proves too light.[157]

The dreamer realizes that he is not ready for this wedding. He comments that he'd only have gotten drunk during the celebration; that is, he would have become less, not more, aware.

The war invalid whose motorcycle grazed him is "the other" within him, his dark brother who had sustained internal rather than external wounds during the war. For some time the dreamer had been able to forget him, but the invalid is a part of him. He shows that he is back by his dangerous driving.

With this dream and the following one, the analytic work comes to a provisional closure. Up to here discussions have focused on assessing and clarifying the dreamer's external situation and his internal distress with its origins in family structure and childhood. The dream of the sunrise foreshadows a new development. The dreams of the royal couple show the dreamer his distant goal. The dream of the old man indicates a spiritual improvement caused by removing the source of pus. After the decrease in tension following the sunrise-dream, the dreamer is grazed by a war invalid's motorcycle at the end of Dream Seven. His shadow from which he seemed to have freed himself has caught up with him again. His hectic style of living is obviously associated with a psychic trauma suffered in wartime that continues to endanger him. In spite of the old man's recovery, the dreamer still carries within himself an invalid whose cure is not an easy matter.

Dream Eight: The Hand-Spun Coat

"I put my new hand-spun coat around my sister's shoulders. It turns into a warm cloak."

This dream concludes the first phase of analysis. The hand-spun coat symbolizes the dreamer's new orientation. This coat is not a factory production. Care and empathy have spun its thread. The dreamer will be able to approach his sister with greater warmth when he visits her the next day. While discussing this dream, he realizes that this sister is his Anima, a part of himself he is searching for and which will make him complete. The insight that the Anima is no longer projected on the mother, but meets him now in the person of his sister, fills him with joyful enlightenment. The Anima had appeared first in the tiny picture of the royal couple (Dream Four) and later as the queen of Abyssinia (Dream Five). In the latter the queen still represented the image of the Anima which the mother shapes in the child's soul and which unconsciously influences the son's way of life. The king embodied the leading spiritual principle, which the father awakens and which influences the child and the later adult without his awareness. The unconscious tie with the parents, especially with the mother, is indicated by the son's uncritical acceptance of everything traditional, that is, everything that was believed at home, including beliefs about emotions.

Now that the dreamer has transferred the inner image of the Anima from mother to sister, he will no longer be the child who still expects satisfaction of his wishes from women, who fears maternal strictness, and who attempts to escape the demands of an overprotective mother. He can now change from a mother's boy to a brotherly comrade who not only takes but also wants to give and be considerate. He becomes aware of his personal responsibility towards women. The transfer of the Anima-projection to the sister represents a first, important step in the Anima's development.

Up to this point, the dreams followed closely one upon the other. Due to outward circumstances, the next dream was only recorded about nine months later. This long interruption may not have been altogether accidental. Like growth in nature, the development of the unconscious is slow. Often it takes several seasons, as does the development of the human fetus, before an insight is born into the reality of life.[158]

Dream Nine: The Horses Bolt

"With my brother who is slower and weaker, I'm standing in a stone-paved yard surrounded by a wall. It is open on one side. On another side, there is a smaller opening onto a rocky terrace which drops down hundreds of yards into the sea. Two black horses that have bolted away gallop through the yard. I fear lest they go beyond it and plunge into the sea. I run and catch one by the halter. My brother catches the other. The horses rear up and kick, but I manage to still them. They are saved."

The intuitive person's horses have taken off so wildly that he is in danger of being dragged into the depths, but beside him stands another, his younger brother. Being the older one, the dreamer had looked down upon him, but in the dream he is able to withstand the horses' onslaught only with his brother's assistance. Alone, his consciousness could not have held out against them. Because it is identical with extroverted intuition, it would have joined the onward rush. Yet his shadow-brother, usually a disparaged or unappreciated side of his being (reflecting one of his auxiliary functions), comes to his aid and saves him. Immediately after the discussion of this dream, another follows.

Dream Ten: Riding

"The next night I dream I am riding a wild, brown mustang. I'm sitting in the saddle. The horse makes the wildest leaps, but I have the wonderful feeling of remaining on top."

The dreamer is now capable of bridling his impulses. His horses, symbolizing his anger and desires, still bolt too easily, but it is a good feeling when he can subdue and guide his instincts and be carried by them.

In the analytic phase now beginning, the focus is no longer on clarifying the external situation, understanding family dynamics, or finding causes for his being the way he is, but rather on developing internally. Now he must come to terms with his "animals," that is, his nature and instincts. He will meet on a different level those inner conflicts that were at first represented by an ugly louse and bug.

Dream Eleven: The Heath-Cock

"I'm sitting in the clearing of a forest. Ahead of me is a group of mighty firs. On the ground between the trees a heath-cock makes his mating call. A group of girls sits behind me whispering, snickering, and laughing. I'm angered because the heath-cock becomes suspicious. He stops his call, stretches his neck and flies away. A second one appears from between the trees. The same thing happens. Finally a third one comes. I get him into the sight of my rifle and am about to pull the trigger. I realize it is a hen, which one is not allowed to hunt. I put down the rifle. I realize that it isn't a hen either, but a little, shriveled-up, bearded woman with long, grey-white, stringy hair which partly covers her face and hangs all about her. She comes towards me slowly. I tell myself, 'Thank God I didn't shoot.' I awaken."

The two previous dreams dealt with horses that could be used for labor; that is, they dealt with more or less domesticated instincts. Now the dreamer finds himself in the forest, in nature which is not directly subject to his will. The heath-cock makes his mating call by instinct. He is temporarily deaf and blind to danger. Behind the dreamer's back, girls whisper and snicker at the blind instinctuality of animal nature and at the aggressive hunting instinct of the dreamer. The latter feels somewhat ridiculed by the women because of his instinctive reactions. The laughter startles the cock, and the hunter is not able to fire. The same thing happens with the second heath-cock. The third one, however, changes into a hen right in front of the hesitating rifleman. His conscience stops him from firing. Female game must be spared. As he continues to hesitate, the hen transforms into a troll. Intense anticipation and hesitation change an exclusively instinctive animal into a nature-spirit with human traits. It is nature-like but not instinct-bound.

Such miraculous transformations can be found in the sagas of the swan-knights.[159] In the Germanic epos, swans become swan-maidens who turn back into swans and fly away when hunters try to grasp them. If a knight succeeds in capturing a swan-dress, the maiden stays with him and bears sons who, because of an evil destiny, are again changed into swans. A similar metamorphosis is attributed to the white hind. She evades the hunter and leads him into distant, forlorn hunting grounds. As he approaches her, she turns into a radiant young woman. The passion for hunting pursues as game the shy, hard to find, hard to grasp nature-soul; it pursues the fleeting contents of the unconscious which promise fulfillment of one's deepest longings.[160]

If the hunter in this dream had fired prematurely, he would have permanently fixated his understanding of his instincts at an animal level. An assertion like "after all, it's only sexuality" would characterize a person with this fixation. The girls' mockery forces the hunter to reflect and evaluate himself. They mirror his still impersonal and indefinite Anima. His hesitation causes his impulsive-masculine aspect to be replaced by a passive-feminine, instinctual one. The latter is represented by a near-human nature-spirit with whom one may converse and establish human contact. The troll is a clearly defined figure in contrast to the vague, indefinite quality of the girls. In the next dream, the dreamer achieves the transformation he had observed in the third heath-cock.

Dream Twelve: The Bathing Suit

"I see hanging a woman's bathing suit which looks like a skin. When I put it on, it fits my larger body. I sense that I'm now simultaneously male and female."

The dreamer slips into the "skin" of the owner of a bathing suit. By identifying with a woman, with her attitudes and ways of reacting, he discovers that he is feminine as well as masculine. He finds that he is able to be passive-receptive. For the first time, it becomes clear to him that he must seek the feminine, not only outside in a woman, but also in himself. This decisive insight will help him to reclaim his Anima-projection. This dream is an anticipatory experience of his own wholeness.

It is important for the ego not to allow itself to be seduced into identifying permanently with the Anima, inasmuch as this would cause the man to become effeminate.

Dream Thirteen:
Young Hart, Poacher, Earth-Mother and Variegated Field

"Armed with my rifle I walk upward on a path through forests and meadows. Suddenly at a turn in the path, I see a young hart who has died of a gunshot-wound. Since it is illegal to shoot such a young hart, I call the foresters. We search through the forest until we find a dilapidated hut. We rush in with drawn weapons and arrest a surprised poacher. He is led away, and I leave the house with the arrested man's wife. At that moment a neighbor, an old, grey-haired, shriveled-up woman, comes out. She assumes that the poacher's wife will want to get rid of her property since her husband has been arrested and offers her $3000 for it. The offer seems quite high to me, and I ask her why she is willing to pay so much for a neglected hut. She answers, 'I need a variegated field which is on her property. It is worth it.'"

The heath-cock that changed into a hen is joined here by a young hart. Among the Germanic tribes, the hart symbolized the dying and resurrecting sun of New Year.[161] In alchemy a *cervus fugitivus*,[162] a fleeing hart, symbolizes an early, transitory form of spirituality. The goal of alchemistic skill was to transform the hart into the stone, symbol of the sun or the king. Unfortunately, before he can transform himself, the hart in this dream becomes a poacher's victim. This poacher represents the inconsiderate, lawless aspect of male activity. He breaks into foreign preserves and appropriates things which are not rightfully his. In his greed, he is as blind as the heath-cock during his mating calls. Lawless masculinity, the opposite of male courage and enterprising spirit, is arrested by consciousness and put behind lock and key.

After the poacher's arrest, the feminine side of the dreamer reappears. As in fairy tales, the troll of the previous dream appears, a bit more humanized, as the old earth-mother. For good money she acquires the poacher's property. Contrasting with the poacher in her willingness to pay for what she desires, she makes an offer which seems excessive but is commensurate to the value of the variegated field. The dreamer explains that this field could produce a wide variety of fruits and plants. The field had belonged to the poacher, but instead of caring for it he had only exploited it. This field could produce several times more fruits and flowers if only it were cared for by the right person. Now it passes from the hands of the poacher and his wife, who represents primitive emotions associated with him, to those of this old woman who has detached herself from animal nature and from mere drive and instinct. The field will now serve a higher purpose.

Let us consider the poacher more closely. Among the Germanic tribes, poachers were accepted and rewarded by the god Odin who himself became a wild hunter.[163] Odin would attack men violently in order to turn them into either heroes or berserk people.[164] This "wild" masculinity was repressed, but not fully subdued, by Christendom. It continues to dwell in human nature in the guise of a shadow or "devil." A substantial part of psychotherapeutic discussions are devoted to the task of becoming conscious of the shadow.[165] Knowledge of the shadow becomes more important as one approaches deeper layers of the unconscious and the archetypal images found in myths, fairy tales, and ancient religions. The shadow is dangerous if it is not recognized; however, it contains energies without which we cannot attain the wholeness of our being.

The poacher is a universal shadow-figure. Faust,[166] for example, ails because he does not recognize Mephisto as his shadow, that is, as a part of himself. He is too willing to let the devil and his three wild companions—Fighthard, Robsoon, and Holdtight—comply with his wishes and projects. Their actions must, in the end, fall back upon Faust himself. Our dreamer, similarly, had not allowed himself to see that he was succeeding easily only through the poacher's assistance. Now he must take a further step and assume responsibility for his shadow's actions. Faust, convinced that he is an idealist with no evil intentions, yet becomes a poacher where Gretchen is concerned. At the end of the second part (of Goethe's work), he allows the devil and his cohorts to execute his plans for reforms, even though they cost the lives of Philemon and Baucis, a genuinely pious couple. To the very end, Faust wishes to claim new land, unaware that he is allowing his own grave to be dug.

In our time, Faust's quest has been repeated on a grand scale.

Obsessed by a Faustian urge, Germany made imperialist plans whose execution involved, as with Faust, Mephisto's helpers Fighthard, Robsoon, and Holdtight. Pious citizens were murdered. Their possessions, like those of Philemon and Baucis, were confiscated for the sake of "greater projects." Trenches turned to graves. Along with grave-diggers came "Want," "Worry," "Guilt," and "Misery," the somber personalities who afflict the blind Faust at the end of his life. Faust is, then, the symbol of Nazi Germany and of those of us who, driven by the Faustian impulse, ignore our shadow's actions.

Faust is rescued from hell through the intervention of the beatific penitents, women who show him the penance for which he never found time during his active, willfully masculine life. In heaven he is first changed by the example of the loving Patres into an admiring boy. Then the presence of his early beloved, Gretchen, pulls him upward to the Virgin, Mother, Queen, the epiphany of the eternal-feminine which will heal him through grace and love. Only now may he experience the *present* as fulfillment. This late fulfillment occurs in an otherworldly heaven, that is, in hidden strata of the unconscious, but leaves life on earth unchanged. A man will remain a victim of his untamed impulses and unlimited greed until he integrates the eternal-feminine into his being.

The feminine, however, does not approach him, in the beginning, in her heavenly glory, but as a modest, homely creature. For example, she appears in this dream as a troll; to Faust she first comes as a witch. We find in this dream the earth-mother of traditional fairy tales and ancient nature-religions. The Greeks called her Demeter, goddess of Eleusis. Her daughter was beautiful Kore. In the Eleusinian mysteries a ripe ear of corn, the golden fruit of the field, was presented as a sign of wealth and fertility. Corn and wheat became symbols for death and rebirth to new and eternal life. In agriculture the earth-mother teaches human beings to fulfill their needs through industriousness and effort.

Variations of this Great Goddess are Cybele, Anaitis, Astarte and Isis. The goddess is a mother or sister of a son- or brother-lover who dies and resurrects each year. In this sense, she is an early form of the Virgin Mary, whose godly son offers himself as a sacrifice for humanity. With the appearance of the earth-mother, one adopts the work of cultivating one's own field and waiting for the ripening of sowed corn, while sacrificing aggressive masculinity, hunting instincts, and eagerness for combat. Among the priests of Cybele, this sacrifice took the form of self-castration. In the Catholic church, it is represented by the priest's renunciation of marriage and his obedience, even in thoughts and beliefs, towards the Mother Church. It requires of each Christian the imitation of Christ. This sacrifice is a denial of one's will as well as a renunciation of the ego's presumptuousness in favor of the superior impulses of the Self.[167]

In this dream the dreamer gains insight into his shadow and renounces primitive, masculine impulsiveness. In the following dream, he succeeds in remaining a passive observer and consequently discovers how nature, when allowed to follow its own ways, finds new solutions.

Dream Fourteen: Mouse and Corn-Hawk

"I'm walking along a broad forest trail. To my right and left are tall firs. Just behind me walks a feminine figure, possibly my sister. Ahead of me runs a mouse or mole. Along the path, above and slightly behind me, flies a bird of prey which I identify as a rare corn-hawk. I feel that he wants to aim towards the mouse but cannot see it, as I'm between them. I also have the impression that the mouse would like to be eaten by the bird of prey. I talk with my sister about that. The bird is quite colorful, as if he had blue and red laces or flowers pinned on his wings. I think that things would certainly work out if the mouse were decorated in the same way. I look at it again, and I notice that the mole, or mouse, now has colorful dots and lines, like those of the corn-hawk, in its pelt. At that very moment the bird of prey swoops down and grabs the mouse. Oh, thank God, all of us, including the mouse, are redeemed."

The awakening of the dreamer's feminine side is illustrated by the transformation of the heath-cock into a troll (Dream Eleven), the identification of the dreamer with the swimsuit's owner (Dream Twelve), the earth-mother's acquisition of the variegated field in the last dream, and now the Anima's transformation into an inward, sisterly companion. The mole or mouse represents chthonic nature, the soul's impulsive, instinctual aspect. The corn-hawk represents a spiritual aspect of the instinct. It is not holy but rather wild, dark, and nature-like. In this dream the earth-bound instinct—the mouse—and soaring spirituality—the hawk—desire to become one. The union of drive and spirit is obviously longed for by the mouse. Earth-bound instinct has an innate drive towards the spirit by which it wishes to be recognized, grasped, and understood.

The approach of these opposite instinctual forces is mediated through the red and blue flowers and laces which decorate both hawk and mouse. Obviously, the variegated field of the last dream has brought forth blue and red blossoms. Blue may represent here the sky or rays of the spirit. Red may represent warmth, heat from a fire, or blood. Color as an expression of feelings is the mediating factor between seemingly unbridgeable contrasts. In this dream, the mouse is simply devoured, but a universal sigh of relief signals the correctness of this event. The fact that the mouse was devoured tells us that for the time being the spirit will be dominant, not by going its own ways, alienated from nature, but by feeding upon the chthonic instincts. The next dream will show how impulsive energies can now benefit scientific thinking and research.

Dream Fifteen: The Circus Athlete

"I'm in a circus tent. A female companion is right behind me. There is no audience. Up in front an athlete exercises on a high horizontal bar or trapeze. He's young and strong and has a pointed beard. My companion whispers to me: 'This is a scientist who does gymnastics here.' Two little boys, about four or five years old, work out with him. They lie on mattresses suspended in the air. The man swings the mattresses, and the boys must then make contrary motions. The child closer to the athlete repeatedly loses a rope, almost falling off. The other child has no problem and is no longer observed."

Dream Sixteen: Rotary Motion

"When I fall back asleep, my lady companion tells me, in connection with the boys' movements on the mattresses, that if I constantly turn from my back to my stomach, I will be able to solve the scientific problem that has preoccupied my waking life. Then I dream I'm in a room with three young men whom I know from either high school or college. Each one of us lies on his own mattress. Before we have rotated ourselves ten times, I suddenly realize, 'Now I'm finished—I have solved the problem.'"

These two dreams demonstrate that the sharp-eyed bird of prey of the last dream anticipated an aptitude for scientific thought. In Dream Fifteen an athlete, whom the Anima-companion designates a scientist, hovers on a trapeze in a circus tent. Beside him are two boys on suspended mattresses. This arrangement is reminiscent of Mithras, the sun-god of the Roman legions, who is often pictured between two boys who may symbolize his rise and fall. With his pointed beard, the athlete/scientist calls to mind Mephisto. Thus, the scientist practicing gymnastics apparently is more than just a human being: he may be intellect manifesting itself as a demoniacal force. Thinking, as one of the dreamer's unconscious functions, is affected by the demoniacal aspect of the unconscious. The circus tent, with its round, enclosed form, is a first, though unstable, container for the roundness and wholeness of the Self.[168]

In Dream Sixteen we find four young people, including the dreamer, upon mattresses. They must practice the scientist's exercise in order to solve the scientific problem which actually preoccupied the dreamer at this time. Movements of the unconscious, represented visually by shifting bodily positions and counter-positions, reach consciousness. Now he is not simply the victim of opposites as in Dream One. He is learning to include opposites and move between them. Thinking in terms of contradictions still seems to him a circus trick; but it brings tangible results in his scientific work.

Three men exercise in the circus in Dream Fifteen. In the following dream, four men turn around on their mattresses. In this transition from a threesome to a foursome and in the tent's roundness, an approach to the wholeness of personality is expressed.[169]

Dream Seventeen: Spanish Riding School

"I'm riding a well-saddled horse. Then I see, in the guise of a tiny picture, the best horseman from the Spanish riding school on a white stallion."

Dream Seventeen concludes a series which began with Dream Nine. In the latter, there was a bolting black horse, but here the dreamer is on better terms with his instincts. He goes to work with greater interest and confidence. As a distant goal he envisions riding a white horse perfectly. The white horse illustrates the fact that his instincts have undergone a process of spiritualization, and spirituality can now become a supportive reality in his life.

The next dream is an epilogue to this series.

Dream Eighteen:
The Anima Warns against the Eleven Crows

"I was at a wedding. The couple, whom I know, and the other people were fairly well-off but primitive, uncultivated. We drove noisily in horse-drawn carriages to the inn where the wedding feast was held. In the midst of the crowd, I suddenly saw a woman who fascinated me. Looking at her with desire, I offered her a drink and a piece of cake. She declined politely but responded to my glance openly, without sensuality. I was again impressed. I realized that my approach was useless. Then the scene changed. I found myself in the office of a modern, neutrally styled house (or hotel). The door opened, and I stood again in front of this woman. She was well-dressed, unobtrusively elegant. She told me very intensely: 'You must always revile the eleven crows. They eat seeds and are to be chased away. You must always revile them.' (In the dream it was clear to me that, whenever I got angry, it was better to revile birds than people.) Then she left. I wanted to go after her and ask where I could meet her again. Just then she returned and said: 'If you need me, you can simply knock at my door. I live upstairs.' I was deeply impressed by her appearance and manners."

The dream had been triggered by a discussion about women

with a friend. Their talk is mirrored by the uncultivated wedding
guests. Evidently, the feminine figure who had been following the
dreamer for some time was also present during this discussion.
Possibly because the dreamer was gradually able to respond properly, the Anima now appears to him for the first time in her
distinguished, superior guise. He realizes that his covetousness will
not accomplish anything. She cannot be reached by this type of
behavior. Her influence is of such force that the dreamer finds
himself transferred to a neutral setting, the office, where he
discards his original, uncultivated viewpoint. Now, for the first
time, the Anima exhorts him. Emphatically, she tells him of the
eleven crows which eat all the seeds. In the dream he realizes that
he must not revile people, when he loses his temper, but the crows.
In the parable of the sower (Matt. 13) the Bible reads: "Look, a
sower went out to sow. And as he was sowing, some seeds fell
alongside the road, and the birds came and ate them up." The
Anima wishes to remind the dreamer that the good seeds cannot
grow roots because they are always swallowed by the black birds.

Black crows are dark thoughts tempting the dreamer to blame
others instead of himself. Martin Ninck mentions the twelve
berserk men of the Heidrek-saga and the twelve friends of Hrolf
Kraki, the crow.[170] The berserk men are possessed swordsmen,
followers of Odin. This Germanic god had, as companions, two
ravens. For the Germanic tribes, the raven was a sign of battle and
victory, as well as death. The crow was a messenger of bad news,
and its name was a term of abuse.[171] The black birds of misfortune
signal evil thoughts and primitive aggressiveness and depression.
They are associated with an era in which disagreements were settled with weapons.

More difficult to explain is the number eleven. It can be seen as
being made up of ten plus one, thereby pointing to a new beginning on a higher plane. Or it may indicate a tendency towards
twelve, just as three tends towards four and seven towards eight.
The two viewpoints need not exclude each other. Strangely appropriate is the following, seemingly farfetched association. The
eleventh card of the Tarot, the ancient symbolic game of the gyp-
sies, shows a beautiful young woman, richly dressed, wearing a
pilgrim's hat. With her hands, she alternately opens and closes the
jaws of a lion leaning against her. The card indicates self-
assurance, self-confidence, trust, strength of character, triumph of

spirit over matter, courage, a good woman's influence, and patience in trials and sorrows. The lion symbolizes either refusal of masculine violence in favor of womanliness or animal nature kept in check by ethics.[172]

In the fairy tales of the Seven Ravens, the Twelve Brothers, and the Six Swans, we find common elements: bewitched brothers who have been transformed into birds and a young sister who redeems them by sewing shirts. In all three stories the sister is not allowed to utter a word for the several years in which she carries out this task.

A comparison between these tales and the present dream is instructive. In the fairy tales, the brothers are transformed back into knights only through their sister's silence. In this dream, the dreamer's Anima instructs him to keep silent when he feels tempted to revile others. She teaches him to come to terms with his anger and to humanize his spiteful, instinctive reactions (symbolized by the crows). She then tells him that she is always available as she is living in the upper story, the realm of the heart and spirit, as opposed to the lower realm of impulse and affect. The Anima indicates to the dreamer that she belongs to him. In fact, she is his own soul, but in order to integrate her refinement into his being, he will have to get rid of his concupiscence and change his wrath and anger into self-criticism and chivalry.

The dreamer had met his lower Anima in a previous dream in which she had begged him for protection in order to keep from drifting back to her earlier existence as a whore. At another time—the dreamer could no longer remember where these two dreams fit in the series—he heard a wonderful voice from a church altar singing the Magnificat: "My soul praises the Lord, as he has looked down upon the lowliness of his maidservant." The Anima of Western man is, as shaped by Christendom, split into a refined woman who has high, pure ideals and a primitive woman who is licentious and worldly. Instinctual compliance would jeopardize the development and transformation desired by the "whore-Anima." It would cause her to return to her former, primitive worldliness. Ignoring the whore-Anima's expressed wish would have been a tragic error, not only because it would have undone what she had already achieved, but also because primitivity is dangerous to the soul. It misleads people, especially men, to casually assume that they are moved only by instinct and not by love. Such a misunderstanding occurs so easily, because in men feeling and instinct are two distinct, often irreconcilable realms. The resulting double Anima has been represented by a saint and a whore, by the madonna and by a cold-blooded nixie with a fishtail. Such an Anima does not have a human heart yet. In a double sense she is heartless. Fairy tales often state that she can gain a heart and an immortal soul only through sacrifice and suffering.

In *The Love-Dream of Poliphilo,* Poliphilo meets at the beginning of his journey a large number of nymphs.[173] At an early stage the Anima, because of her indefinite nature, is projected onto nature. At this stage she appears in the form of many kinds of women, such as the nymphs mentioned above. She may appear unexpectedly in new shapes as game. We find this, for example, in many fairy tales and in Hofmannsthal's *Woman without a Shadow.* Faust is at this early stage when he is rejuvenated by the witch, and Mephisto comments, "After this potion, you soon will see Helen in every woman."[174] In our dream-series, this initial stage of internal development is indicated by the heath-cock transformed into a hen and by the forest girls who snicker behind the dreamer's back (Dream Eleven).

In order for the Anima to transform herself and develop spiritually, the religious significance and value of her spiritual side must be recognized. As long as his Anima remains a vixen or a nymph, a man is justified in doubting whether that which he feels is truly love. If he persists in behaving in a primitive-masculine way, he will convince himself that his eros is nothing but instinctual hunger and thereby cheat and betray his soul which, like the whore-Anima, wants to love and be loved.[175]

One often finds two aspects in men: a "nature-boy" and an ascetic or spiritual man. If the "nature-boy" has been dominant, it is important that the spiritual aspect be developed in the second half of life. On the other hand, if the man has suppressed his natural masculinity, he has probably also disdained his Anima (inasmuch as she represents nature and life) as "evil." Because of this inner constellation, he has been tempted to regard himself as superior to women. He has felt that women are incapable of reaching his spiritual heights. Women have been branded as serpents and seductresses who are responsible for any arousal of his inferior nature.

When Mephisto states that Faust sees "Helen in every woman," he does so in the guise of "the force which wills evil and furthers good." Man looks for his lost nature-soul which, in antiquity, dwelled among the gods and was called Selene, Aphrodite, Psyche and, among the Gnostics, Sophia. According to the Gnostic tradition of Simon Magus, Helen was a "virgin of light" descended from heaven. She is at once goddess, moon, ennoia, idea, and prostitute. She is the divine soul which originated in heaven, was banished, infused into a woman's body, and lost on earth.[176] Man seeks his ancient soul. He longs for immersion in nature, for lost piety which venerated divine powers in nature, and for eternal ideas embodied in various goddesses. He seeks his ancient soul to compensate for, and to heal, his modern, one-sided consciousness. For this reason Faust descended to the netherworld of antiquity and returned with Helen.

There was, however, another reason for the revival of antiquity in Goethe's time, namely, the rediscovery of ancient art. The relationship between Faust and Helen is, therefore, a somewhat literary affair, from which Euphorion is born. Euphorion is full of fiery enthusiasm, but his life is short. His body disappears, and only his dress, coat, and lyre are left. For Faust poetry, in the form of an ancient garment, remains, but the reality of his experience of his feminine soul escapes him again when, after a brief period of intoxication, he embraces Helen for the last time. From her, too, he keeps only a dress and veil.[177]

Dream Nineteen: The White Bull and the Three Girls

"I'm inside a glass pavilion. I see an oversized, white bull running towards me. I'm frightened, aware of my vulnerability. The mighty bull snorts, stamps his feet, and lowers his horns in a threatening manner. Just as he is about to storm the glass wall, a wide glass door opens and he enters. A little girl appears and easily leads the bull outside. I'm saved. Then, I find myself in a spacious hall where young women are dancing. Three women approach me. I accept their offer, filled not by desire but by tenderness which I still feel upon awakening."

The glass house in which the dreamer lives symbolizes the structure of his ideas. The fact that it is made of glass and is, therefore, transparent indicates both vulnerability and spirituality. Though the house is more solid than the circus tent, the first container of his wholeness, he still cannot feel safe in it because of the gigantic bull which, snorting and stamping, threatens him.

In Mediterranean countries, the bull was venerated as a godhead. He embodied generative power, health, and fertility. Fertility flowed from the sacrificial sun-bull upon Mithras's altars.[178] The Egyptian Pharaoh, or god-king, was thought to be identical with the Apis-bull (also known as Ka), the incarnation of divine creative power. As "Ka-mutef" (bull of his mother), he procreates himself from his mother, the bull-god's wife.[179] Pasiphae, the queen of Crete, disguised herself as an artificial cow in order to conceive the Minotaur, the bull-god. Hathor is portrayed with the head of a cow. Hera is called the cow-eyed goddess. As a bull Zeus abducted Europa, and as a bull Dionysus was revered by his priestess. Being giant and white, the bull in the dream is, doubtless, a god against whom human knowledge and will are impotent. Thus, as if by magic, a large glass door opens before him. But then a little girl is able to take him by the bridle and lead him outside.[180] The virginal Anima succeeds where the man and his consciousness would fail. She leads the wild bull away as if it were a tame ox, thereby saving the man's newly-won spiritual stance.

The three women in the second half of this dream represent the feminine principle. They incarnate the three phases of Hekate (or Selene), the moon-goddess: growth, wholeness, and diminution. As the moon-goddess embodies both nature and the soul, this threefold succession indicates that both nature and emotions are subject to changing phases. When the fullness of life has reached its highest point, it must vanish in order to reappear like the moon's sickle in the evening sky. The three ladies offer themselves to the dreamer. Because the impulsive bull, the generative god of antiquity, had allowed himself to be led away, we find that the dreamer's instinctual impulsivity is replaced by trustworthy tenderness.

The white bull has still another aspect. Like the white stallion (Dream Seventeen), and unlike the brown stallion (Dream Ten), he represents a force of light or spirit. Like the Egyptians' Ka-mutef,[181] he embodies the universal, spiritual, creative force which operates in nature and spiritual realms. Natural creative power and spirit are about to differentiate themselves. When the dreamer is able to avoid the impulsive violence of the god, his spiritual side emerges. In dreams that follow this one, but are not written down, he is brought into a new relationship with his father, the first effective spiritual factor in his life. He discovers new feelings of tender gratitude for his father whom he lost too early, but who, in one of these missing dreams, saves his life.

Because we have reached an essential developmental level, let us quickly review our dreamer's progress thus far. In Dream Eight he had turned with new warmth towards his sister, his Anima-projection. In subsequent dreams, he succeeds in withdrawing the Anima-projection from her. In the bathing-suit dream (Dream Twelve), he realizes that, although the Anima has appeared in the form of a woman, she is part of his own being. Therefore he is able to act in masculine ways and, psychologically, in feminine ways. Once he has withdrawn his Anima-projection from his sister, he is confronted by his animal side. At first the dreamer learns to tame his horses, so that they obey him when bolting. In a following dream (Dream Eleven), he is in a forest where he meets a still to-tally unconscious, instinctual aspect. There, his hesitating, careful attitude allows a heath-cock to change into a hen. This animal soul turns into a troll who later (Dream Thirteen) acquires, as earth-mother, an uncultivated field, an as-yet-unused part of his interior self. She plans to grow colorful flowers and fruits—namely, feelings and sweet nurture—on this land that had previously belonged to the poacher, the dreamer's shadow.

In the following dream (Dream Fourteen), we see how his dark, chthonic instincts allow themselves to be seized by the corn-hawk, his spirit in the form of his intellect. With this, a new spiritual movement sets in. The dreamer learns to think in terms of op-posites (Dreams Fifteen and Sixteen). In Dream Seventeen he foresees the time when he will achieve harmony with his spiritual instinct. His soul has now followed him for some time in a sisterly guise. Then, in the dream of the eleven crows (Dream Eighteen), she presents herself as his higher, spiritual Anima. She emphatic-ally warns him of his tendency to attack others angrily and ad-vises him to seek errors in himself. So strong is her influence that, in the next dream (Dream Nineteen), the dreamer is promoted to a higher, spiritual level, the glass house. Now the Anima is able to stop the onslaught of the nature-god, the overpowering bull. Male impulsiveness is kept in check by emotion and feelings.

Meanwhile, the dreamer is able to rejoin his family. His wife, always his good comrade, now enjoys with him a loving closeness which he would never want to lose.

The girls in the forest (Dream Nineteen), symbolizing the nature-soul's indefinite quality, have been replaced by a sisterly Anima-figure through whom the dreamer is able to experience love as human relatedness. What had been instinctual ties can now become personal caring.

A few months later a new phase of development begins which is introduced by a super-personal Anima-figure and symbolized by a banner.

Dream Twenty: The Woman-Commander

"I'm looking at an Asian woman-commander. Behind her, to her right, stands her general. He is also Asian. She reviews her well-disciplined troops as they parade past her. I cannot see the troops. I only hear their steps and sense their enthusiasm and their dedication to their commander. The commander is tiny and neat. Her hair is black, her face round. She wears a silver-plated armor which half-covers her breasts. She also wears a precious, white bolero which reaches below her breasts. I'm exploring her face in order to figure out what it is about her that fascinates her troops, but I don't see anything noteworthy. In her right hand she carries a white and blue banner. With her left hand she grasps the upper end of the cloth and holds it tightly against her body. Only her head appears above it. When she puts her chin forward and stands at attention, I hear her troops seized by a fanatic enthusiasm. Meanwhile, her general has moved to the other side of the street. I hear him giving sharp orders. After a while, the commander plants the banner's pole into the ground and begins to pace back and forth, or in circles, with short, nervous steps. Occasionally, she draws figures in the soil with the tip of her foot. Then, her general stands again beside her. I become aware that it is improper to continually stare at her and leave with a female companion who stands behind me. Before leaving, though, I turn around once more and nod farewell. The commander and her general acknowledge this gesture by nodding in a formal way."

The Anima in her personal aspect stands behind the dreamer, as she had in previous dreams. Now she seems to mediate the vision of a super-personal figure. Similarly, Gretchen draws Faust, Beatrice draws Dante towards a vision of the queen of heaven. The Eastern church has a song in which Maria is glorified as an army-commander.[182] The *High Song* reads: "You are beautiful, my friend, like Thirza, lovely like Jerusalem, fearsome like legions." To be sure, the dream's super-personal Anima is not a heavenly queen, but an Asian ruler and an Amazon.[183] She wears a silver-scaled armor. In alchemy, silver is regarded as feminine, moonlike. The scales remind one of the Anima's origin in the sea of the unconscious, the realm of fishes and vixens. The silver-scaled armor also implies that she is a moon- and war-goddess. Above the armor she wears a precious, white bolero, and in her hand she holds a blue and white banner. The latter has the light colors often found in paintings—Murillo's, for example—of the Maria Immaculata. The commander, however, has both feet on the ground. She rules the anonymous masses of Asia, not the saints.

The dreamer remarks that, for him, Asia represents "the other side," the anti-Christian world. Ever since the war, he has been terrified by the violence found in Asia. Because it encompasses the non-Christianized soul, Asia is for him a symbol of the collective unconscious. This realm, still foreign, is ruled by the feminine principle—a powerful, super-personal woman—and her general. One often hears that the East, Russia and China, has an *Idea,* and this *Idea* can move the masses. In the present dream this idea, embodied in the banner, is carried by a woman, the Anima, who stimulates imitation and enthusiasm. Mediator of super-personal, irrational ideas which oppose rationality, she has the power to exacerbate unconscious energies until they erupt into the Western world, that is, into consciousness. She is powerful because, like Haggard's She, she also represents the male Self, the still-unconscious male image of God. The general, her subordinate, is a shadow-figure of the male Self, under the Anima's spell. As emotional might, the commander is able to mobilize the compelling, impulsive energies of the dreamer and the masses. She acts as a foreign power, opposed to consciousness, as long as consciousness does not approach her and display interest in her idea embodied in the banner. Later, the dreamer commented that the commander made him aware that it was time for him to learn about the East.

The blue and white banner combines the blueness of the sky and the whiteness of unrefracted light. Blue is the color of the heavenly sphere that encompasses and overlooks the world. This overview and knowledge of the world is linked with the logos, the white light of the cosmos. Knowledge of the world is transformed into detached insight, while, in an opposing direction, the light of heaven penetrates the earth. Like Prakrti and Sophia, the Anima is a mediator through whose being eternal ideas affect the world. Like the Chinese spinner or weaver, she actualizes destiny. However, she is also, like Mary and Kwan Yin, an intercessor who elevates human action and thinking into spiritual knowledge. Silver, blue, and white appear on earth with a feminine figure. That distant realm in which Murillo's Immaculata floats above the earth descends and moves the world. The goddess-soul moves the world through her quality of inner reality. She sets things into motion, with or without consciousness, knowledge, or approval. The general only transmits orders which originate from the woman-commander.[184] The dreamer comments that the general reminds him of the Korean Nam Il, a young man who represents, not tradition, but dangerous, impulsive actions. The dreamer's vision, then, extends beyond his personal problems to world events.

The flag indicates the dreamer's main concern. It announces, and symbolizes, a higher level of consciousness. In Tantric Yoga, blue and white belong to the visuddha-chakra,[185] the mandala located in the throat above the storms of the heart. The symbol of this chakra, a white elephant, is reminiscent of the white bull in Dream Nineteen. Jung reports that in this chakra ideas and concepts are integrated into one's own inner experience.[186]

Because the therapeutic goal, until now, had been differentiation of the ability to relate, the dreamer had progressed quickly. He became capable of relating with genuine emotion to a differentiated, cultivated woman who would expect a differentiated relationship. The next step, foreshadowed by the impersonal Anima figure dressed in silver and white, and by her blue and white banner, is far more difficult because it cannot be attained quite as directly. It involves sacrificing part of the dreamer's newly-achieved personal relationship in favor of impersonal, spiritual contents. Relationships, at this stage, no longer exist for their own sake. They must lead to eternal ideas, to archetypal images, such as the truth about ourselves, and to the experience of God. We must now look differently at our friends and our enemies. We dislike our enemies only because we see in them the shadow that we refuse to recognize in ourselves. That shadow, the enemy within ourselves who places obstacles in our way and crosses our conscious intentions, is more dangerous than any external enemy. He is the "splinter in one's own eye" which impedes any agreement with the 'other.' Questions of acceptance or rejection will now move into the background. The only thing that matters is finding what we really are and how we will come to terms with our problems. Whatever happens to us can no longer be dismissed as accidental. Even the accidental event will be understood as providential and challenging.

Because every external event has an inner significance, the dreamer can no longer avoid even his fear of Asiatic people. He must seek their cruelty inside himself. This new, impersonal orientation will lead to a deeper understanding of the shadow.

The dreamer greets the strange, Asian woman from a distance, and by nodding her head she acknowledges that she, too, has noticed him. Yet there is an abyss between her Eastern way of being and his Western consciousness. However, unconsciousness is reaching consciousness. This is indicated by the quartet formed by the commander, her general, the dreamer, and his companion. Jung describes the "Wedding-Quaternio" as a symbol of wholeness.[187] Two pairs are linked within themselves as well as with the other pair, expressing the linking of opposites: the conscious with the unconscious and the masculine with the feminine. To be sure, the four persons in the dream are not yet linked sufficiently. The Europeans and Asians must approach each other, and the general is still subordinate to the commander. A genuine *quaternio* will be found only in later dreams.

Dream Twenty-One: The Sword of the Ancestors

"I'm walking through a grey city where misery reigns. I'm constantly approached by old beggars. On their backs they carry sacks filled with precious family heirlooms, such as ancestral swords, which they offer for sale. I don't want to hurt their feelings, but I don't own anything with which I can pay them. I also fear that they may attack me in desperation. At a street corner I turn to the left. At the next corner, I turn to the right. At the end of this street is the house in which I dwell. I enter. In order to save electricity, I climb the broad, worn stairs in the dark. I reach a vestibule which leads into several apartments. My door is the last one on the right. It is a wide-open double-door. The light is turned on. Comfortable warmth exudes from the tile-stove. An old man who also has a sack with a sword over his shoulder is busy cleaning up. I'm genuinely happy that he has found work, and, thereby, warmth and food. The room is oak-paneled. Against the walls are antique chests. A small section of the room is set apart by a writing desk. This is my space, although it is only a small part of the entire room. The rest of the room belongs to my father. In the middle of my father's space, a large, evenly-grown Christmas tree stands on a table. It is decorated by numerous, elongated tin vases and two porcelain vases with designs of green leaves. As I turn one of the vases around, I see an inscription in gold letters. It is the name of the city of my father's ancestors."

The dreamer finds himself in a grey city plagued by misery. Wandering beggers try to sell heirlooms. Such widespread misery indicates a collective, rather than a personal, problem. The beggars offering heirlooms, particularly old, precious swords, for sale are unemployed souls of ancestors, psychological contents of the past which seek reacquaintance with people living today. Because no one takes an interest in them, they are in misery and, therefore, dangerous. The sword used to be an expression of the dignity and power of a family and an instrument for independent, masculine defense. For the dreamer, it is also the sword that Sigmund had to pull from a tree in order to begin his god-given destiny as a hero.[188]

The dreamer then finds himself in a pleasant, old-fashioned parlor, free from the sufferings of the war-ravaged modern world. Only a small part of his room is designated as his space. He is but a link in the chain of his ancestors. His ego is just a small, late-born descendant, a little segment of the unconscious Self which encompasses all his ancestors. The sword is still owned by an old man, now employed as a house-spirit. The old man, no longer dangerous, is helpful and has a function with respect to the whole. His proximity allows the property of the ancestors, particularly their instrument, the sword, to gradually become the dreamer's conscious property. The sword represents an ability to make independent decisions and to judge for himself. By using the sword, the dreamer's consciousness should take over the unconscious functions of the Asian woman in Dream Twenty.

In the chamber of his father, that is, the chamber of the ancestors and the Self, is a wonderful, evenly-grown Christmas tree, symbolizing quiet, patient, even development; growth on barren ground; calm in the storm; light in the darkest periods; and union of naturally developed symbols with Christian tradition.[189] The tree is decorated with vases made from the metal used by the ancestors for their vessels. Vases are feminine symbols of receptivity and bearing. They are tangible forms of unconscious contents. Their golden inscriptions reveal the name of the paternal city. Love is thus channeled from woman, through the feminine vessels on the lighted tree, to the city, to which the dreamer would like to return some day. By means of the sword which endows him with the ability to make conscious decisions, he is to continue his father's and his ancestors' lives.

This dream redirects the dreamer's energies from the Anima to his spiritual and professional activities.

Dream Twenty-Two: The Little Daughter with the Ball

"I dreamed today of the beloved woman. I was enamored of her daughter, a child who playfully threw a soft, white ball towards me. I couldn't catch it, and it rolled into a neighbor's garden. At this instant the girl's dog, a playful, snow-white fox terrier, rushed and fetched it, but brought it back only to the border between the two yards where I picked it up myself. Then I was lying on a lawn chair. Ahead of me was a grove of mighty oaks. The woman sat at the end of my lawn chair, and I told her how utterly happy I was. I was filled with a sense of happiness and contentment which I had rarely experienced in actual life. The intensity of my emotion was reminiscent of the tenderness I felt in the dream of the bull and the three young women [Dream Nineteen]. On my left, by the way, was someone I was aware of, but whom I didn't see."

This dream occurred almost nine months after the dream of the bull. In some intervening, unrecorded dreams, the dreamer rediscovered his father who had died early in his life. Now, nine months after his encounter with the "three young women," he has become the father of an "inner" daughter. The sister-Anima is completed by a daughter-Anima. The sister-Anima feels and thinks like his real sister, but the daughter-Anima has her own spontaneity, immediacy, and lack of concern. She is joyful and lively like her little dog. She wants to play and to tempt the mature man to be childlike. By throwing the ball back and forth, she hopes to establish a mutual relationship between consciousness and the unconscious, between thinking and feeling. The dreamer, however, is clumsy and allows the ball to roll into a neighbor's garden. Maybe he unconsciously expects his neighbor, his shadow, to take on the troublesome, playful interchange with the little Anima, but the small dog, the newly-awakened playful instinct, does not allow this to happen. It knows exactly where the ball is and re-engages its master in the game.

After the quiet episode on the lawn, the dreamer finds himself in front of old oaks, sacred trees of destiny. Here he experiences happiness and satisfaction. He feels redeemed from problems that have troubled his family for generations. He now experiences the presence of feelings as an almost tangible inner reality. In Plato's *Symposium*, Diotima states that Eros would no longer be rough and barefoot if, like the dreamer's feelings, he could transform himself into a conscious, inner reality. Then he would no longer be the constant companion of need, a powerful, scheming hunter. Instead, he would be an enduring, inner acquisition, available when one is loved, when one desires goodness, beauty, or wisdom, and when a fellow human being is in need. Eros thus would obtain his rightful position, his home. He would be able to unite conflicting interests in the world of the discriminating and separating logos. Emotions would no longer be in opposition to Christian love as described in the first letter to the Corinthians: "Love does not behave indecently, does not look for its own interests, does not become provoked. It does not keep account of the injury. It does not rejoice over unrighteousness, but rejoices with the truth. . . ." The beginning of this transformation was first experienced in the dream of the three girls (Dream Nineteen). If the dreamer continues to care for his little dream-daughter, this transformation will, through her, gradually become an integral part of his being. The following dream occurred eight months later.

Dream Twenty-Three: Bow and Arrow

"A youngster had laid down his bow and arrow as they didn't seem to function properly. They looked fairly miserable. As I lifted them up, they suddenly turned out to be very large, larger than myself. The arrow was as long and slender as a spear. It was made of soft, rough wood. I recognized the bow as an Australian aborigine's bow. It seemed to be made of antelope horns or of some special kind of tortuous wood. The youngster and a woman watched me as I bent it. I intended to pull hard and fast and to let the arrow fly. But then,[190] recalling the instructions of Zen Buddhist archery masters, I began to slowly bend the bow to its point of maximum tension. At this point my fingers let go by themselves. As in Zen, "it," not "I," shot. The arrow, made entirely of wood, without even a metal point, kept on flying for an infinite distance. I was quite surprised. It flew across the tops of a long row of trees before falling into a faraway village made entirely of straw-huts. I looked for the youngster and the woman, largely to gain recognition for my long shot. However, my pride was soon mixed with concern that someone in the village might be wounded. I told this to the woman, who was quite indefinite. She thought that no one was injured."

This dream reveals further progress towards less egoistic action, a development begun in the dream of the commander with her blue and white banner. Zen masters regard a quiet, calm state of mind, unaffected by success or praise, as exemplary. The masculine consciousness of the dreamer takes over the youngster's toy, his childlike wishes. In the man's hands, the bow and arrow become the wonderful instruments of our stone-age ancestors, the "original bow." The man now treats the bow and arrow not impatiently, as a boy would, but with complete calmness according to the dictates of Eastern wisdom. For a Western success-oriented person, this progression, made possible by familiarization with Zen, represents a great gain. The arrow reaches an unknown, distant goal, a far-off center. The following dream, which occurred several months later, brings the dreamer into a close relationship with the Eastern Anima.

Dream Twenty-Four:
The Chinese Girl in a Blue and White Dress

"A young Chinese girl, dressed in blue and white, was waiting at a bus stop. I stood beside her. My hip touched hers. She returned the light pressure. The bus arrived, full of people. We let it pass by. I left the bus stop. I sensed that the Chinese girl was following. Then I noticed that two people, a Chinese girl and woman, were following. A truck arrived. We climbed on. Several women sat in a circle around me. When I first saw the Chinese girl at the bus stop, I felt love, intimate tenderness for her. I felt as if I had finally found her. Now she was sitting on the floor of the truck, leaning her head against my left knee. There was infinite intimacy in her attitude and touch. I longed to kiss her, but, because of the other women, I could not. The Chinese woman sat on my right, loving me with cruel intensity. I felt no conflict between the two Chinese women. In order to be allowed to kiss the Chinese girl, I had to kiss all the others first, so I made the rounds. Among the women was a sinful, pretty blonde. The Chinese girl kissed me but briefly—she didn't want anyone to notice anything unusual—but with such longing that we both knew that we belonged together and would be together. I woke up."

In the past one could barely mention China to the dreamer because of his intense, largely war-related fear of that foreign, hostile country. He had to confront Asia for the first time in the dream of the feminine army-commander. In that dream, the Eastern Anima appeared as an overwhelming military power. Now she approaches him in a peaceful manner. He has, in the meantime, come closer to her by developing an interest in Eastern thought. Until relatively recently, China did not, like the West, focus upon casuality and upon controlling nature. It attempted, instead, to fit human beings meaningfully into nature, time, and the cosmic rhythm.[191] Eastern people attend to nature's uniqueness.

They perceive maxims of life by which they feel supported and against which it is dangerous to resist.

In the Chinese girl, the dreamer now finds the Oriental sense of life which he experiences as his long-sought inner complement. The girl is even more, because the shadow which surrounded the woman-commander is set apart as an elderly woman. The dreamer did not at first describe the older Chinese woman as the embodiment of cruelty and lack of restraint, the qualities which led him to fear the Orient. Only later did he reveal that the love of this older woman seemed to him cruel and dangerous because of its lack of moderation. To him the older Chinese woman appeared as the negative side of nature, as the perilous representative of the ruthlessness and cruelty which occur in Chinese novels and in war reports from all races. In the young lady, however, he encountered the blossoming femininity which is part of an ancient culture unfolding uninterruptedly from nature, a feature in which the East excels over the West. The older woman, on the other hand, represents the danger of lawlessness and barbarity of that collective unconscious that looms also within the dreamer. The young lady is the long sought-for bride, symbol of the forthcoming *coniunctio,* and a promise of inward confluence. She will eventually vanish as a figure and will become part of his psychological make-up.

The woman and the girl are opposites, but, paradoxically, they are also one. They are the one ancient and eternally young, dark and light soul. Sitting in a circle with the two Chinese are many other women. The dreamer must kiss all of them in order to reach the one he seeks. All, even the blonde, sinful, little woman, represent different aspects of women. The dreamer experiences the entire gamut of the nature-soul, from the ruthless cruelty of the older Chinese woman to various encounters and, eventually, to the tenderness of the young lady in the blue and white dress.

Eventually, he may reach that last step where the Anima can be withdrawn from his projections and become his soul's content, his inward completion. At first, however, the dreamer will have to confront many times the dark, dangerous side of the Anima and her shadow. As he gets closer to the collective unconscious, he is also more directly exposed to the collective shadow. As he gets in touch with impersonal, collective powers, it is imperative that he build dams against their negative aspects. He must deal again and again with the shadow. First, however, we must briefly discuss a second dream in which the dreamer attempts to incorporate aspects of the Anima into his masculine being.

Dream Twenty-Five: The Runner

"I'm in a crowd, watching a runner. Enthusiastic over his performance, I go with a British officer to meet him. The officer asks what he must do in order to run as well. The runner demands to see the officer's feet. They are tightly bandaged and quite stiff. It is obvious that the officer tries to use them like machinery, to make them obey and run. The runner, however, insists that the bandages must be removed, as they are but an artificial cramp, that the foot must become soft and elastic, and that the movement of the muscles must occur playfully. With a touch of irony he adds that the officer is not likely to be able to learn this, since he's already too old and should have begun sooner."

Every experience communicated by the Anima is followed by its masculine counterpart. The dreamer now experiences, in a masculine form, the informal, open nature of the Chinese girl. Such male dream-figures as the runner or, earlier, the athlete in the circus tent demonstrate to him qualities that he should appropriate. In the bow and arrow dream, the arrow intuitively attained the distant goal which he is now to reach by himself. He must travel by foot, not by such modern means of transportation as the bus. What counts is the running, not the goal.

The victorious runner reminds us of runners in primitive tribes who, like animals, are one with their bodies and with nature. He wins, not because of an athletic feat, but because of natural elasticity. He is freed from cramp-like will because he does not force himself. Instead, he allows any performance to be as playful as the little Anima-daughter (Dream Twenty-Two).

With the feet we touch the ground of reality. The foot must be quite soft and elastic in order to adjust itself to any unevenness. For an intuitive person like the dreamer, it is extraordinarily difficult, only partly achievable, in fact, to adapt directly to concrete, present reality. He is inclined to neglect the commonplace present with its many details in favor of presentiments and future possibilities. The dreamer had to force himself, both in military service and in his profession which required a great deal of precision, to acquire a self-discipline foreign to his nature. He wanted to advance and achieve high goals. He could not afford mistakes or negligence. These efforts and his ambitions created a cramp-like tension.

As a people, the English are predominantly sensation-oriented. Thus, the British officer is well-suited to represent the sensation-function. British officers in the colonies were frequently entrusted with distant posts and with the responsibility for heavy tasks. They were forced into tense individual performances and into a somewhat stiff formality. Thus, the officer in the dream may portray the dreamer's over-strained sensation-function. He admires the runner, but it remains doubtful whether he will ever be able to equal the runner's natural relaxation and flexibility.

Dream Twenty-Six: The Rats

"I see a rat come out of a pipe. It attacks our little dog, bites it, and kills it. I am disconsolate. I notice two women, one clad in black, the other in red. I know that they are the rats. I shoot them."

Rats multiply extremely quickly. They can barely be eradicated in their hideouts. They can become a frightful plague, both because they attack live animals and human beings and because they transmit illnesses. The rat in this dream is a seemingly insignificant, light-shunning, but extremely dangerous instinctual impulse. It is dangerous because of its greed and its tendency to invade domestic territory. In the dream the rat endangers the dreamer's dog, a cheerful, domestic, instinctual component. Undomesticated greed is about to kill the lively, charming aspect of instinct which benefits the family.

Then the dreamer has the sudden insight that two women are rats. As he is aware of their danger, he shoots them. Both women emerged from the older Chinese woman in Dream Twenty-Four. They are the gruesome and immoderate shadow of the Anima and of the instinctual nature that now manifests itself. Years later, the dreamer still vividly recalled the malevolent, venomous red cloth of this dream-figure. In her he sees a perilous form of provocative sensuality. The woman in black impresses him as a threatening eruption of the shadow. He compares both women to the "Great Whore of Babylon," the symbol of unbridled covetousness in Revelation. He also compares them with "Everywoman" of the Middle Ages, who was portrayed, on one hand, as seductive and, on the other, as replete with sickness and vermin. The dream shows him that he must defend himself against a certain type of woman, namely, against this side of the Anima. As a result, he shoots the dream-figures. For the time being, he can protect himself from regressing to the level of the whore-Anima only through radical measures.

Dream Twenty-Seven: I Overtake My Mother

"I'm racing in a large sleigh. I'm supposed to win, but I find myself alone on the street. Then I notice my mother on a small sleigh ahead of me. I have to pass her on a curve without running over her and without being thrown out of my sleigh. I succeed. After overcoming a number of obstacles, including a bus, a skier, and a fence for animals, I realize that I'll reach my destination. It occurs to me that I will win first prize. At the same time I tell myself that this is entirely unimportant. The main thing is that I have done well and reached my goal."

Because of his earlier decision to fight the Anima's shadow-aspect, the dreamer is able to enter the race and reach the goal which he previously had been able to attain only with the far-flying arrow of his longing. Now, after overcoming the rats, the dark Anima, he is able to overtake his mother, the first bearer of the Anima-image, without disturbing her journey. In order to reach his new goal, the dreamer must leave his mother behind him. The mother represents the longing for childlike security from which the son's consciousness must become free. This time he succeeds in directing his attention entirely upon his task and his goal, without being distracted by ambition or desire to win.

The following dream portrays his personal struggle with super-personal, religious values.

Dream Twenty-Eight: The Church Collapses

"I meet an old professor, my former teacher, in a railroad-station. We exchange a few words. He leaves through a door with another old gentleman. With many other people I go along a hallway to a door. The Dictator was standing behind this door. I thought it was idiotic for him to stand there when his enemy was right outside the door. I entered and found myself in an enormous hall in the basement. My things were stored in a corner. I gathered them in order to climb out of this hall. Everyone else wanted to do the same thing, to escape from impending events. We reached the upstairs and found ourselves in Rome's cathedral of St. Peter. An officer yelled at the people and tried to chase them back. I swore at him. Suddenly I noticed some men in the cupola desperately trying to secure the bells and the bell-tower with ropes. Their strength left them and the bells plunged down, crashing through the floor and probably crushing people in the basement-hall where we had been. Then the cupola began to collapse. We turned and tried to get outdoors. All the walls began to crumble. I broke one of the church windows and managed to jump out. Just before I reached the door of a fence, walls collapsed behind me. A stone hit me in the neck. I still hoped to escape with a final leap, but square stones fell all around me. I realized I was trapped. I was crushed by stones before reaching the door."

After leaving his pious mother, the dreamer finds himself in a railroad-station, a new point of departure. There he meets a former teacher who soon departs with another old gentleman. The appearance of the old professor identifies this starting point as a place of men, of professionals, and of traditional conscious values. But the dreamer is moving beyond this place. He must distance himself, therefore, from his mother, his former teacher, and his scientific father. With many others, he now finds himself in a basement below St. Peter's Cathedral. Here the dictator stands, looking out for the approaching enemy. St. Peter's Cathedral is the spiritual structure beneath which, in the unconscious, a power struggle between opposites (for example, between the lion and dragon portrayed by alchemy, between greed and might) takes place.

At the end of this dream, the dreamer sees himself transposed back to the end of World War II. He discovers that a power struggle between human consciousness, represented by the dictator, and primitive instincts, represented by the enemy, continues to rage within himself. At the same time, he discovers that his conscious world has been a netherworld. He has subconsciously drifted, with many others, away from the healing truths of the church, from that which the church signifies and presents as an ideal. But when he tries to escape the enemy, the eruption of unconscious powers, by seeking refuge in a church, he finds out that the church can no longer protect him from the enemy nor withstand an outbreak of primitive instincts. Worldwide political upheavals have undermined the grandiose structure of the church within the dreamer's soul. Within the church walls, he feels a lack of protection and an increased threat of collapse.

He had had a dream in which a church collapsed once before. In that dream he was able to save himself by fleeing in spite of his pious mother's pleas to stay. He was then able to avoid religious problems by not looking at them. How would he ever stand alone against the spirit of the age or find a remedy for its distressed condition? Was he not but one of the many victims of historical events? Was he not without a calling as religious reformer? In this last dream, however, flight is useless. Religious crises hurt him personally. The torch of the Second World War has revealed the power of the Antichrist. Subterranean conflicts have eroded the church's image. This is made clear by an earlier dream which we will discuss now.

Dream Twenty-Eight A: The Bomb

"I'm standing before a modern highrise building. Through a door I can see a court surrounded by residential buildings. A bomb hits the area behind this passage, and the buildings collapse. I know that my apartment and all my property, which I acquired through great hardship after losing everything in the war, have been destroyed. I think of how hard my wife had to slave for our belongings. At that moment a priest in vestments comes out of the passage. Obviously, he has been with the wounded and dying. He carries the extreme unction with him. Suddenly, I'm overcome by rage against the cruelty of fate and God who controls fate. I raise my fist. I threaten the priest and curse God. Though I know that this is a horrendous sin, similar to that of the Titans, I continue to hate and to curse wildly and angrily. I am oppressed by my anger for many days, but I am also relieved that I have expressed it for once."

The trauma of war goes on. After people have re-settled in modern, utilitarian buildings, the peace and quiet are destroyed. A bomb may fall any time out of the clear sky and shatter everything. In his dream, in contrast to his real-life situation, the dreamer is simply one of many tenants of a large apartment house. The bomb affects him and all the others, destroying the calm, the peace, and the fruits of reconstruction. The dreamer's rebellion against God, who allows or causes such things to happen, and against the blindness of fate had been suppressed, but now it finally breaks through. He curses the priest, the sacrament, and God. He knows he is committing a mortal sin.

He internally confronts a problem which he had faced externally during the war. The highrise building, the modern, utilitarian apartment house which he inhabits in the dream, reflects his practical, modern attitude which he tried to accommodate to the world. But now this attitude no longer protects him. An internal bomb explodes his newly acquired peace. He must once more radically restructure the edifice of his views. His war experiences have finally driven him to the side of the Titans, towards rebellion against the gods in heaven. His suffering breaks down his Christian attitude, and he opposes the God-father of his childhood. He loses his sense of security. In the dream of the collapse of St. Peter's Cathedral he finds himself, therefore, between Scylla and Charybdis, between the dictator and the invading enemy, in a camp of mutually destructive forces of the Antichrist. Flight into the security of the church fails because deep down he left the church long ago. The men who make a last, strenuous effort to hold up the bell tower represent his desperate attempt to sustain the edifice of his former Christian views. Bells are reminders which summon one for prayers and church services. They are the church's live voice. Falling, they act as the crushing Christian conscience. A similar function is found in the legend of the child who refused to go to church on Sunday and was, therefore, pursued by a bell.

The church is made up of a community of believers. In *The Shepherd of Hermas,* an apocryphal New Testament text, Hermas has a vision of the construction of the church. An old woman, personifying the church, explains to him the meaning of stones used for construction. White, square stones that fit together are the saintly, pure apostles, bishops, teachers, and deacons who live in conformity with God's holiness and who work for the benefit of God's chosen people. Broken, discarded stones are sinners. Those which are not discarded far from the church tower are likely to be useful for construction once they have made penance.[192]

The disintegration of this community strikes the dreamer with deadly force. The stone which hits him in the neck is his own, not yet hewn, self, his not yet resolved religious problem. He is not yet polished enough to fit into a religious community and help build it. His own religious problems overtake him and hit him hard; but what slays him is the failure of those whom he believed reliable but who, like himself, dropped out of the community.

That which, until now, was the highest, though not always obeyed, authority for him collapses. St. Peter's Cathedral is the symbol of the one and only *mater ecclesia,* Mother Church, built upon a rock. It is a visible symbol of the unification of opposites: the all-encompassing, protective Mother and the spiritual authority of the great Father, the Pope. Just as the individual stones in Hermas's vision symbolized the faithful, St. Peter's Cathedral symbolizes the fortitude and security one finds in the orthodox community. Until recently, religious questions were resolved by the Roman authorities. Now they are vital, personal concerns.

The dream of the church's collapse marks a radical change in the dream series. Up to now, personal problems—such as affects and emotions, approaches to the Anima, and differentiation of the latter's being—have been in the foreground. In the beginning, the relationship to the Anima was understood as a personal concern. There have been occasional attempts to experience the Self as an impersonal inner center—for example, in the dreams of the circus athlete (Dream Fifteen), the lady commander (Dream Twenty), and the Christmas tree (Dream Twenty-One).

The collapse of the church, however, reveals that until now the dreamer still identified with the church and felt contained by it. With the cathedral's collapse, his "old Adam," his "old ego" must die once more. Because God has been nicely settled in heaven, and religion settled in church, the dreamer has been free to shape his life according to his own pleasure and traditional, local moral standards. Unconsciously identifying with the church, he believed himself to be personally free. However, with the collapse of the church, his sustaining and protective spiritual and psychological authority, he is confronted by religious problems. The following dreams have an increasingly open character. The inner dialogue centers more and more on the search for genuine religious insight. The death of the old ego, shown in the dream of St. Peter's Cathedral, at first hovers over the dreamer like a vague threat. Only gradually does he realize that this death signals the final relinquishing of an overly youthful, unreflective way of life. His unawareness must die in order to build the new, live world view of a responsible, free-thinking adult.

Dream Twenty-Nine: The Field on the Mountain Slope

"High in the mountains, surrounded by forests, there is a field on a grassy slope. It is filled with bushes and weeds. A man, possibly my brother, and I try to clear it. He digs up the bushes with his shovel, and I plow the field. It is hard work, but the result is a field of healthy, glistening, dark soil in beautiful furrows. Knowing that there is further work to do, we pass through a hedge to a field closer to the edge of the forest. This field, in contrast to the first, is well maintained. It is filled with various fruit trees planted in rows. The trees are relatively young. At a man's height their trunks are cut neatly, so that only the lower branches, some with apples, remain. All the trees lack tops. The other man states that, although it is a shame to dig the trees out, it would be better to do so. Being the stronger one, he begins to dig out the trees. We then become aware that there are rows of thick, heavy root-stocks of firs, cut about three feet above ground, between the thin stems of the fruit trees. This is going to be a tremendous job, but I now recognize that the work must be done. The man tells me, 'When all the trees are removed, we will have a better shooting range. Also, we will be able to see deep into the forest.' I see only this second man, but I *know* that another man and a woman are here. At last the field is cleared and plowed like the other one. The four of us discuss what is likely to grow. We are full of confidence that there will be a good sowing. We don't sow, we leave this to the forest and the wind. When the field is ready, we find a dead mouse. It is as big as a rat. I think it *is* a rat. We know that this animal was killed by switches as it came out of its hole. We are glad that it is dead."

The field high up on a slope is probably the same as the colorful field in Dream Thirteen which was owned first by the poacher's wife and then by the old earth-mother. Now it is the dreamer himself who cares for this field. If the mountain symbolizes the highest goal attainable in this world, then caring for the field represents the dreamer's higher tasks. The front part of the field, full of bushes and weeds, reminds one of the parable of the sower (Matt. 13): "Other seeds fell among the thorns, and the thorns came up and choked them. Still others fell upon the fine soil and they began to yield fruit, this one a hundred-fold, that one sixty, the other thirty."[193]

The field is the soul. A good seed may not grow in it if there are many weeds. The field is an example of unadulterated, but also uncultivated, nature. It will yield a rich harvest once it is cleared and plowed. Behind the hedge, hidden and closer to the forest's edge, is another field with rows of trees. All the trees are cut at a man's height. The motif of topped trees is found in alchemy as a counterpart to the lion with cut paws.[194] It suggests a painfully incisive sacrifice. It is likely to suggest an additional meaning when it arises in an intuitive individual. Intuition induces the extroverted person to pursue new possibilities. What is new is more attractive to him than what is old, already-known, and close at hand. He lacks patience to wait until his trees bear fruit. Whatever has been started is truncated for the sake of a new goal. Because of his varied interests, and also because of pressing circumstances, the dreamer has changed his place of work and his career. He has given up what he has achieved in order to continue his education. His versatility, restlessness, cosmopolitan skills, and lack of material success are both his strengths and his weaknesses. The truncated trees point to the repeated interruption of his development. The life flowing from the roots never achieves its crowning.

The roots of the firs between the fruit trees are reminiscent of the mystery of Attis. Every year Attis was carried in the guise of a hewn fir into the shrine of his mother who would weep over him. The remnants of the fir trees indicate that the dreamer lives his life as the beloved son of the mother-goddess and that he sacrifices his life over and over again for her. His consuming ambition is, ultimately, a concession to his mother. Her son is to accomplish that which her deceased husband was not able to do. He is to reach the highest rung of the professional ladder.

In the back of the field are two kinds of trees, firs and fruit trees. Not only Attis but also his mother-goddess was worshiped in the tree on the mountain. Jung quotes from the *Gnosis of Justin:* "The trees of the Garden of Eden are angels; the tree of life is the angel Baruch, the third of the paternal angels; and the tree of knowledge of good and evil is Naas, the third of the maternal angels."[195] The different trees correspond to these angels: the firs to the paternal ones; the fruit trees, bearing apples (like the tree of knowledge) and other sweet fruits, to the maternal ones. Growth of professional development as well as of the Anima has been repeatedly cut short. The truncated fruit trees represent a manifold Anima-experience which never allowed the fruits of knowledge to ripen. Even here, the intuitive individual keeps chasing different possibilities without realizing that he is caught in the mother-goddess's garden of Paradise.

We mentioned before that, as long as she remains in the natural state of paradisiacal ignorance, the Anima can be projected upon many kinds of women. Every possibility that appears on the horizon seems to promise the fulfillment that has been longed for since early childhood. Every attempt at becoming aware of the Anima is pushed aside by a new, false hope. The tree of internal growth was again and again truncated, and a new one was planted beside it. The dreamer never went beyond natural growth, devoid of insight and knowledge. What is missing in the dream is the upper part of the firs, the part that embodied Attis and was brought to his mother's sanctuary, and the upper part of the fruit trees, the manifestation of the grieving or bridal mother, companion of her beloved son. The growth of the natural soul, depicted as an orchard, is halfway arrested. Denied maturity and fulfillment, it is incapable of growing into the spiritual regions. Spirit and nature remain separate. The church manages the spirit. In it the spiritual symbol is at home, but nature is not included and, therefore, must forego spiritual fulfillment.

Often alchemical work included caring for and growing one or more trees. The alchemical, or philosophical, tree must be planted in a well-protected garden into which nothing foreign may penetrate. This garden is the carefully purified inner earth, the "cleansed Mercurius."[196] It is said of the alchemical tree that whoever eats of its fruits will never be hungry.[197] Thus, alchemy replaces natural growth by planting a spiritual tree in the spiritual earth. Its prototype of this tree, according to Jung, is the paradise tree which bears moon- and sun-fruits instead of apples. These fruits allude to king and queen, the quintessences of masculinity and femininity.[198] The magnificent Christmas tree which the dreamer found in his father's apartment was also a kind of Paradise tree (Dream Twenty-One). It was both a legacy from his father and a happy childhood memory. Now he must plant a spiritual tree in his own inner garden.

The collapse of traditional, religious views forces the dreamer to turn towards his own "soul-garden." He discovers that it is full of wild weeds. A man, possibly his brother, shows him that his field must be cleared and plowed, if anything worthwhile is to grow in it. The earth within one's own soul is the *prima materia* that is transformed into "cleansed Mercurius." Four figures, three men and a woman, work in the garden. The dreamer comments that, although they are different figures, they may all represent himself. They portray those aspects of his being which, until now, he has not been able to differentiate.[199] As in the dream of the army-commander (Dream Twenty), the four figures indicate wholeness. This time, however, the male aspect predominates, since clearing the field represents a conscious activity requiring male initiative and man's spiritual capacity for discrimination. The dead mouse or rat discovered by the gardeners would then represent the greed of the impure *prima materia,* the tenacious gluttony which, in Dream Twenty-Six, appeared as the Anima's addiction. This greed has been expelled, as shown by the rat's death, by self-discipline.

The four persons, representing four different soul-forces, are hopeful that the forest and wind will bring forth good seeds. The forest, the unconscious, has predominantly feminine qualities; the wind, predominantly masculine qualities. The dreamer can prepare the soil, but he must leave the sowing to God or to the forest and wind, that is, to nature. He cannot rationally and willfully choose the right seed. His further development cannot be consciously predetermined, but the alchemical analogy of the garden with the sun- and moon-tree suggests that the dreamer's goal is attainment of the two lights, sun and moon—that is, the quintessence of masculinity and femininity, the union of spirit and soul.

The cut firs between the stems of the fruit trees show that the dreamer's immature spirit maintains an unrecognized, unconscious connection with the mother-goddess. When spiritual values were based in the church, he remained, as son, attached to unconscious nature. In the front part of the field, where male trees, symbols of his spiritual growth as a man, belong, only weeds prosper. Disorder and confusion have reigned here. This problem affects others than the dreamer. In Dream Twenty-Eight he was with others in the basement below the church. *Many* were buried by the collapsing, and *many* tried to flee with him. The people in the basement are the masses who are either not yet or no longer affected and guided by the church's eternal images and who, therefore, unconsciously lapse into paganism. They lead a life defined only by materialistic terms. The remedy for this state consists in cleaning up one's own soul-garden. This dream effected a change, a purification in the dreamer's everyday life. He decided to give up his heretofore superficial relations with women.

Dream Thirty: The Eagle

"I stood in a large room in a multi-story building. Below me I could see the tops of firs. Suddenly I saw an eagle rushing by, playfully shooting downwards and re-ascending. The eagle's wings were steel-colored with white tips. A boy was in the room and I called him to the window so that he could see the eagle. I protected him with my arm and we were standing behind the window, so that the eagle, soaring downwards, its wings rushing in the wind, could not grab him. The eagle overtook a flock of birds but did not grab any of them. I was surprised. Then the arm of a crane moved swiftly out from the flat roof of the skyscraper and overtook the eagle. At first I thought that he had been captured, but then I realized that he submitted voluntarily. When he was brought into the room I noticed that he had his legs tied and was able to walk only with small steps, and was, therefore, unable to grasp the birds with his claws. In order to live, he had to allow himself to be captured."

The eagle is the larger relative of the corn-hawk in Dream Fourteen. He was Zeus's bird and abducted Ganymede into the clouds. He might prove dangerous to the boy at the window. He could carry the still weak Self of the dreamer up to the gods, alienate him from his daily tasks, and thereby turn him into an eternally immature companion of the gods, living on an unworldly Olympus.

Father Zeus is not mentioned, but the bird with his dark wings and white tips suggests a union of light and dark, good and evil. In ancient Egypt the Horus-falcon was the symbol of the highest celestial god. As a sharp-sighted and all-surveying celestial spirit, and as a manifestation of destiny, he corresponds to a concept of god more ancient than that found in the Old Testament. We find in Ezekiel (17:3) a riddle in which Jehovah also compares himself with an eagle. It reads: "This is what the Lord Jehovah has said: 'The great eagle, having great wings, with long pinions, full of plumage, which had color variety, came to Lebanon and proceeded to take the treetop of the cedar. He plucked off the very top of its young shoots and came bringing it to the land of Canaan; in a city of traders he placed it. . . .'" In his positive aspect, the eagle is an all-surveying, all-knowing spirit. As Horus-falcon he has the sun- and the moon-eye, a celestial consciousness, the precious gift which the dreamer needs to complete and crown his garden (Dream Twenty-Nine).

However, the eagle is also wild, sharp-eyed, greedy, predatory, presumptuous, and physically superior to the human being. His feet are tied in the dream. In order to live he must descend into the human realm, as he is no longer able to catch his own prey. It was probably the clearing of the field in the last dream which resulted in this restriction of the previously autonomous, knowledgeable, knowledge-hungry, instinctive spirit. In that dream, we found that the dreamer cleared out all wild growth. He also killed the rat or mouse which had been the bird's food. This clearing of reality has restricted the freedom of the bird of prey, the rapacious instinct, and forced him to give himself up to the human beings. The bird is overtaken by the crane, by means of psychological control. Whereas the dreamer has experienced his life as subject to the whims of his curiosity and thirst for knowledge, he is now able to decide consciously what he wants to do. His hunger for life and knowledge will be subordinate to the conscious ego, to human responsibility.

Dream Thirty-One: The Woman in the Furrow

"War! I'm in a battle. I'm under cover in the furrow of a field. I notice a nude woman lying in the same furrow ahead of me. Then I find myself in a house with the same woman, and I'm told to marry her as she has only a few minutes to live. We are led into a room and married. Then the woman appears to be dead."

The dreamer finds himself again in war, in an inner conflict. His only protection and cover is the furrow he himself has plowed. He discovers a naked, unfamiliar woman in this furrow. The furrow is the open womb of the earth; the naked woman incarnates this earth. From above a celestial spirit, the eagle, had been approaching; from below appears the embodiment of earthly reality. The woman symbolizes unprotected, exposed life, nude and poor when deprived of all ostentatious garments. She is as bare as his field after he has cleared it of all weeds, trees, and incomplete growth. She is as poor as a soul deprived of all the benefits of the church. This woman is his life reduced to bare, human, natural facts. He is to affirm this reality and wed himself to her. His saying yes to her means saying yes to simple, untrimmed, and inescapable human nature. He accepts her, and thus she becomes his own truth. She dies in order to become a part of him.

Maybe the naked woman in the furrow is more than a human being. She may be the goddess whose dark aspect the dreamer has shot in the dream of the rats (Dream Twenty-Six). She is probably also a transformation of the mouse found by the dreamer clearing the field (Dream Twenty-Nine). As a rejuvenated goddess emerging from the furrow, she is also like a seed. She is the grain of wheat which through many transformations must die and resurrect.

Dream Thirty-Two: Divine Service in the Grotto

"I'm climbing up the side of a rock. Halfway up I reach a grotto. With great difficulty I pull myself into it and sit on its edge. Inside, numerous people are attending a religious service. I am surprised because they are also singing folk songs. They sing:

> With great longing
> I went to the Lord:
> May I, may I, may I,
> May I love the maiden?
> But of course, he says and laughs,
> Just for the boys I've made the girls."

In Dream Thirty a celestial spirit, in the form of an eagle, descended to the dreamer. In Dream Thirty-One the dreamer united with the earthy Anima. In this dream, the dreamer moves upward. The steep rock represents a great difficulty that he must overcome. In the course of the dream, it becomes clear that this difficulty is his distance from God which he must overcome. By his climb he reaches a point where a divine service, in which a question is addressed to God, is taking place. He has reached the level of a pre-Christian cult, a nature religion whose content and attitude have been preserved in a folk song and, by extension, in the folk consciousness. In the first two stanzas of this well-known song, a young man asks his mother and, later, his pastor: "May I love the maiden?" Both answer negatively. The mother believes he's too young for love. She wants to keep him for herself. The pastor, the representative of religion, would condemn the young man if he professed himself in favor of love. The community in the grotto sings only the third stanza which addresses the question directly to God. In the song, God answers that he has created the woman for the man. God accepts the dreamer along with his love. At this point, the formerly distinct realms of nature and spirit begin to approach each other. The nature-soul has spent its life in the garden with weeds and truncated trees, and the dreamer has lived two lives, one Christian and one pagan. But the dreamer sets out to reach the level of Christian consciousness. The following dreams will tell more about this quest.

Dream Thirty-Three: The New Church

"A new church is being built. So far, only the scaffold has been completed. The church is going to be quite simple and modern. It will have a main ship with a high, slender tower on each side. The towers will be made partly of steel plates similar to those found in erector sets for children."

The dreamer has now also climbed the other half of the rock in the last dream. He is no longer in the cave, but in a place where a church can be constructed. The dream reveals a beginning attempt to build a new church, to reach a new understanding of religion. So far, only a scaffold exists which is to be gradually enclosed by walls. The two towers flanking the main structure are equivalent poles linked with each other, possibly logos and eros. This church is to replace the dome-like structure that collapsed in Dream Twenty-Eight. This dream is the direct consequence of that one.

Dream Thirty-Four: The Tabernacle

"I saw a tabernacle made of precious white and golden brocade. On top it had a border like one finds in tents.[200] When its curtains opened, I saw something resembling a bale of cloth in large folds flowing downwards. This material was grey and laced with silver. I was told, 'The tabernacle is the exterior life; and what it hides is the interior life. You must strive for the latter, taking care that it doesn't come outside.' I kept working on the material, lacing it with silver."

After the construction of the new church, its contents are to be understood in a new way. This dream, like Dream Thirty-Two, is concerned with the integration of nature and spirit. It states, "Your outward life is the tabernacle, and within it is contained, like the holiest of holies, your interior life. Though it sometimes seems to you toilsome, miserable and worthless, this external life is the precious wrapping behind which the secret of your interior life is to remain hidden." In keeping with the dreamer's male consciousness, the external life is symbolized by white and gold. Gold represents the spirit's sun-quality; white represents the clarity of consciousness with which one strives for what is rational and morally good. The dreamer's inner life, however, is not represented by a silvery paten or the chalice, but by a silver and grey cloth, a symbol of the feminine aspect of the man's soul. This cloth is the vessel into which God descends. The dreamer intends to enrich the dark soul-material with silver, that is, with psychological insight. He is warned that this darker material must not become visible to the outside. The Anima's dark sides, her struggles, her depressions and irrational ideas, must not be visible on the outside. They must remain hidden behind a clear, correct, and conscious exterior attitude.

This dream locates the problem of the Anima in the dreamer's interior. The Anima becomes the inner reality, the content of his life. She becomes both the content of the tabernacle and the vessel for the incarnation of the living spirit. The dream sharply distinguishes between inside and outside. The outward life is laced with gold, with spiritual awareness, while the inner being is embellished with silver, with moon-quality, according to alchemy. Both the inner and the outer life are placed in relation to the most important mystery of the church. The dream elevates the human being and equals it to the central religious symbol.

Dream Thirty-Five: The Sapphire Ring

"I found myself in a large party with the British Queen and Prince Philip. However, they only spoke with each other. Later I could only see them through a pane of glass. The queen allowed me to choose a present, either a brooch with white and rose-colored rings, intertwined like those of the Olympics, or a ring with a setting of white pearls and a beautifully cut blue stone, which I could pick up outside the large window. The ring was too small for me, but I chose it anyhow, thinking that my daughter might be able to wear it. Only later did I discover that the ring was contained within a sphere of golden filigree, a magnificent work of art."

At the time of this dream, the queen of England and her husband were in the news. In them the god-pair, sun and moon, take on human shape even though the queen of England outranks her male partner. The fact that the royal pair is removed behind a pane of glass suggests that they are a part of the inner, spiritual realm and are not yet within reach for the dreamer. One of the queen's presents is a brooch with white and rose-colored rings. Red and white, according to Jung, are the alchemical colors which correspond to sun and moon.[201] The interlaced rings thus symbolize the *coniunctio* of sun and moon, that is, the intimate, nuptial union of spirit and soul. This union is within reach of the dreamer, but he cannot yet grasp it. These two rings anticipate the next developmental step. The dreamer chooses the other piece of jewelry, the ring with the sapphire and crown of pearls. Jung quotes Rulandus in regard to the sapphire: "Its specific virtue consists in rendering the wearer pious and constant. In alchemistic medicine it was a heart medication."[202] These are the exact qualities that the Anima needs. The blue of the sky is crystallized into the solid, transparent sapphire.[203] This blue stone, spirit turned into a substance, reminds one of the heavenly throne of sapphire in Ezekiel's vision (Ezekiel 1:24) which is the seat of the divine, higher human being. We have previously mentioned, in discussing the woman-commander's blue and white banner in Dream Twenty, the blue and white vishuddha-mandala of tantra-yoga in which a white elephant personifies the spiritual drive that confers substance and concreteness to ideas.[204]

What is meant by the pearls? In the fairy tale of the goose girl at the fountain, we find that her tears shed during banishment turn into pearls. When she is delivered and has again become a princess, she receives her transformed tears as a dowry from the old earth-mother. These pearls then are the tears of princess Anima. When she was entangled in the world, she was forced to perform menial tasks. The salt of her tears and the bitterness of life which she tasted during this time, however, are later transformed into a softly glowing jewel. Alchemy speaks of the "pearl of love."[205] The ring with the sapphire and pearls is not meant for his sister-Anima but for his daughter. The dreamer feels far more responsible for the latter than for the former. The ring symbolizes his connection with the daughter-Anima. The dreamer's relationship to women has undergone an additional change. From now on he will be able to meet women in a fatherly, responsible manner.

What appeared first in the guise of a banner and later in Dream Twenty-Four as the Chinese woman with a blue and white dress becomes the property of the daughter-Anima. She is to become the bearer of spiritual reality. At the dream's end, the dreamer notices that the ring is contained in a golden, filigree sphere, indicating that it belongs to the tabernacle. This dream reaches the acme of consciousness of the vishuddha-mandala. Subsequent dreams need no longer deal with blue and white. Now the dreamer must acquire the interlaced rings or produce the red and white stones. The white pearls are precious, but they have not yet attained the hardness and crystal-clear transparency of the alchemistic stone, or of the diamonds and rubies that decorate the royal rings. Alchemy speaks of the red slave and white woman who must be dissolved, purified, transformed, and united in the alchemical operation.[206] We already know that red stands for blood, fire, and passion. How can passion be transformed into a red stone? How can the nuptial union of the red and white essences take place? We do not know, for each and every individual's journey is new and unique. All we can do is entrust ourselves to the paths and wisdom of the unconscious.

Dream Thirty-Six: Brandy

"I was with many people in a church. I was in front, close to the communion rail, able to observe everything. The old bishop passed his office on to a younger one. Both were filled with profound piety, and I was deeply impressed. The service proceeded in the following way. The old bishop lifted the host, worshiping during the transubstantiation. He passed it to the new bishop who accepted it, full of reverence. At that instant, a priest with festive, priestly vestments came out of the sacristy. He held a chalice, into which he had poured a bottle of brandy, and passed it to the people who knelt down for communion. Soon, most of them were drunk and began howling. I went back to my bench where I knelt down between two acquaintances, a woman and a man, and cried as I was horrified."

The dreamer finds himself in the church, a suprapersonal realm. He's in front, near the communion trellis. He is with the laymen, close to the priestly interchange that takes place in the interior room but which concerns him directly. The old bishop, the shepherd of the flock, has just lifted the host as he does during the transubstantiation. Thus, the dream starts at the center of the mass, the holy moment when God becomes present at the offering.

If we ask ourselves where and how the rites which preceded this high point of the holy service took place, we discover that previous dreams correspond, albeit in an individual and not easily recognized way, to these preparative steps.[207] In the dream of the rats, the dreamer shot the black and the red Anima, thereby sacrificing some of his former attitudes. As a result, he was able to overtake his mother in a race and reach a new goal (Dream Twenty-Seven). When he overtook his mother, he discarded a life without direction and began working deliberately on his problems. As a result, his former concept of the church as protecting mother collapsed (Dream Twenty-Eight). His new, increasingly aware, attitude led him to examine himself, to clear his field of weeds, and to plow rooted-out soil (Dream Twenty-Nine). In short, it led him to a cleansing of his life, which involved a sometimes painful process of letting go of old habits. Three men and a woman participated in rooting out the field. The number of workers suggested a four-fold differentiation or division of his being, as by a cross. (In the mass the priest makes the sign of the cross over the host.) In Dream Thirty the dark bird appeared with which the spirit is carried from nature into the human realm. Dream Thirty-One showed a woman lying in a furrow, a fruit of the field who must die in order to resurrect. After the dreamer's union with the sacrificial offering, he climbs a steep rock and is accepted, along with his natural aspect, by God (Dream Thirty-Two). This acceptance indicates nature's approach to the spirit. Like the first elevation of the bread during the mass, it suggests the spiritualization of nature.

A new church is built in Dream Thirty-Three. In this dream is gained a new concept of the church in which opposites balance each other. Dream Thirty-Four portrays the dreamer's outward life as a tabernacle which contains his inner life. Thus the dream links his ówn inward experiences with the traditional symbols of the mass. In Dream Thirty-Five the king and queen appear. In alchemy they represent Sol and Luna, the god-pair. The terms *godfather* and *godmother* refer to this hidden meaning. Indeed, the queen and her consort appear as the communicant's godparents, his spiritual or divine parents. They give him a sapphire ring with white pearls, but he is not yet capable of accepting the intertwined rings, symbolizing the union of red and white, which they also offered. The daughter-Anima will receive the blue ring. As a virgin, as kore in Eleusis, and as rejuvenated fruit of the field, she corresponds to the sacrificed and prepared bread. The sapphire ring is the transformed substance offered by the divine parents, the pearls transformed tears, reminding us of the moon's soft glow. The sapphire, as solidified celestial blue, symbolizes a spiritual body. The offering of the ring signifies that insight into the nature of the unconscious can now occur, becoming hardened conviction and solid knowledge as symbolized by the sapphire. Eternal laws, archetypes, and religious truths will now become visible through various events.

Let us return to the present dream. The older priest passes the transubstantiated host to a younger one. The first part of the mystery, the transubstantiation of the bread, occurred in the series of dreams that we just discussed. Now something horribly sacrilegious happens. Another priest in full vestments emerges from the sacristy and pours brandy instead of wine into the chalice. Instead of giving the chalice, as is proper, to the priests, he passes it to the laymen. This brandy coming directly from the sacristy is not prepared by the ritual, expiated, mixed with water, or spiritualized. Moreover, it is not wine but highly concentrated alcohol. The laymen suffer the evil influence of this unholy beverage.

In his study of "The Symbol of Transformation in the Mass," Jung states: "Just as bread is the substance for physical existence, so the wine represents the substance for spiritual existence."[208] During the mass, wine transforms itself into Christ's blood. To partake of this wine is to be filled with Christ's spirit. Brandy, the soldier's restorative, however, has a devastating effect in this context. It produces drunkenness and a low spirit which profoundly saddens the dreamer. He returns to his seat and kneels between a man and a woman, the disunited opposites of his being. He realizes that drinking this impure, unholy spirit will produce intoxication and loss of ego. He could try to reassure himself that this was but a diabolical temptation. Anyhow, the wine should be offered only to the priests. With such an explanation, he would abandon the solution of his next problem, the synthesis of red and white. (In the ritual this synthesis is illustrated by the mixing of wine and water.) However, because the priest appears in full vestments and approaches the laymen with great solemnity, we must surmise that this dream points to a future task for the dreamer. The following dream will confirm this possibility.

The older bishop passes the host to a younger one. The former represents a father, the latter a son. In a child's life, the father represents a phase in which spiritual tradition is blindly accepted as rule and law. As the son grows up, he learns to separate himself from his father and to confront him with his independent thoughts.[209]

After the collapse of the church in Dream Twenty-Eight, the time of the Father ends, and blind acceptance of spiritual tradition is no longer possible. In Dream Thirty-Three we witness the construction of a church with two towers. This construction symbolizes the separation of opposites. Psychologically, the phase of the son has begun. The son who no longer blindly subjects himself to his father's authority must now choose independently between good and evil. As a consequence, evil becomes more prominent. The third priest, representing the seduction of evil, reveals the contrast between good and evil. As carrier of an inebriating potion, he is a counter-priest and Antichrist. While the wine fills the priests with Christ's spirit, the brandy awakens the laymen's primitive, unredeemed, pagan nature. In the Dionysian mysteries, drunken emotions were incorporated into religious expression. In drunken states, people may try to burst the narrow limits of their existence. Alcohol, opium and other intoxicants are tempting because they promise transcendence of the everyday ego. The third priest attempts to awaken the impersonal depths of emotional nature in order to draw the laymen into the religious realm. His attempt fails because of their weakness and inadequate preparation. They lose their poise as well as their awareness of the solemnity and importance of the church. The potion effects a lowering of the mental level, a descent below the level of profanity.

The dreamer is not alone with his problem. About one year

later, he saw a movie which portrayed the same problem he saw in his dream. How to heal one's spirit, transform one's primitive, emotional nature, and unify one's self are not personal, but universal, human questions.

Dream Thirty-Seven: The Transition

"1. With many others I was standing in a church at the communion rail. In place of an altar, there was only a plain wall with many cracks. An older and a younger man stood on ladder-like wall-hooks trying to repair the cracks while new ones appeared. I feared lest they lose their balance and fall. I turned towards the people, mostly youths and uneducated persons, and began to preach. But my sermon was more like a lecture on physics or technology. It ended with a metaphor: 'A missionary must be like a sailboat which sails with full sails out into the dark sea.' A white-haired old man suddenly stood beside me. He told me that he had liked what he heard, especially the metaphor of the sailboat. Then he added that I better begin to preach, since I had promised it.

2. Near the small city in which I worked, one could cross a river by means of a ferryboat. On the other shore was a border-city named Nordlingen (Northlingen) where there was rich, Italian vegetation, with cypresses and Baroque churches. I wanted to visit. A man went with me. Inside the churches, there were museums with collections of prehistoric tools kept in glass closets. After viewing one of the collections of prehistoric tools and old wood- or wax-seals, we went to the ferry in order to cross the river. The old man sat in the front of the boat filled with people. He alone was allowed to row. Suddenly a motor started and propelled the boat. We hit a small ledge of sand which we had to cross on foot. The old man walked to my right, and beside him walked a younger woman. At first I wanted to lean on him as I was barefoot and my feet were hurting, but then I realized that it was up to me to support him."

A new threat to the church follows the disastrous distribution of brandy to the laymen in Dream Thirty-Six. The altar has disappeared. It is now necessary to seek behind it, behind all ecclesiastic symbolism, for the meaning of one's life. The wall behind the altar, which separates the church from the world, is disintegrating. An older and a younger man, who probably represent, as in the preceding dream, a father and son, try to repair it. The dreamer, however, fears lest they fall down from the wall-hooks, the concepts, which sustain them. Thus he himself turns towards the waiting crowd, mostly young or uneducated people, and begins to preach. It is the younger and less educated ones, within himself and within the world, who sense deficiency and seek a new orientation. The dreamer's sermon is restricted by his natural-scientific schooling and his listeners' range of interests. He tries to convey some of his religious convictions through scientific parallels. He concludes: "A missionary must be like a sailboat which sails with full sails out into the dark sea."

His sermon, this last expression in particular, meets the special approval of an old man. It is not enough for a person to journey alone. He must take others with him. His insights must be transmitted in order to become alive, grow and deepen. If he feels called upon to help others, he must have the courage to let his own little lifeboat be driven by the wind (the *pneuma*) and to expose himself to the darkness and danger of the sea, the collective soul. Three events in this dream—the dreamer's sermon, his statement that missionaries must be like sailboats in a dark sea, and the old man's appearance—reveal a new developmental step. They show that the brandy, in contrast to its superficially horrendous effect in Dream Thirty-Six, has broadened the dreamer's consciousness. He speaks as layperson to the crowd about the necessity of allowing oneself to be moved by the spirit (*pneuma*). At that moment appears the old man, whom we may surmise is an archetypal old, wise man who embodies knowledge and wisdom accumulated through centuries of human experience. The appearance of the old wise man always signals a significant step in development.[210] Through him a man gains his personal spiritual orientation. After the old wise man becomes his companion, the dreamer relies more and more on his own "inner court." While he had previously been driven by his need for life and experience, he will now be motivated by his search for the meaning of his experience.

As long as the man is susceptible to his Anima's fascination and superior power, he must resist her seduction into fantasy and blind thirst for experience. Only conscientious execution of concrete tasks, careful consideration of professional obligations, and genuine commitment to marriage and family can protect the dreamer from his Anima's inordinate demands. By the dreamer's gaining insight into her nature and limiting her demands, the Anima is induced to submit herself to the old wise man's guidance. A new attitude towards one's profession and everyday life, therefore, becomes necessary. The Self's suprapersonal archetype, the old wise man, confronts the dreamer with extensive possibilities which, if experienced as obligations, may become too demanding.

What is searched for but unknown always appears, at first, as projection upon the outside world. A man, especially an extroverted person, immediately believes that he must find the new values in his profession. He therefore attempts to improve in this area. He must, however, seek a much deeper meaning. In fact, in order to follow the path indicated by the old wise man, he must limit his outward activity and let go of everything inessential. He must also become less rigid in regard to rational rules and collective norms. If he does not fulfill these obligations, new insights will not prevail. The plenitude of new possibilities may also physically demand too much of the dreamer. He can protect himself only by a strict limitation to essentials.

In the second part of the dream, we find the dreamer on the shore of a river. Luxuriant Italian vegetation and Baroque churches are on this shore. On the opposite bank is Northlingen, which represents, to the dreamer, the Spartan poverty of the North. In other words, on the dreamer's side is Christendom, the good, the conscious world. On the other side is unknown darkness, the unconscious and its perils. In the North, according to Biblical tradition, the devil dwells. The Old Testament (Jeremiah 1: 14) reads: "From the North comes the boiling evil to the country's inhabitants." In the North, pagan gods dwell. At the North Pole, "behind the North Wind," is the castle of Arianrhod (silver-wheel), where dead pagan heroes and kings are placed, in contrast to ordinary dead people who wander disconsolately through its frozen grounds.[211] The next dream will take place in the North, the realm of evil, of dethroned gods and of lost masses.

In this dream the Baroque churches are museums. They are significant only as places where ancient symbols are stored. Remnants of ancient rituals do persist in the rites and customs of the church. However, the dreamer does not tarry in these museums. He must find the meaning that has, for him, disappeared from the church.

The old wise man manages to ferry him across the stream. Crossing the island, the dreamer wishes to lean against the old man because the pebbles hurt his bare feet. He is painfully exposed to hard reality. He has lost his former attitude but has not yet found a new one. He tries to lean upon the wisdom of the unconscious, but realizes that he himself must fortify the ancient, though new to him, meanings that are still weak and uncertain. Consciousness cannot simply rely on help from within. It must provide enough active support so that the newly emerging contents can grow strong and expand.

Dream Thirty-Eight:
The Lay Priest and the Three Wart Fellows

"The rear of a large, empty hall is closed off by a wooden partition. I hear the sounds of wild jazz coming from behind it. I enter through a door and find myself in a room filled with people who are singing along with a recording of the crazed music. The people jerk their arms upwards in time to the music. A small area is fenced off by a rough table. An older man, obviously the lay priest of this community, stands behind the table and blesses the people. Three gigantic, muscular men stand beside the priest. Their naked torsos are ugly, covered with warts. They control the people by their glances. I don't participate in the singing or dancing. I don't want to. After all I do not have anything to do with it. One of the muscle-men looks at me piercingly and threateningly, but I withstand his glance and refuse to participate."

The dreamer has now crossed the river of Dream Thirty-Seven. Primitive dancing ceremonies channel instinctual energies into such activities as hunting, warring, cultivating the soil, harvesting and healing. Here in a hidden corner of the soul, energy is being produced as it has always been created in primitive cultures, but, as the frenzied music shows, it has become degenerate and dissonant through misuse. Whenever such energies are divorced from their ritual, religious contexts, they discharge themselves in other ways and are easily converted into various excesses. The lay priest who blesses the activities seems to know that they were originally religious rituals which he would like to restore through his benedictions. The three muscular fellows beside him are devils. Their horrid warts remind one of dinosaurs and reptiles. The muscle- or nerve-energy that motivates the crowd's jerking movements derives from that part of the unconscious realm which is still related to reptiles. We have seen a manifestation of this level of the soul in the brandy dream. The dreamer refuses to take part in this excess and pretense. The three muscle-men who request this of him contrast too sharply with his consciousness and culture. The horrid, wart-covered figures also recall the masked devils who played crude pranks during Italian carnivals. These figures date back to the Saturnalia.[212] They are late caricatures of satyrs and fauns. These primitive, pagan energies were channeled by the Catholic church from carnival festivities into penitence and religious meditation during Lent.

Beyond the river, or behind the wooden partition, is a foreign world into which the dreamer enters, and into which a priest advances with his benedictions as a missionary who dares to sail alone into a stormy sea. He enters the devil's sphere where the wild, excessive dances and rituals take place. The dreamer discovers that which is directly opposite to the church, the heavenly sphere and the trinity. In the unconscious he meets a diabolical threesome. In *The Divine Comedy*, Dante, too, opposes to the heavenly trinity the three-headed devil of deepest hell. In the dreams, human beings are carriers of archetypal, divine and diabolical principles. As a representative of the higher principle, the old priest descends into an inferior realm. He attempts to bridge the two worlds which are now separated by a wooden partition.

The dreamer sees the dancers with their flailing arms impotently longing for happiness. The crazier they act, he comments, the more convinced they are that they can force benedictions. The primitive crowds try to achieve happiness, blessings and deliverance through excess and eccentricity. They will fail. Ancient wisdom dictates that deliverance can be achieved only through sacrifice, purification, transformation, and the placing of oneself in a religious discipline. When the old priest's religious images and concepts fail to persuade the crowd, the dreamer turns away and refuses to participate.

The dream portrays the clash of consciousness and the unconscious abyss. It expresses a degree of over-excitation and strain which consciousness cannot assimilate. This unresolved stress causes complete exhaustion and an illness detailed in subsequent dreams (Thirty-Nine through Forty-One).

Dream Thirty-Nine: The Woman in the Violet Dress

"I'm at a party with many people. Our hostess has black hair and wears a violet evening gown. She is grossly sensual. Suddenly, the royal pair arrives. They are incognito, in plain clothes, but everyone recognizes them and bows. Everyone, that is, but the hostess, who turns them away because they were not invited. The queen orders a servant to have their coach driven up to take them home. The guests and I are aghast. We know what a frightful surprise it will be for our hostess. When she sees their coach, she finally realizes what an asinine thing she has done. All the guests begin to leave quickly."

The hostess in violet is equivalent to the red and black figures that the dreamer spotted and shot in Dream Twenty-Six. That shooting had stopped the immediate danger which threatened from without, but it did not resolve the dreamer's inward problem. The woman in violet is one more manifestation of that realm across the river or behind the wooden partition. She symbolizes the wild behavior which the dreamer rejected in favor of a cultivated consciousness. The rejected shadow now affects the Anima. Instead of being a helpful companion, she is a crude woman like the Whore of Babylon. Consciousness could not relate to this aspect of the unconscious which therefore refuses to subordinate itself to the royal pair, the ruling principle. The last dreams have uncovered a crack in the personality which cannot be immediately healed. As a result, subsequent dreams are gloomy.

Dream Forty: *The Explosion of the White Powder*

"Boxes filled with white powder are brought to a faraway place. They explode, producing a high, white, mushroom-shaped cloud. I find protection in a shed. I expect a few nearby horses to panic, but they remain calmly in place."

Dream Forty-One: *Volcanic Eruption*

"I am dangerously close to a volcanic eruption. Again, I do not have adequate cover. Ahead of me is a swarm of bees flying in perfect formation. As long as the bees are not disturbed, I am also protected."

What progress had been made is now threatened. The attempt to integrate red and white has failed. Both dreams reveal dangerous affective discharges that accompanied an illness with high fever. The calm of the horses and the perfect flight-formation of the bees allow us to surmise, however, that deeper instinctual levels were not affected by these disturbances. The next dream discusses a first attempt to deal with the opposite behind the wooden partition.

Dream Forty-Two: *Faust and Mephistopheles*

"We were at once two men and one person. The other was slightly older and heavier. We were performing *Faust* on a large stage. I was Mephistopheles, and the other was Faust. I knew, however, that we were one. He performed and spoke magnificently. I tended to stand on one side of the stage and to restrain myself. It was clear to me that he was better and more important. The enormous theater was sold out. We received stormy applause, but I know that it was mostly *his* achievements that deserved applause. We then went to celebrate our success. In the garden of an inn he sat down nonchalantly. He seemed to have the rough, friendly manners of my paternal, peasant ancestors. As soon as we had poured our drinks, people left the garden because of a police curfew. We were angry. The other man called for the host, an unsympathetic, cunning type. To my surprise, my companion was on a familiar, first-name basis with the host. He complained, but the host did not yield. Then the other told him something very strange. He said that for once he would have liked to celebrate with me, his *dictator.* Suddenly, there was a large, black dog in the garden."

The dreamer and another man are in a colossal theater, obviously the theater of the world. They enact *Faust*, but their roles are reversed. The other plays Faust, the hero; the dreamer plays Mephistopheles, the shadow. A personality's dissociation into different characters is dangerous, though possibly essential to self-knowledge. In *Faust*, Goethe portrays an insatiable hunger for life.[213] Aware of his great abilities, Faust at the end of his life colonizes the world, barely conscious of the great responsibilities he is assuming. He is successful, thanks to his intelligence, his yearning for eminence, and his lack of consideration. His success is applauded. The dreamer enacts the story of Faust. He has not created the play himself, but has found the script and taken it over from his rough, friendly and ambitious ancestors.

During one's youth, one tends to identify with heroes and conquerors. One finds one's place in the world by adapting to collective ideals and expectations. One thereby becomes capable of channeling one's forces exclusively into one's purposes and goals and of accomplishing a great deal. As one becomes better in this role, Mephistopheles, the secret puller of the strings, the dark shadow of the collective ideal, becomes more dangerous. Faust starts to feel uneasy as he begins to recognize that the devil, his other ego, is his dictator. His name alone (Faust = fist) should alert us to the "rule of the fist" *(Faustrecht).*

Mephistopheles is our animal aspect paired with clever intellect. He represents given talents and skills such as drive and intelligence. He embodies physical impulses. He is also the despotic devil who craves power through possessions and knowledge. Because he represents drive and its extension, compulsion, he is a *dictator.* Goethe's Faust is aware only of his guiding ideals, but Mephistopheles knows the egotistic purposes they hide.

When the dreamer identifies with Mephistopheles, he becomes aware of his guilt. He is nearly crushed by the world's guilt which, through this identification, falls upon him. If he blindly strives for success, he is bound to become overwhelmed by guilt during a depressive phase. Therefore, he must now separate both from Faust, the success-oriented person, and from his shadow, the devil.

Mephisto seduces through love as well as through power. In Goethe's *Faust,* he changes into his feminine counterpart when he dresses up as Phorkyas and when, after Faust's death, he becomes enamored of male angels. He shares with his brother, the alchemistic Mercury, a hermaphroditic nature.[214] He is dangerous in the same way as the power-hungry She. His ambition, greed and passion are consuming.[215] His is the danger of pleading life according to collective demands for inconsiderate self-affirmation and unconscious, instinctual impulses. In this dream, evil manifests itself, not as a quality of the Anima, but as a collective, male shadow figure, that is, as self-knowledge and insight into human potentials. It is this knowledge that keeps the dreamer from celebrating the theatrical success. It is police curfew. Faust's day is definitely ended. The host, without whom one cannot settle the bill, is the true shadow whom even the stage-Mephistopheles must obey and who announces Ash Wednesday, the end of the masks' festivities. Behind the host, a black dog, the poodle which Faust first encountered, appears. The dog is animal nature which the dreamer first recognized in the black and red figures, in the rats; which he rejected in the three warted devils (Dream Thirty-Eight); and which he finally repudiated in the violet hostess (Dream Thirty-Nine). Now his dark nature meets him as the shadow.

Faust, Mephistopheles, the host, and the black dog form a male quartet. The dreamer's ego, his consciousness, is overcome by the dark side. In spite of his earlier opposition, the dreamer has entered the realm of the three devils of Dream Thirty-Eight. In this dream the devils are differentiated into Mephistopheles, the host, and dog. Through the dreamer's identification with both collective roles, with Faust and Mephistopheles, his human ego is charged with the superhuman responsibility of the world's guilt and torn into the extreme opposites of good and evil. In the conscious, Christian conception of the world, good prevails. Yet here, on the side of the unconscious, evil prevails. The remedy for the painful condition into which the ego has drifted includes separating from the archetypal figures and defining one's limits with respect to the collective role. The ego must look within itself and accept its own personal guilt, moral problems, and its obligations towards its own weaker sides. It must accept itself as a limited human being with limited possibilities. The ego is neither Faust nor Mephistopheles, but only the servant of the two superhuman, basically divine, figures. It only realizes the impulses that come from its light and dark sides.

This dream is significant for the dreamer's confrontation with the problem of *morality* through his identification with Mephistopheles and Faust. He must go one step beyond Faust and recognize that he is responsible for Mephistopheles's success. To identify with Mephistopheles is intolerable. However, identification with Faust is equally so. Mephistopheles is a figure of the collective unconscious, and Faust represents collective consciousness. Now, rather than continue the collective roles, the dreamer must modestly accept responsibility for his actions and claim the shadow, namely the host and the dog, as his.

Dream Forty-Three: Aida

"*Aida* is to be performed in an opera house with seats like choir chairs. I show several ladies to their seats in front. They invite me to sit with them. I gracefully decline and sit in the back of the hall with the crowd. I wear a white, flowing dress, reminiscent of the ancient Greeks or Arabs. It is made of fine white wool. It looks like a Dominican habit, but it is looser and more open. I think that the people will find it strange and effeminate, but, after some hesitation, I become indifferent to their possible criticisms."

Sometimes it is unusually difficult for consciousness to understand an inner necessity. In such cases, a dream may take the form of a play which shows and explains to the dreamer his next task. The place in which the play is performed is an opera house with choir chairs. It is half-profane and half-ecclesiastical. The dreamer doesn't exactly know where he belongs. The ladies ask him to sit with them, as if he were a woman, but he decides to join the ordinary people. He wears a strange dress, a version of a monk's habit, which strikes him as being somewhat feminine. A monk wears his cowl (like the Galloi of Cybele, the Great Mother) to show that he has sacrificed his masculinity. Just as the consecrated follower of Cybele renounces his primitive, masculine nature in order to assume that of the mother-goddess, so the monk renounces his masculine nature in order to approach God with a receptive, feminine attitude. This attitude places the dreamer on the side of his unconscious. He no longer identifies with Mephistopheles, but partly with his feminine side, the Anima. Even the opera that is to be performed has a feminine name.

Aida is the story of the royal couple's death. Thus, the dream foreshadows the ritual death of the royal couple, one more conscious sacrifice of what has been achieved. If integration is insufficient because essential parts remain disparate, the current psychological-spiritual attitude, the royal pair, must die once more. In *Christian Rosencreutz's Chymical Wedding,* three royal couples and a Moor, representing their shadow, appear. They must all die once more in order to be melted into one pair through alchemy.[216] In his monastic outfit, the dreamer could be one of the Egyptian priests who sentence Radames and Aida to die. The white dress puts him in contrast to evil and draws him into the play.

In his white monastic outfit, the dreamer has cleansed himself of the world and evil, distancing himself from Faust and Mephistopheles. As a result, the religious problem reappears now in his dreams.

Dream Forty-Four: Three Priests and a Priestess

"I wish to attend a small, simple church in the country. Many people stand outside. Inside, many people stand in the hallways, but the pews are empty. I prefer not to sit down since I will have to get up and cede my place, maybe to a woman, when the rest of the people come inside. Also, I am not sure which side is designated for men and which for women. Everyone looks at me. I walk through the crowd all the way to the front. Here, the high mass is celebrated at the altar. The priests are in white and golden vestments, but, to my surprise, they are not, as customary, three priests, but four. The fourth is a woman. I wonder why a fourth priest was added, and why a woman priest. I think this situation is an earthly reflection of the situation in heaven. As is customary, the older priest is the main celebrant. He and one of the younger priests are turned towards the altar. The other young priest stands on the side of the steps, his face turned towards the two in the center. On his dark head with short, trimmed hair he wears a small, golden crown. He sings the Epistle and the Gospel. The priestess stands in the middle and faces the public. In her hands she carries a large, white and golden book containing the Gospel and hands it to the priest with the crown to read and sing. She is joking and laughing. This bothers me, and I think that one should not have allowed women to participate in the service."

The dreamer enters the church, and the religious problem is explored further. He does not sit down because he does not know which side is the women's and because he would eventually have to give up his place to a woman. Thus, he feels uncertain about where he really belongs. His uncertainty about belonging to the women's side is a symptom of his remaining identification with the unconscious, the Anima, from whom, however, he is now able to distance himself.

Turning away from the women's side is also supported by the fact that the dream takes place in a church in which, because of the three priests, the male element predominates. Comparing it with the dream of the brandy (Dream Thirty-Six), we may notice some progress. In Dream Twenty-Six, the third priest played a most questionable role. Here he sings the Gospel and the Epistle; he has a function in the ritual. In comparison to the dream of Faust and Mephistopheles (Dream Forty-Two), we also find a great change. In that dream only one positive male figure, Faust, appeared, in contrast to two negative male figures (Mephistopheles and the unpleasant host), as well as the black dog.

In the present dream, there are three positive male figures, as well as a feminine one, who represents nature over and against the spirit. The third priest's crown signals a spiritual kingship. The dreamer associates the priestess, before her questionable behavior, with Maria, the heavenly queen. Later, however, her inappropriate behavior introduces darkness into the spiritual realm, almost as a complement to the old priest's bringing blessings from heaven down into the realm of darkness.[217] The dreams, thus, show a slow interpenetration between the two realms. The three priests represent the masculine principle of the logos; the priestess introduces the feminine principle of eros. The mixture of evil, previously expressed as the pouring of brandy, reappears, in milder form, in the priestess's irreverent behavior. She takes the place of the grey-silvery cloth in the tabernacle's interior which would not blend properly with the white and gold of the priestly vestments (Dream Thirty-Four).

The four priests have different functions: the first, intuition; the second, feeling; the third, introverted thinking; and the woman, sensation, which, for now, is identified with the Anima.

Dream Forty-Five: The Adoration of the Queen

"I was part of a crowd, arranged in ascending circles, which was paying homage to the queen. I was quite close to the front, but I couldn't see the queen as I was kneeling and bowing with everyone else. A black man scantily dressed in native garb stood in front of me. He bowed his head all the way to the floor. I wanted to do the same, but, thinking it wouldn't be appropriate, I bowed less deeply. When we raised our heads, the queen was gone and a priest in a black cassock stood in her place. His back was turned towards me, and his arms were extended like those of a conductor. He made a quick, sweeping movement and the cheering stopped. He suddenly no longer had a head. Only a white collar protruded from his cassock. He left.

Next, I found myself in the black man's room. He was a student. He wasn't a black now, but a mulatto. We sat on the edge of his bed. I felt deep friendship and love for him, and I was sad that we had to part. The thought of returning to primitive conditions in Africa did not please him. He went to his washbasin in order to clean himself. He expressed the hope that we would see each other again."

In this dream the dreamer is on the side of the feminine and the shadow, yet he does not identify with these figures. The feminine principle, symbolized by the queen, is worshiped by a crowd. This dream occurred at the time of the papal letter proclaiming Mary as heavenly queen and mistress of all creatures. In his dream the dreamer participates in the celebration worshiping Mary as queen (in fact he did so before he had actually heard of the papal declaration!). In his jubilation, he and his simpler nature are united with the crowd.

The horrid jazz music of the cosmopolitan city (Dream Thirty-Eight) has vanished. The beautiful black man with his genuine humility before the queen emerges from it. He may also be a precious aspect of Mephistopheles's black poodle (Dream Forty-Two). The dreamer shares this shadow-figure's humble and cheerful adoration of the queen. Mary, the queen of heaven, includes his inner, archetypal picture of the queen. The black man is "primitive" only in the sense of "spontaneous" and "genuine." As a primitive, he focuses upon that which is essential and practical. He is the dreamer's simple, unadulterated sensation-function. His European studies connect him to European consciousness. He has the runner's ability to relax which the officer in Dream Twenty-Five admired. The black man returns to Africa, his natural home. The dreamer, unfortunately, cannot stop him. Only during vacations (the dream occurred at the end of the dreamer's vacation) does the black man come into his own. During periods of work, he is exiled to Africa, the unconscious. The disappearance of the priest's head may mean that recognizing Mary as mistress of all creatures is not a task for the intellect. The crowd's rapture was a spontaneous experience that preceded the papal formulation of the new, dogmatic content. The dreamer is carried by this rapture, and thus linked to the black man with his genuine piety.[218]

Dream Forty-Six: The Convent with the Throne Room

"On overgrown paths I reached a magnificent old abbey, hidden in a garden. To my right is the path to the church's interior. Straight ahead is the entrance to a hall that looks like a treasury or museum. I enter through the path on my left. In the hall's foreground is a wonderful, large, white and gold throne. Moving on, I reach the cloisters surrounding a neglected, romantic garden. The sunlight which fills the garden and flows into the cloisters creates a unique, dusky-green setting. Proceeding in the arched hallway, I see, across the garden, the roof and tower of a church. The tower is large and impressive. At the end of the hall I meet a father. I'm a guest who desires to study and write. He shows and offers to me several rooms. The first room, on the ground floor, is large, sunny and almost ostentatious. I don't want it because it is too grandiose and distracting, and because too many people will be walking through it. The second room, in the upper story, is very small and modest. I don't want it either, as it is musty like a prison cell and too dark and dusty. The third is a fine, medium-sized room with a window from which one enjoys a great view of green hills. I take that one."

Immediately the dream recurs in a slightly different form:

"I'm on the same path to the abbey, but I'm driving a mechanized vehicle which pulls small wagons filled with teenagers and children. I'm forced to drive very carefully as I must manage many curves in the road and pass underneath low tree branches. Then we are before the abbey and take the middle path into the hall. I want to guide the children towards the left in order to show them the beauty of the cloisters; I walk ahead and see the cloisters and the tower again. I turn around and find that no one has followed me. I return and find some of them in the hall. I feel a strong desire to sit down on the white and golden throne, but I don't. I want to show the children the beauties of the museum, but they disappear again. I look for them in the church interior. I enter a bright, high-ceilinged cathedral with white and golden columns. The boys are noisily entertaining themselves in a corner. The girls, on the other hand, have all climbed the stairs to the altar. From below I see them devoutly standing so close together before the altar that they wholly obscure it. They all wear the same white dresses and small red jackets. Meanwhile, the boys have left the church and are walking up a broad stairway to an adjoining room. It occurs to me that they should get something to eat. I plan to order some food, but I find that they are already eating happily and noisily in a dining hall. I'm just about to tell some of the big ones to watch out and keep order when it occurs to me that everything will be all right. All the boys are loud and cheerful. I don't need to do anything."

Here, the dreamer finds his way into a convent, a place of Christian meditation. The extroverted dreamer withdraws into a positive introversion. He discovers an inner place which was cultivated, later neglected, by the ancestors. When the dreamer avoids the first, ostentatious room where he would always be interrupted by outsiders, he renounces an attitude that would induce him to work only for the sake of outward appearance. He also refuses the gloomy cell, the ascetic, depressive withdrawal, which he has also known. He chooses a room with an open view where he is free to work. This retreat is suitable and meaningful.

His free decision to immerse himself in introversion and meditation on religious matters brings with it a crowd of children: young, promising forces to whom he wishes to show the beauties of the old convent. He would like to seat himself upon the magnificent throne of the children's presence, but he resists the temptation. His ego renounces the king's place. This renunciation is of great importance and shows progress from the dream of Faust and Mephistopheles (Dream Forty-Two).

The children don't stay in the museum. They don't remain in the past. They live in the immediate religious experience. The boys display a youthful spirit of enterprise. They pass by the religious paintings without showing much devotion. The girls, however, stand devoutly around the altar. They retain the childlike openness and piety that are enhanced by the setting and by the hidden meaning of paintings. They are dressed in white and red, the union of soul and spirit, which was destroyed in Dream Forty and Forty-One, but which reappears with new freshness in these girls. This union is understood by the little Animas. They direct their warmth and immediacy towards the altar, the place of the holiest of holies.

The boys, the renewed spirit of enterprise in religious matters, soon find themselves in an adjoining room where the church offers them spiritual food. Since the dreamer renounced the tempting throne, he is now able to renounce the urge to impose order upon the boys. He realizes that he can allow their youthful eagerness freedom. He does not need to interfere; he can let things happen.

Dream Forty-Seven: The Round Church

"I'm in a church or a mosque. A central room is linked by open arches to similar rooms. I believe Constantinople's Hagia Sophia was built this way. One of these side rooms is an apse, in which the altar is located. The altar is invisible to me, but I know it is there. In the middle of the central room is a horizontal wheel which almost fills the room. It moves clockwise very slowly. It has many spokes upon which many people, including myself, sit. As the wheel turns, I move, against my wishes, away from the altar. I look through the arches of the central room into the various side rooms. Each is built in a different style (Roman, Indian, Arabic, etc.). All religions are represented in these adjoining chapels. Finally, I come closer to the altar. I'm now at the periphery of the wheel. When I'm facing the altar, the wheel stops and slides, as if floating towards the altar. I'm completely immersed in the light of this apse. I'm quite close to the altar which is still invisible. Light flows over me and I hear a wonderful, tender music, similar to Christmas carols. I'm experiencing infinite devotion and bliss."

Dream Forty-Seven marks a high point in the dreamer's inner journey. In the previous dream he renounced the throne. Thus his ego became subordinate to a higher principle, an invisible center. In this dream, that higher principle takes the form of a wheel upon which the dreamer sits with many others. In its roundness the wheel represents perfection. Its circular shape is an ancient symbol of the godhead which manifests itself in the universe. The center is the invisible godhead; the circle represents the godhead's emanations in space and time. According to Plotinus, the soul turns in a circle around its center, the divine principle from which it emanates.[219] The nave of the wheel symbolizes the divine Self in the human being, the principle that is higher than the ego and encompasses opposites. As a symbol of the godhead's realization in creation or as a symbol of the Self in the human being, the wheel encompasses more than one individual human being.

All human beings belong to the Self. Our egos are but a tiny fraction of the infinite expressive possibilities available to the divine. In Buddhism the wheel symbolizes the doctrine, its proclamation, and the impulse for deliverance. In the dream the wheel turns clockwise, from unconsciousness to consciousness, and from ignorance to knowledge, reflection and self-awareness. As it turns, the wheel offers the dreamer insight into the world's religions and shows him that they all are related to the same midpoint. At first the dreamer is dissatisfied because the wheel's motion carries him away from his goal, the altar. As he views the side-chapels, however, he gains the tolerance and universality which he is seeking.

The memory of the dream elicits from him a deeply satisfied exclamation, "Ah, indeed everything is here!" He now understands that he must distance himself from the faith of his childhood in order to experience the validity of all religious expression. The wheel carries him to the altar where he breaks through to another, hidden reality, one about which images speak, but which itself is beyond images. It is formless light, music, devotion and inner fulfillment. The altar of his religion and the Christmas songs remind him of his childhood's most blissful experiences. The piety of the girls in the preceding dream becomes, here, his own.

Dream Forty-Eight: Four Speeches

"I am supposed to give a speech at a large Christmas celebration. I propose instead that four speakers, including myself, present brief, but thorough, discussions of Mary to a small, select group. I suggest the following topics: (1) Mary, the virgin—a theologian is to discuss this topic. (2) Mary, the mother—this presentation is directed primarily to women. It should speak to the heart. (3) Mary, the queen—I reserve this topic for myself. I will include in my presentation a discussion of the dogma of Mary's bodily ascension and coronation. (4) Mary, the working woman—I insist that this topic also be included. This presentation should address workers and portray Mary, the wife of Joseph the carpenter, and the miserable conditions under which she gave birth to and raised a child. It should focus upon that part of her life which is hardly mentioned in the Bible. I emphasize that the portrayal of this important aspect of Mary has previously been neglected."

The preceding dream reawakened childhood memories of Christmas. Now, in celebration of the mother of God, Christmas is to be understood in a more conscious and profound manner. In place of a conventional party at which he would have been the sole speaker, the dreamer hopes to substitute a celebration during which urgent theological questions will be reflected upon and discussed by four speakers, the dreamer and three other men. He no longer identifies with the unconscious, nor does his ego aspire to the throne. The four suggested speakers will discuss the four functions of Mary in order to arrive at a complete, comprehensive understanding of the Anima-problem. The first theme, Mary the virgin, is to be discussed by a theologian, that is, by the theologian who is inside himself and who his mother wanted him to be. Mary's eternal virginity is an irrational, supernatural phenomenon. It cannot be discussed rationally. However, intuition which grasps the meaning of dogmatic or symbolic statements can do it justice. The virgin birth of the savior is already anticipated in the great goddesses of the Near East.[220] It is found again in the many contemporary dreams which involve a virgin, or abandoned woman, who gives birth to a fatherless child, with the attributes of the mediator and the hero-savior. If we understand Mary as the Anima's archetypal image, we see that her "virginity" points to the ability to listen inwardly and to be fructified by the inner spirit.

The dreamer explains that the second speaker must address women. He addresses the problem of femininity through *feeling*. From early childhood, Catholics hear prayers to Mary in which she is presented as an example to and educator of mothers. A young girl can orient her behavior in accordance with that of the God-mother. Mary, the *mater dolorosa,* guides the girl through the joys and sufferings of motherhood. She takes her from possession to sacrifice and renunciation, from natural to spiritual motherhood. Men also experience these phases through prayer. Their feelings for mothers and their empathy for motherhood are imperceptibly developed. Viewed inwardly, Mary, the mother, dedicates herself with patience and devotion to the soul's rebirth. She embodies constant love and care for its inner growth.

The dreamer himself wants to discuss the third theme—Mary the queen. He attempts to complement knowledge acquired through *feeling* with knowledge acquired through *thinking*. He wants to learn the meaning hidden in Mary, the exemplary divine Anima. As queen, Mary wears a crown. Hers is the crown of human wholeness. The man who learns to worship her is no longer subservient to the discriminating logos only. He also submits himself to the heavenly queen, and by extension to the feminine principle, the forgiving and reconciliatory eros.

As queen of the earth and all its creatures, Mary shall, according to dogmatic pronouncements, overthrow Satan, the master of this world. She will lift all creatures up to herself and will ascend bodily into heaven. Even the body, with its instincts and biological processes, will be deemed worthy to enter heaven. Matter will rise into the realm of the spirit. In Mary the entire material world wants to set out for the *coniunctio* with the spiritual realm. The split between spirit and nature need not persist forever. The human being is not forced to keep any part of himself separate. There is nothing so dark that it cannot strive towards the center and be understood by the spirit, and nothing so nonsensical that it cannot be transformed into meaning. By taking on the discussion of this theme, the dreamer attempts to grasp the eternal truth of contents that were formerly projected upon women. He seeks their archetypal, religious meanings that are valid independently of the particular woman in which they manifest themselves. Every individual woman is but an incomplete reflection of the queen, the archetypal image that is sought for within the soul.

The fourth theme is unusual. It outlines a future task. The dreamer meets some resistance when he proposes it, and the speaker's identity is unclear. This theme requires the dreamer's fourth function, *sensation*. This speech, addressed to laborers, is to describe Mary as one of their own. The dreamer comments that quiet, hard work is to be celebrated. The speech is also addressed to the people behind the wooden partition who suffer the surveillance of the three devils (Dream Thirty-Eight). In order to discuss this topic, a speaker must focus upon immediate reality. This discussion, neither abstract nor metaphysical, is concerned with human beings' relation to the eternal symbol of the heavenly queen. When Goethe's Faust addresses Mary as "Virgin, Mother, Queen," she seems unattainably distant. Here, however, she is addressed "Virgin, Mother, Queen—*and* simple woman." She is accessible for everyone. She is not in a distant beyond but can be found in the here and now.

For the dreamer, this means that the eros-principle must find access to his daily work. Even his occupational performance will require the participation of the *whole* human being. No longer are religious symbols confined to the church. They now transform everyday life. The *inner* child is born during everyday toil. The human being is the bearer and executor of the dogma. This dream paraphrases and amplifies the one in which the tabernacle represented the external life and the interior, dark, silver-laced soul-material represented the Anima's activity (Dream Thirty-Four). If he learns from this fourth speech, the man will no longer require a "queen" who can speak to his feelings. He will be able to experience and worship the Anima in an ordinary woman. This is a parallel to Seuse, the mystic, who greeted the mother of God in every poor, little woman.[221]

Dream Forty-Nine: Riding Lesson

"The young imperial prince rides ahead of me. I'm unable to follow him at the same speed because my stirrup is knotted. I dismount and try to saddle the horse again. I notice that I cannot completely straighten the stirrup. I mount and continue to ride. The horse is young. It has a wonderful, soft coat that is brown like honey. I fear lest the young animal be unruly, but it allows itself to be guided by the slightest pressure of my thigh. On the street it trots softly. On the meadow it accelerates to a rocking gallop. It is just wonderful to ride this horse. Suddenly, I have two companions riding close to my left and right. They are imperial princesses whom I'm to instruct in horsemanship. Since I'm able to ride my horse without using the reins, I put my arms to my left and right around my companions' shoulders. I lift them in the rhythm of the trot and, thus, easily teach them proper, rhythmic riding movements. I feel uncomfortable since the imperial parents watch us from behind, incognito. They might notice that I can use only the left stirrup as I have only limited use of my right foot. Nevertheless, the ride continues easily. The princess to my left is older and more mature; the one on my right is younger and more childlike. I am most interested in the one on my left. She is friendly but unapproachable. The younger one on my right responds quickly to the slightest pressure of my hand upon her shoulder. After riding various types of paces, we finally stop. Carefully, I help the princesses dismount. I notice that the knotted stirrup became unknotted sometime during our ride. The entire saddle is in good shape now. I feel light and happy.

Later, I find myself in a large hall. There is a garden in front of the building from which one can see the front of a beautiful, new house. I know that the imperial family is visiting this house. I see them at the window and, later, the balcony. Two imperial princes (one rode ahead of me at the dream's beginning), the two princesses and their parents are there. I salute. They wave back.

Then I find myself in a room with three other men. I can see one, but I know the others are there. The one I see wishes to either drink, celebrate or play a card game. I explain that we cannot do this because we have to go to work. He argues that we can always be reached by phone. I insist that we go to work, and we do."

The young imperial prince riding ahead of the dreamer represents the renewed and rejuvenated leading principle which is now embodied in the son, not the father. It is distinct from the traditional (paternal) spiritual attitude, but, because it is the *son*, it is closely connected to it. It is the organic continuation of the paternal world. That which in the church-dreams was expressed in the images of priests is now transferred to the secular world where emperor and princes are the leading powers. The renewal in the spiritual sphere has brought with it a renewal in the instinctual sphere. A wonderful young horse now carries the dreamer towards life. The velvety, soft coat of the young animal indicates health. Life forces have renewed themselves after an illness. The dreamer fears lest the animal be unruly, but it allows itself to be guided by the soft pressure of his thigh. A new accord and interplay between consciousness and instinct has been reached. As spiritual understanding changes, so does instinct. The instinct is no longer gruesome and destructive (as it was in the first dream) nor nervously overwrought (as in Dream Nine of bolting horses). The saddle-gear is still somewhat knotty, indicating a lack of agility and sureness in his new way of life.

Now the dreamer is to give riding lessons to the two princesses who appear at his sides. The two Animas are to learn to move in harmony with the instincts. The dreamer teaches them various riding paces. His own feelings are correlated with the movements. They don't bolt, limp behind, or get lost. The extroverted, intuitive man does not shoot beyond his target because of male capriciousness. He takes care that empathic feelings can keep in step. The dreamer is not identified with the imperial family nor with the Anima. His conscious ego establishes the pace and watches out for the unison of the different sides. He does this in sight of the imperial parents. He feels responsible to the superior court of the Self, where the imperial, crowned couple represent the union of opposites.

He harmonizes easily with the younger princess. The youthful side of the Anima allows herself quite easily to be carried by the instincts. The older, more mature Anima, riding to his left, is more difficult to convince. The younger one may represent the youthful, personable, nestling feelings, whereas the older may manifest the type of relationship that has come up in the later dreams—for example, in the worship of the queen (Dream Forty-Five), the devotion of the girls at the altar (Dream Forty-Six), or the four speeches about Mary (Dream Forty-Eight).

In the course of the ride with the two positive Anima-figures, the knot in the stirrup disappears spontaneously. What initially seemed insoluble can straighten out by itself with the proper rhythm.

Later we find the dreamer back at work. The imperial family has settled in the beautiful, new building. Now we have three pairs—the parents, two princes, and two princesses—indicating that the dreamer's new masculine, spiritual attitude will benefit his profession and will be accompanied by appropriate emotional attitudes. This attitude, once attained, still depends on the proper understanding and "pacing." In other words, it must be practiced and maintained in everyday life.

The dream's postscript shows the other side of the picture. In place of the emperor and his two sons, the dreamer now has as companions three men who induce him to drink, feast and play cards. They try to seduce him into accepting the lower spirit. They are not demonic, like the three "wart-men" (Dream Thirty-Eight), but indolent. The emperor and the two princes represent their opposite. The dreamer as a *fourth* member stands between the upper and the lower threesomes. His ego remains free to choose his commitments.

Dream Fifty: The Hart

"I am the strongest hart in the entire forest. I'm lying down on soft moss, my legs drawn underneath myself. I'm protected by firs. At my side lies a hind. I stand up on my four legs. I wish to roam through the forest and drink water from a brook. The hind warns me that the morning is already advanced and I must look out for human beings. I shake my antlers and feel them hit the tree branches. In order to get out from under the low-hanging twigs of the firs I must stoop. I walk around in the woods between the tall stems, but I soon return to the hind, because it has become light and I fear the hunter. Later, in the guise of a human being, I reach a trough below a stand of firs. I recognize the place. (After awakening, I know it was the same place where I have been as a hart.) I clear the ground of bark and twigs. I arrange the wood neatly so that something will always be at hand for making a fire. It is a good feeling to have this hideout and to know that I can return to it at any time."

In Dream Thirteen a young hart was killed by a poacher. Here, the hart is alive again, and the dreamer experiences his own nature by identifying with it. This extraordinary dream is a deep experience for him. Rarely do adults perceive their oneness with nature so intensely,[222] but a similar empathy was revealed in the dream of the riding lesson. The Anima, too, has become a hind. She does not pursue her separate, all-too-human path (as she did in the dream [Thirty-Nine] of the violet hostess). The dreamer and his unconscious soul journey from urban life to nature. He descends into the body's pre-human, animal nature and connects consciousness and instinct. Buddha suggests such connection in himself when he mentions his ability to recall prior incarnations as animals. As a result of education, civilization and culture, human consciousness has separated from its instinctive roots. In this dream, it is reconnected with these roots.

Later, the dreamer returns to the forest as a human being. He is happy to be able to find protection here. His fusion with his animal soul was so thorough that he actually *felt* his animal body (including his legs and antlers) and feared human beings. This fusion is a memory from which he can derive peace and protection. The dreamer's return to nature is highly significant. Many excesses and errors result from deviations from the laws of nature. The vivid experience of oneness with nature will lead one back to the laws of nature, provided that one listens carefully to what goes on inside oneself.

By examining the preceding dream of the riding lesson, we find how the hart and hind fit into the dream-series. In that dream, the imperial parents appeared with the two princes and princesses on the balcony of a house. The princes and princesses are siblings linked to each other as same-sex and male–female pairs. Whenever two such pairs appear at the end of a fairy tale,[223] a satisfactory solution, an inner equilibrium, has been attained. This pattern of equivalent pairs, where one is closer to nature (the younger princess) and the other embodies a spiritual attitude (as expressed in the distinguished reserve of the older princess), finds two complements in these two dreams, a spiritual one in the parents and an earthly one in the animal pair. The imperial parents of the previous dream are above their children whose *spiritual* origin they represent. From this origin, the dreamer's renewed and widened inner structures have shaped themselves.

The hart and hind of this dream, then, portray both the *natural* origin and conclusion of the new pattern. They are its origin much as the nature-like Anima evolved from the heath-hen; they are its conclusion as the dreamer became a hart. The new internal structures which encompass the upper parental pair, the two princes and princesses, and the lower animal-pair represent a manifold link of *sol* and *luna,* king and queen, and white and red. That which was only alluded to by the intertwined rings has now become, in the four pairs, a living, inner symbol.

The dreamer has attained in this dream the quartet of pairs and, thus, the eight-fold link of the opposites. Now he must incorporate this wholeness into his waking life.

Dream Fifty-One: Your Will—Your Way

"I'm asked to speak at a meeting. My theme will be 'Your Will—Your Way.' I neither consent nor decline. Instead I wonder whether I have properly understood the meaning of the theme. Should it be 'your will—my way' (as in, quoting the Lord's Prayer, 'your will be done')? If so, my speech would be about the submission to God's will which determines one's path. Or does the theme 'your will—your way' mean that everyone is the forger of his own fortune? In that case, everyone would choose and follow his own path. These reflections continued beyond the dream and throughout the next morning. At first I considered the first version, adapted from the Lord's Prayer, more likely. Eventually, however, I concluded that 'your will—your way' was correct. Therefore, my speech would not be a discussion of God, but a personal, direct appeal to my listeners."

Human beings possess the dangerous gift of free will. In contrast to animals, they are able to act against instinct. As a result, they must continually learn to submit to God's will and to recognize it in their fate. By doing this, they will be able to accept themselves and their fate and to understand life as meaningful. The first part of life's task may be expressed by the short phrase "your will—my way." In other words, "Let me recognize your will, so that I may choose my path accordingly." However, because the dreamer has reclaimed his instincts in his identification with the hart and experience of unity with nature, his task is reversed. After long reflection, he concludes that he must speak to his audience about a second phrase, "your will—your way." He recognizes that this formula emphasizes a human being's free will and personal responsibility. He has grown beyond the child's blind trust in God. He can no longer load his burden upon God; he must carry it himself. He must make a conscious decision and choose his own path. He must recognize that what happens to him from now on is a consequence of his own thoughts, decisions and actions. He can no longer accuse God nor argue with Him because he knows that what has happened to him in the past, what he experiences now, and what the future will bring are his destiny and responsibility.

But the phrase "your will—your way" can be understood in another, deeper sense. God's will, which expresses itself in the soul, is God's way, as expressed in the actions of human beings.

The next dream shows the dreamer a new path.

Dream Fifty-Two: Deliverance from the Water Tank

"I'm a prisoner. Escape to the streets is impossible. I must use the river. I and the 'Other' stand in a large, semi-circular water basin from which four rivers are flowing: two powerful ones to the right and two small ones to the left. The one on the far right is partly dammed up. The river on its side is a roaring torrent. The thin brooks to the left run through wooden culverts and pipes which carry very little water. I find myself swimming in the basin. I try to swim to the right, but I'm constantly thrown back by a whirlpool. I'm totally exhausted. Suddenly a window opens in the dam. I hold on to its lower edge. Behind it are an old woman and a young girl. Both are quite friendly. The old woman gives me bread for refreshment. She advises me to seek passage through the small brook on the extreme left. I thank her and bless her. This makes her happy. I let go of the window frame and swim back to the point from which I began. Then I walk to my left on the edge of the basin. The 'Other' had remained on the rim of the basin without ever jumping in. He had wanted to go left from the beginning. Now we choose the path to the far left. The stream is quite shallow but rapid. It moves downhill in sharp curves through canals and wooden culverts. I am afraid, and in one of the sharp curves I cling to the rim. At that very moment a window opens before me in the wooden wall. Behind it are the old woman and the young girl again. The woman tells me to take off my shoes so I can swim better. She wraps the shoes in a package for me. I become aware that I am, strangely enough, wearing evening clothes. They look quite silly above my bare feet. I take off my white tie and give it to the young girl as a keepsake. As I have no gift for the old woman, I hope that she too will take pleasure in the tie. I continue to swim but lose the package with the shoes. At first I regret the loss, but then it loses its importance. The main thing is to escape successfully. The water flows through a covered canal. I wonder whether I'll get through. Happily, I do. On the other side, the river is large and quiet; I know I am now in my homeland, though not yet out of danger. I get out of the water. I want to continue on the road, but people I meet warn me that a checkpoint is ahead. In order to avoid it, I have to get back into the water and swim. Now the river is an offensive sewer. But there is no way out. In order to pass the checkpoint I even have to dive. Then, I am safe. The country is green. There is sunshine. The birds sing. I am free."

This dream returns to the dreamer's traumatic wartime experiences. These experiences, however, are presented as contemporary images. He has been imprisoned, and now he must free himself in order to survive. The escape which he attempts in this dream is as necessary, as difficult, and as vital as his escape from wartime captivity was. The dream reveals to him that he must follow the natural flow of energy. The old woman offering him refreshments is the earth-mother. Her daughter represents life and promise for the future. The old woman advises him to follow the shallow brook on the far left, not the powerful river on the right. In other words, she advises him not to follow the path of the primary function—the easy, habitual path of intuition—because it is blocked.

The dreamer immediately accepts the interpretation that the four rivers may represent the four functions. He concludes that he must follow the tedious path of sensation, his fourth function—the path of accurate, factual observation—since his intuition no longer allows him to get ahead. The fourth brook is poorly contained. It is rapid, though shallow, and replete with turns and dark canals. The dreamer must entrust himself to his sensation even though it has poor foundations and little of the water of life. In the previous dream, he became one with his body, in the form of a hart. He must now do the same with the reality function close to his body. In the extroverted, intuitive person, this reality function, sensation, has an introverted or subjective connotation. Because of this connotation, he must painfully work through all the subjective sensations and fears that are evoked by external difficulties. And he must do so without knowing beforehand where this troublesome path will lead.

In his fear he clings to one of the curves, and the earth-mother and her daughter reappear. The woman advises him to take off his shoes—that is, to give up his former ways—in order to swim better. Only now does he notice he is wearing evening clothes, characteristic of the correct social attitude by means of which the extroverted, intuitive person tries to master his tasks and difficulties. This attitude is not appropriate here. Without hesitating, he gives away his white tie, the hallmark of a fine society dress; and when he loses his shoes, he shows little regret. What matters now is, not the proper, conscientious, social attitude, but the ability to endure in the fight against obstacles. Just when the canal leads into a large, quiet river and the dreamer assumes that his life will continue quietly and safely, he must dive into the water once more and traverse a disgustingly polluted section. Nothing is spared him on the path of the inferior function. But, finally, he reaches the green, sun-bathed, promising land: freedom.

This dream proved to be true even in its details. The struggle for survival became so hard that the dreamer had to temporarily give up the fine social life to which he was accustomed. Deprived of all means of support, he eventually attained an independent professional position commensurate to his knowledge and skill. Finally, just when he thought he had reached his goal, a new delay with bitter privations was introduced.

By mentioning these details of his life, we are jumping ahead in our story. We mention them only to show that this dream of deliverance from a water tank anticipates external, professional deliverance. The homeland, the life-situation which is appropriate for him, symbolizes a return from constant tension and struggle to himself and his family. The end of the dream shows that escape was imperative and that the goal is promising. This dream gave the dreamer the strength and initiative to use his sensation-function as reality-function. It also showed him that perseverance was worthwhile. He concluded from this dream that from now on he had to develop his sensation. Doing so required restraining his intuition, basing his scientific work upon precise observations, repeated checking of details, and careful formulation. In order for him to adjust to life, developing his sensation-function meant keeping strictly to givens.

Dream Fifty-Three: Imprisonment in the Rocky Cliff

"I assume an unusual role in this dream. On the one hand, I'm an active participant, and on the other hand, I'm a spectator observing the various participants, including myself. I see three people. I am in the middle. To my right is a woman who belongs to me. We are quite fond of each other. To my left is a dark-skinned, muscular Egyptian. He walks about half a pace behind me. It is obvious that he is a constable. He urges me ahead, not forcefully, but I'm obliged to comply. I know that it is senseless to resist. I have done something that is against local customs and for which I am now being led to prison. With a white, cotton towel, the Egyptian dries his glistening, sweaty torso, arms, and face. In his movements I detect his superior force. The woman knows my fate and stands by me. She is such a calming influence that I don't even think of resisting. I see the three figures reach a vertical rock wall, and at the same time I experience this in the role of the prisoner. On the side of the rock, there is a small quadrangular opening

On the side of the rock, there is a small quadrangular opening through which I barely manage to crawl at the Egyptian's behest. Behind it is a cave. I can see through the small window that someone is inside. Simultaneously, I am inside the rock cave as a prisoner. Only this small window allows a view. On the floor of the cave, there are chains which the Egyptian orders me to place around my feet. I hear the chains' rattling. At the same time, I'm outside and the Egyptian is the prisoner. Once more he stretches his hand through the opening of the cave. Since he proffers it to me, I'd like to grasp it; but I fear lest he pull me inside and overwhelm me. However, I know, or trust, that he wouldn't do that, and I give him my hand. The events from the point where I cease to resist to the point where I give my hand to the Egyptian happen timelessly and simultaneously. No time distinctions can be made, though various themes can be separated. From this moment on, the process of deliverance begins. My cave in the rock is drilled into from both sides. Obliquely from the outside, the entire front of the cave is removed. Many drills and hammers are working. Soon, the cave will be, at best, a shallow deepening in the cliff wall. I admire the fine technical preparation of my rescue. I experience all this both as spectator and as prisoner."

According to the dreamer, the previous dream of his rescue from the basin referred to his external, professional life-situation. In contrast, he understood the dream of his imprisonment in the rocky cave as referring predominantly to a personal problem. The present dream shows him that, if he is to become professionally independent, he must submit to an inner judge. He sees that the journey to inner freedom requires insight into his personal guilt and voluntary submission to the decreed punishment. Imprisonment, then, is the beginning of deliverance. We are free only when we accept our finitude.

The split caused by the fact that the dreamer is both participant and observer is necessary because the dreamer must confront his empirical, acting ego. He must distance himself from his ego in order to recognize that this ego is the Egyptian's prisoner. The dark-skinned, muscular constable is reminiscent of the muscular men in Dream Forty-Five. At the beginning of the *Chymical Wedding,* a Moor lives with princess Anima in concubinage.[224] In our present dream, however, the Anima does not enter into a pact with the shadow. She is clearly focused upon the conscious ego. The vigorous Egyptian represents the superior power of nature to which the ego may succumb. He embodies the dark shadow-side of nature and the danger of nature-religions. The situation in the dream is paradoxical. An error is condemned by an inner court. The dreamer must recognize his breach with traditional morality and allow himself to be imprisoned by the Egyptian.

However, it is his constable who is really the prisoner. Only his identity with the Egyptian in the rock prison keeps the dreamer captive. The handshake, by means of which he declares himself jointly responsible with the prisoner,[225] and his confidence that the shadow will no longer overwhelm him begin the process of deliverance. The cave in the rocks reminds one of *Aida* (Dream Forty-Three). In *Aida* Radames is buried alive with Aida, but here the dreamer is sentenced, as he says, alone to three years in prison. Three years of voluntary renunciation is a long time, but it can be endured. The Anima faithfully waits outside the prison. Psychological relatedness will outlast this period of suffering. Having renounced the arbitrariness of the ego, recognized his guilt, and accepted his punishment, the dreamer starts a period of submission to an inner court. The numerous drills mobilized to liberate the prisoner symbolize the spiritual activity of penetrating and understanding the supra-personal problem of matter and nature.

Several dreams follow in which the dreamer feels persecuted. He is called into court and condemned to be hanged. The ego hesitates when it is called upon to submit to the inner judge and accept restrictions of freedom. Accordingly, the dreams become threatening and speak of death by hanging. A radical change, symbolized by a state of suspension, is demanded.

It is said of Odin:[226]

> I know I hanged
> in the windswept tree
> for nine long nights,
> wounded by the spear,
> consecrated to Odin,
> myself to myself,
> on yonder tree
> whose root's unknown
> to everyone.

They offered me
no food nor drink;
Deep down I bent,
picked up the poles,
raised groaning them,
then down I plunged.
I began to wake up
and to thrive well;
Now I became wise;
Word led me to word
and another word.
Work led me to work
and another work.

Consecrated to himself, Odin, the roaming, captivating god, hung nine days from a tree. Tied to nature, prevented from roaming, he loses the ground under his feet. He must persevere, though pained by uncertainty, until he finds the right runes and attains wisdom through them. By remaining quiet and persevering, by renouncing the possibilities of the outer world, and by tolerating his own hindered nature, he achieves a state of concentration in which he uncovers the symbolic meaning of restlessness. Saint Nicholas of Flue was similarly stopped on one of his roaming journeys by a vision. He then returned to his cell where he transformed his urge to roam into inner reflection and spiritual meaning.[227] Hanging, not unlike the death on the cross, suggests self-sacrifice and, simultaneously, elevation and spiritualization.

The ego may continue to reject limitations on its freedom. It may not patiently accept any sort of suspension or heed the call to sacrifice willfulness and patiently wait and persist. If that happens, the symbolic dream-image could become an obsession. During the dirge for Attis, a picture of the young god was fastened to a fir or pine which was then cut and mourned as a god.[228] Death-masks of Dionysus were also fastened to trees. Both Odin and Dionysus are gods of intoxicating ecstasy who can lead human beings to their deaths. Both are also masters of the dead. Attis, the epitome of luxuriantly flowing life, dies, like them, when nature begins to wilt. He is sacrificed to the mother, and this sacrifice guarantees new life and fertility. Whoever is seized by the gods' ecstatic life must also accept, as conscious sacrifice, their end. Happy is he who is able to take off the mask of a god and hang it, as a symbolic sacrifice, on a tree. When he returns her son's picture to the divine mother, he can recognize himself again as a human being, an actor in the god's mystery play who returns to his limited, everyday existence after the rite's performance. He who does not recognize as symbolical the wedding and the sufferings of the god, but instead identifies with the gestalt that seizes him, may fall prey to the compulsion of the death-wedding's archetype. He falls into a trance and, finally, death.[229]

Dream Fifty-Four: The Taming of the Anima

"In a jeep I'm driving with an old physician to an old woman's house. I carry with me the upright stem of a tree. A fox has killed hens here, but we cannot catch it. Then four foxes look up towards us from below the street. Later, I ride a fine red horse on a path beside a field. The horse is magnificent and large. It has a lot of pep, but with me it is quiet obedient and disciplined. Then a man comes riding behind me. He is leading another red, slender horse by the halter. This one rears up and is quite unruly. I had anticipated that my horse would behave in the same way, but I notice that it responds to me unconditionally. It is a pleasure to ride. I tell the man: 'Only one thing will help. You must hit this obstinate horse.' At this instant the horse turns into a nude woman. I am about to whip her across the back when she runs up a slope and threatens to hit me with a club if I come near her. She is just as unruly as the horse and needs to be whipped. In spite of her threatening attitude, I ride up the slope and manage to strike her just as she tries to duck. To my surprise she responds: 'Thank you!' She really means it and seems relieved. It is as if we were in a fairy tale and I had freed her from a spell. Another rider joins us. He is an Englishman riding excellently on a fine red horse. The woman has dressed herself by now. She is quiet and polite." (The dreamer added: "Maybe my Anima needs to be tamed.")

The dreamer's delivering the tree trunk to the old woman's house indicates his willingness to bring the sacrifice requested of him. This truncated tree symbolizes Attis who is carried as a fir trunk into the sepulchral vault where he will be mourned by his mother. Instead of a priest, a physician accompanies the dreamer. He is the wise old man in the guise of healer. With the god's death and the sacrifice of the overflowing libido, all life sinks back into the grave. Even the dreamer's developed functions revert to a primitive condition. As in Dream Ten of the heath-cock, these functions take the form of shy, wild animals, in this case foxes.[230] Foxes confront consciousness rapaciously. They don't allow themselves to be ordered around.

But a new development is rapidly taking place. Barely has the dreamer looked at the foxes when one of them is transformed into a horse whose origin is betrayed by its color. The horse is a magnificent, well-disciplined animal on which the dreamer ascends. The instinctual energy that had regressed to its natural condition becomes again a supportive, adaptable, effective force that carries the dreamer towards his professional goals. His shadow-brother follows him on horseback. He brings with him a slender and unruly horse whose origin is obviously that of a hen-stealing type of fox. This unruly aspect of the instinct is also transformed by the dreamer. It becomes a nude, unruly woman, a primitive Anima.

Energy from the Anima can be utilized, but it brings an element of uncertainty to the inner economy of the man. The third horse, symbolizing the energy of the unconscious and the feminine soul, can be disturbed at any time by circumstances. If it is, it may derail conscious energies. In the meantime, the dreamer has learned *not* to identify blindly with the Anima or be induced by her to act rebelliously or with animosity. He is willing to tame the feminine side without false pity, but the Anima reveals her archaic nature by threatening the dreamer with a club, the most primitive weapon. The dreamer does not allow himself to be knocked out by her. Instead, he tames her the way he would tame a stubborn horse. And, lo and behold, she is thankful for it. By his firm opposition, he frees her from her dangerous, primitive nature. He achieves a deliverance similar to that in *The Taming of the Shrew* or the fairy tale of "King Thrushbeard."[231]

The transformation of a fox into a woman is a motif found in many fairy tales, especially those of China.[232] In the tale "The Golden Bird,"[233] the fox requests that the hero, whom he assisted in completing his tasks, kill it and chop off its head and paws.

Paws severed from beasts of prey symbolize the restriction of conceit, rage, and beastly nature. In "The Golden Bird," a fox is tamed. At first this fox with its sensitive nose is needed to obtain three treasures: the bird, the golden horse, and the maiden. Once the hero has obtained these treasures, he must sacrifice his own rapacious drives and the cunning of his instinct. In other words, he must kill the fox. The fox, after his death, changes into a prince who reveals himself as the maiden-princess's brother. Fox-prince and princess are variants of the original animal instinct.[234]

In this dream the Anima has again become unruly. She has fallen into the hands of the shadow, the second rider, who leads her by the halter. By being tamed, she is freed from her amalgamation with the shadow. After that happens, a rider with a proper attitude appears. The dreamer is rewarded for his responsible behavior by the restoration of his positive, masculine energies.

The Anima expresses her desire for guidance in this dream. The man recognizes that under certain circumstances he must resist the Anima. In fact, she will be thankful when he does not accept her unruly attitudes. Had the dreamer failed to tame her, the regressed Anima would have maneuvered him again into a primitive relationship. By his opposition, however, he enforces appropriate behavior. Thus he is able to direct the freed energies towards the transformation and spiritualization of his nature.

Dream Fifty-Five: The Communion Rail

"The church is filled with the devout. The priest says mass at the altar. Several men are crowded into the row of benches ahead of me. In order to create space, they carry the kneeler to the middle aisle. One of them pushes it with some zest, and it slips forward and hits the communion rail, which shatters. The priest, who has just reached the moment of the transubstantiation, seems to interpret the men's action as a personal attack and insult. He interrupts the transubstantiation, runs to the men, and starts to beat them. They defend themselves, gain the upper hand and chase the priest from the church. I am aghast. As he flees, I notice that he is bleeding from cuts on his neck below each ear. I run after him in order to help. I take him to his home. There, a very aged priest is sitting at a table. He has been sleeping. He is the wounded man's superior. Dull and feeble, he looks up. I tell him what has happened, but he remains uncomprehending and indifferent."

Like Dream Thirty-Six, this one places the dreamer into the church at the very moment of the transubstantiation. The church is packed; longing for the church's healing truth is great. A few young men are too crowded. The enterprising, questioning, and researching side of the dreamer does not have enough space. Therefore, the young men place the kneeler into the middle passage. Maybe they are unable to show submission by kneeling. One of them pushes the kneeler so hard against the communion rail that it breaks. The dreamer comments that this action was not meant as an attack or insult. It was an impulsive action and an unconscious mistake. By their presence in the church, the young men indicate their interest in the religious service.

Their seemingly inconsiderate, disrespectful and involuntary action also has a deeper meaning. They wish to penetrate the separating wall and participate directly in the transubstantiation. The tradition-bound priest, or the tradition-bound side of the dreamer, experiences this attempted approach as an attack. In the men's clumsiness he can see only aggression and insult, and he retaliates in a most unchristian manner. The scene ends with a misunderstanding and brawl in which the priest is injured. The dreamer is deeply frightened by the young men's action and its consequences. He runs to help the priest. The cuts near the priest's ears tell us that his ability to listen and understand was injured. He is entirely incapable of understanding what is happening. Because the young men are unaware of the hidden purpose of their action, their attempt remains ineffective. Eventually, the dreamer seeks the assistance of the aged priest who embodies intellectual understanding of religion. But this priest is ancient, unrejuvenated. He has not adapted to the times. As a result, he is unable to understand or respond to the burning questions of the present. He is not even aware of them.

The fight between the church-goers and the priest symbolizes the battle within the dreamer's soul. His traditional beliefs conflict with his barely conscious wish to participate directly in the transubstantiation of the wine that takes place behind the separating rail. Like the dream of the brandy, this dream anticipated events in the external world. A few years later, the dreamer heard of a decree of Pope Pius XII in which the symbolic separation of priests and laypersons was abolished and priests and laypersons were addressed clearly as *one* community. This dream, then, expresses a hidden longing of the collective folk-soul, one which eventually received a satisfying response from the highest court. Modern Catholic churches no longer build a separating fence between the choir and laypersons.

Dream Fifty-Six: *Church or University*

"There was a chapel with two doors: one closed, one open. Light came through its windows from inside. I wanted to go in. Beyond the open door was a second door which jammed. It did not open wide enough, and I could not get in.

I had a lot of time on my hands in a foreign city, and so I went to visit an old castle. In the castle's museum, rails—especially church-rails for doors, windows, graves, and altars—were on exhibit. I left the castle and went to a somewhat newer house which belonged to the university. Here I saw a collection of African artifacts, mostly weapons. Just then N came from a side room. He looked like Albert Schweitzer. Before I could speak to him, five blacks arrived. One or two were men, the others women. N spoke animatedly with them in their native tongue. As he spoke, his skin color darkened. I could not understand them, but I listened with pleasure to their fluent conversation with its strange smacking sounds. The blacks were very attentive, spontaneous, genuine, thankful, kind and sympathetic. I enjoyed their pleasure in chatting and their spontaneity."

This is the second time the dreamer fails to enter the sacred space of the chapel, the area of the mystery of transubstantiation. The first door to the church is open to all church-goers, but the second one is jammed and allows an opening too narrow for the dreamer to squeeze through. After this failed attempt to bring his problem into the church and resolve it in the traditional way, the scene changes. Now the dreamer finds himself in a foreign city where he has time to visit museums. He goes to a medieval castle in which different types of church-rails are displayed. The rails have become museum pieces, indicating that exclusion and separation of the individual from the mystery of the transubstantiation is basically a carry-over from the Middle Ages.

The dreamer then visits a modern university which represents the scientific goal of universality accessible to every researcher, including the dreamer. The collection of African weapons which he finds here points to objective, factual interest in other people and their nature. Knives, spears and arrows symbolize the discriminating and penetrating qualities of thought. The collection of weapons thus stands for the natural person's ability to intelligently discuss and defend his or her own viewpoint. Explorer N embodies the scientific spirit of research which focuses on the primitive, natural human being. His helpful, empathic interest in the foreign black race is suggested by his resemblance to Albert Schweitzer. The resemblance also implies a medical attitude whose goal is the healing of conflicts and a Protestant demand for independent thought in theological questions. Indeed, Albert Schweitzer was an author of Protestant theological publications as well as a physician.

This humane, empathic and open-minded attitude of the representative of modern, scientific consciousness produces a change in the unconscious. The inert artifacts of the castle are replaced by lively, alert, sympathetic blacks who display spontaneous joy in chatting. The dialogue which could not be started in the church (Dream Fifty-Five) is now taken up in the university. The researcher changes his skin color in the course of the conversation. That is, he adapts to the blacks with whom he is conversing. The dream shows the process which the British call, albeit with a negative connotation, "going black." In the course of one's contacts with "primitive" people, one is unwittingly affected. By the same token, one's consciousness is changed by a dialogue with the primitive levels of one's own soul. Such a dialogue has important repercussions. On the basis of the mediating attitude of the researcher, an intermediate level is attained.

Dream Fifty-Seven: The Bird Griff

"I'm in a forest, close to the convent-school that I attended as a youth. I am stalking a deer when a large bird, a sort of 'griff,' appears above. He is quite ugly. He has a nude, red neck like a turkey. His body reminds me of the ill-shaped figure of the louse in the first dream. His colors are blue and red. I have my rifle, but I don't want to shoot it. Its horrid body might burst right over me if I did. I would rather that it fly away, and it does when I threaten it with the rifle."

The dreamer finds himself stalking a deer near his Catholic high school. He again tries to deal with his nature-side, but an ugly griff, or turkey-like bird, appears above him. This bird is the negative side of instinctive spirit. The turkey embodies blind rage. The griff (meaning "grasp") represents a dangerous, destructive grasping.[235] This new, disgusting and dangerous bird also belongs to the same archaic realm as the eagle of Dream Thirty. If the eagle is understood as an archaic image of God, then the griff is his negative aspect or that of the natural spirit. In his struggle to integrate his intellect and instinct, the dreamer must watch out for the negative side of nature and of the instincts.

Dream Fifty-Eight: The Cormorant

"The second one, a dark-haired and brown-skinned person, and I are in an unfinished house which is next to some horrible apartment houses. This house is similar to a small Japanese temple in that it has four corner pillars and a roof, but no walls. A black bird approaches rapidly. First I want to shoot it, but I know that I must leave it unharmed. I remember the ugly griff [of the preceding dream] which I couldn't shoot as I feared its stomach might burst. The reason I don't shoot this bird, however, is that it is a cormorant which the Japanese use for fishing. There are stone steps in the small temple. If one wishes to ascend them, one must first enter a pit with manure and garbage. Only from there can one begin the ascent. I hesitate, and the 'second one' encourages me to descend. I go ahead and then ascend the steps. Now I'm sitting with the 'second one' on the uppermost stone slab in the small temple. From here I can see that our little temple is situated on a magnificent bay with clear water and beautiful trees. It is pleasant. I can stay here."

In Dream Fifty-Five the dreamer could not gain access to the mystery of transubstantiation in the church. In the university's collection of African weapons (Dream Fifty-Six), he resumed the dialogue with the blacks, that is, with the spontaneous, natural, primitive side of his being. In Dream Fifty-Seven he searched again for the nature-like spiritual soul. Paracelsus might say he was searching for "the light in nature." In his search, he discovered the darkness that sticks to the natural soul and that embodied itself in the "griff" or turkey-like bird. The rejection of this bird purified his natural soul. The griff reappears in Dream Fifty-Eight as a black cormorant, a positive, helpful bird. Meanwhile, the ugly and dangerous content has settled, as in the alchemical process, to the ground. It lies as garbage and manure in the pit before the small temple.

With his dark-skinned shadow-brother, the dreamer finds himself among horrid apartment houses which are, to him, the epitome of collective mass existence, present in all cities. Since the dreamer has set out by himself to find the inner treasure, he is no longer part of this existence. Before him he sees his own little house which could be a small Japanese temple. Above the garbage-pit, there are a few steps leading up to the four corner pillars. These steps, representing the stepwise increase of consciousness, are similar to the stepwise alchemical process which is based on the planetary steps. The four corner-posts symbolize the four elements or the four-fold and, therefore, total all-encompassing perception of reality. We found this earlier in the cubic form and noticed this already with the four sphinxes of the silver trunk in Haggard's *She*.[236] The roof represents a human construction that unites and surmounts the whole and that offers to the dreamer protection against sun and rain. It represents the basic design for his own world view which also offers protection against historical upheavals and generalizations that lead one into collective existence.

Here a black bird appears again, but this time it is a cormorant which the Japanese use for fishing. At first the dreamer wishes to shoot it, but then he becomes aware that he would be breaking the law since cormorants are protected everywhere. The cormorant is a positive hunting instinct, reminiscent of helpful animals found in fairy tales. The cormorant dives deep into the water for the fish; it brings the values of the unconscious to light.

Only now does the dreamer wish to enter the small temple. To do so, he must first enter the garbage-pit which contains excreta from the bird of the preceding dream. The journey towards individual existence and towards a personal world view includes recognition of the shadow. Understandably, the dreamer hesitates at first, but he finally decides to pass through the garbage. As a result, he is able to reach the steps on which he climbs towards a conscious, all-encompassing view. Now he discovers that the temple offers a wonderful view of a bay with clear water and beautiful trees. The presence of the small Japanese temple in this dream emphasizes the Eastern, Zen-like qualities of natural piety, introversion and meditation in the dreamer's personal outlook. Zen confronts human beings with paradoxes, perils, and unexpected things in order to lead them to wholeness and spontaneity. If the student of Zen can remain calm in the face of any reproach, distraction, or danger, he will be able to live spontaneously. At the end of the dream of deliverance from the basin, the dreamer had to dive into a polluted section of the river. In that dream, he had to confront external difficulties. Here, however, he must recognize and accept human nature itself, in order to ascend towards a comprehensive view of life.

Dream Fifty-Nine: The Flying Hart

"I am hunting a hart who flies across the city like the symbol of a constellation or a wingless Pegasus. The 'second one' beside me doubts whether I'll be able to shoot the hart in motion. I fire. The hart is hit and drops. He falls into a river so powerfully that water splashes high across the city roofs. We run to the main bridge of the city, but the hart has sunk. He is lost. If I had known this would happen, I wouldn't have fired."

The day after this dream, a hunter told the dreamer about an old mountain goat that constantly stood upon the same rocky promontory. It was impossible to shoot him in that position because he would fall into a lake below and be irretrievable. This synchronicity or meaningful coincidence between a dream and external events alerted the dreamer to the archetypal quality and meaningfulness of his hunting dream.[237] Still, the dream seemed largely unintelligible. Only a year later was some light shed on it through an actual hunting experience. While hunting, the dreamer had shot a heath-cock which had caused a lot of damage to other heath-cocks and had evaded rangers' snares for a long time. As a result, the rangers rejoiced. The dreamer, however, was unhappy. He continued to feel deep pity for the dead bird and felt as if his own youth had ended with the bird's life. The dream of the heavenly hart, then, refers again to the sacrifice required of the dreamer. In Dream Fifty the dreamer had become one with the hart and its instinctual, passionate nature. The hart in the sky represents an elevation—that is, a spiritualization and divinization—of this nature.

In the myths of Germanic tribes, there is a hart of the sun and of New Year's standing on the earth whose horns reach into the sky.[238] Waldemar Fenn hypothesizes that the constellation now known as the Big Dipper was the hart in prehistoric astronomy. A petroglyph depicts the hart near the pole at the summer solstice, its antlers formed by the four large stars of the Big Dipper.[239] In addition, a prehistoric cave painting, again above the zodiac at the summer solstice, shows the hart beside the hind. At the side of the animal pair is a human couple, who may represent life and death.[240] The constellation of the hart was above the pole in spring and summer. The descending or falling constellation of the hart clearly indicated fall and winter, the descending course of the year.

After postulating a connection between the hunt of the hart and the ritualistic murder of the king, Robert Graves asserts that the dying or falling hart symbolizes the spring- and summer-hero's death and, thereby, the end of youthful fertility.[241] The dream's end may represent such a sacrifice of the youthful hero. The hart in the sky becomes, through its loss, a sacrificial offering. The transfer of the hart into the sky reveals to the dreamer that what he had viewed as his own, personal instinctual energy is of a super-personal magnitude, placed above the ego. His hunting companion is clearly the dreamer's shadow-brother, the natural human being who would like to prevent the sacrifices that must be made in the second half of life.

In Dream Thirty-Five the dreamer faced the task of the interlaced rings, that is, of transforming blood and passion into spiritual captivation. This task has led to a lengthy struggle. At first, consciousness was not equal to the collision with the chthonian nature of the fourth one, the evil one (Dreams Thirty-Six through Forty-Two). In addition, such a transformation requires broadening and deepening. The dreams of the Egyptian (Dream Fifty-Three) and of taming the Anima (Dream Fifty-Four) introduce the required distinction between the ego and shadow and Anima. In Dream Fifty-Five, the dreamer unsuccessfully seeks access to the mystery of transubstantiation. Here the sacred office is interrupted for the second time at the moment of transubstantiation. The dialogue with the natural side must thus be resumed (Dream Fifty-Six). The dreams of the griff and the cormorant indicate a further purification of that nature later elevated as the heavenly hart, which falls into the river as a sacrificial offering.

Identifications with the images of the unconscious, such as the dreamer's identification with the hart in Dream Fifty, introduce complications for which one is not immediately responsible. In the encounter with the unconscious, one repeatedly finds such identifications. They are essential to some extent. One must identify with these images in order for them to be taken seriously and rendered conscious. These identifications are also dangerous because they distract consciousness from reality.[242] If one struggles against identifying with these images, impoverishment and rigidity of the personality result. If one does allow a certain degree of identification with the internal figures, one must try to grasp their meaning. Only by this conscious effort is it possible to escape their fascination. The hart's sacrifice represents a sacrifice of the hart-nature and an attempt to be freed from unconscious compulsion and youthful instinct.

Dream Sixty: The Picture of the Ancestors.

"In a large, beautiful room, I'm working at a writing desk. On the wall behind me is a large picture in the style of the English portraitist Gainsborough. I'm portrayed as an old, famous, white-haired gentleman, like the old English aristocracy. I'm dressed in white satin and wearing knee-pants. It is an interesting experience. I observe this painting, and, at the same time, I know that I may be this person in some thirty years. It is not a fantasy, but an experience of simultaneity. I do feel at the same time like an old man."

The evening after this dream, the dreamer attended a performance of Strauss's *Rosenkavalier*. In this opera, the Rosenkavalier was dressed in a manner similar to that of the old man in the dream-picture. Synchronicity, then, figures both in the relationship between the dream and external events and within the dream itself where space and time are suspended and present and future, ego-reality and picture interchange mysteriously. In his article "The Spirit of Psychology," Jung describes synchronicity as a psychologically conditioned relativity of time and space.[243] In the opera, the Rosenkavalier, who in fact is a woman dressed as a gentleman, wears a white and silvery suit, whereas the dreamer in the picture is dressed in white satin. The dreamer envisions the possibility of attaining in his old age the kind of purified attitude of which the dream of the white and golden tabernacle (Dream Thirty-Four) seemed to speak. In that dream, the tabernacle represented the external, conscious, masculine life, and the inner, grey-silvery material represented the substance of the feminine soul. The dreamer sees himself with his portrait in a room reminiscent of the official rooms of his mother's ancestors. If he is able to distinguish himself from his Anima and represent masculine, spiritual values, he will be accepted, like his ancestors, as a carrier of his nation's culture.

His professional situation is still unsatisfactory, but this dream brings him consolation and the hope that his patience will not be in vain. The sacrifice of the hart—the sacrifice of his ambition—is here compensated by this vision of the future. The sacrifice of his youthful impulsiveness will help him obtain a spiritualized old age. He himself must change; his own being must, as shown by the picture, be spiritualized and elevated.

Dream Sixty-One: The Church of the Magna Mater

First Part: "I'm with a large party on a somewhat tiresome voyage. At first we travel by railroad on a track that frequently requires repairs and causes delays. Then we continue by bus. Again, there are delays because the streets are often torn up and must be repaired. After a railroad crossing, we reach a parking lot from which a beautiful, large, paved road leads into the far distance. This is the last stop. From here the buses can reach their last station without impediments. After the last stop, we will have a fairly long walk on a level street which should not cause any exceptional hardship. The route of the entire journey—the bus trip and walk—follows a large arc. Our final goal is a well-known pilgrimage church which one can now reach easily on foot. From the last bus stop another path leads through woods and meadows up to the same goal. It is not any longer than the other route, but it is steeper, more arduous and beautiful. I decide to take this foot-path and leave the bus. I ask whether anyone wishes to join me. A young man does and we start out. As I look back, I see that two more people are following. They walk more slowly, and I repeatedly admonish them to catch up with us. Thus we are four. To my companion I point out the beauty of this path from which one has a view of the meadows and hills before the Alps and which runs alongside magnificent, dark oak groves. I explain to him that at a certain point we will see the pilgrimage church above us, a view the others will not see. When we reach this point, we notice that the church is surrounded by other buildings in different styles. Besides the Baroque pilgrimage church there are Romanesque structures, towers reminiscent of the church of St. George in Prague, Gothic elements, and, finally, walls with towers and bat-tlements resembling a medieval castle. All these structures are linked by arches, military hallways, and walls. It seems to be a city of God or a temple-city. As we arrive, we look through various arch-ways. We detect colonnades like those in the Cathedral of St. Paul in Rome or the Alhambra in Granada. Inside, everything is in white and gold. The columns are of white alabaster, and the capitals are golden. I just know that I have seen this temple-city once before. I explain to my companion that the castle contains the graves of such knights and emperors as Redbeard, Karl the Great, and Karl V. Frederick II of the Hohenstaufen, however, was not buried here but in Sicily."

Second Part: "I'm boarding a large, modern streetcar. Ahead of it is another, old-fashioned one with an open platform. I jump off the large streetcar and run ahead. I prefer to ride the small, old one. It will reach my goal just as fast. I arrive at my mother's apart-ment. Though small, the apartment is full of people. The entire family is congregated. All the relatives are here. I sense that the 'second one' is beside me. He is upset that so many relatives have come when there is so little space. I calm him, saying, 'Just leave them alone. Why shouldn't they have come? There will be enough to eat for everyone even though there isn't too much food.' As I say this, I know that everyone will receive a small portion which will satiate them, just as the bread and fish miraculously fed the multitudes in the Bible. It occurs to me that this time I am the one who calms the other. Our roles have been reversed. When I reach the antechamber, the fourth and smallest room, I find three uniformed Hungarians smoking and conversing. They don't pay much attention to me. They have intelligent, noble faces. I assume that they are officers, though they wear the uniforms of enlisted men. The 'other' asks how they got in and is dissatisfied because they do not seem to belong. I reply that one should just leave them there. They make a good impression and are probably refugees who are happy that they could come."

The evening before this dream, the dreamer had expressed the desire to rediscover the faith of his childhood. However, he realized that he had to find the path to religion alone, through his own experiences and reflections. In spite of his many failed attempts to reach the mystery within the church, he still brings his widened knowledge, after each new step, back to the church. He measures his individual experiences against the church's teachings and incorporates them into its comprehensive doctrinal structure. The dream shows him that his goal is basically that of everyone else, but by following the narrow, tedious path he gains a more magnificent and profound insight into the church than those who reach the same goal by the level road. He walks the narrow path with the "other one" and two additional companions lagging behind. Their sluggishness indicates that they are the two inferior functions, thinking and sensation. Their goal is a well-known church of Saint Mary. Here the mother of God is worshiped as the true *Magna Mater* (Great Mother) of the country, and various tribes and races make pilgrimages to her shrine. The Catholic church, then, is presented in this dream as a transpersonal mother who encompasses populations and epochs within her womb. The pilgrimage church of the dream consists of Romanesque, Gothic and Baroque elements, joined into a medieval castle by battlements, towers, hallways and arches.

These elements express the dichotomy of the church's character—defensive and bellicose outside, monastic and other-worldly inside. The colonnades of alabaster and gold from early

Christian cathedrals and the Alhambra remind one of the contribution of Moslem culture to Christianity. The white columns and golden capitals which support the church symbolize the numerous individuals who supported the church and exemplified its teachings in their behavior. White and gold are characteristic of the conscious, masculine spiritual stance. With these colors, he is to be accepted by his ancestors (Dream Sixty) and within the Christian community.

On top of the castle-like structure in this dream was a Baroque section. It is the high point of stormy movement, jubilation, power and magnificence. The dreamer comments that it resembled the city of God, the heavenly Jerusalem descended upon earth. It is the goal of all human dreams, the linkage of opposites, and an image of all-encompassing wholeness realized in the church. In the womb of this great mother are buried kings who figure importantly in the histories of Western Europe and Christianity: Karl the Great (Charlemagne) who embodied European culture of his time and whom the French as well as the Germans claimed as their emperor; Frederick Redbeard who united Germany and Italy and stretched his sword towards the Near East; and Karl the Fifth in whose realm the sun never set and who, as king of Spain, represents a link with the Alhambra and Moslem art.

One emperor was clearly excluded: Frederick the Second, the nephew of Redbeard. He was a great emperor who reigned over Germany, Italy, Sicily and Jerusalem. However, he was equally fond of Eastern and Western spirituality. His concept of the empire did not include a Christian foundation, and Germany was rather foreign to him. When he showed up at the imperial Diet, he brought along foreign goods, blacks and exotic animals. He was battling the papacy and died excommunicated. The three Christian emperors are an earthly reflection of the trinity that dominates the Christian world. Frederick the Second, however—who, in the opinion of his contemporaries, was much too engaged in the Orient, the exotic, and primitive nature—symbolizes the excluded, devilish aspect which has no place in the church.

The dream makes the dreamer aware of the church's openness, its ability to harmonize a vast spiritual scope. But it also reminds him of the limits of this openness. It is a grandiose dream, a peak from which one can only descend.

This descent takes the dreamer from the majesty and splendor of the church and its emperors to the narrow, small apartment of his distinguished but poor mother. He experienced in the church the reunion of the great representatives of nations. Here he finds in his mother's apartment the reunion of his family. All are present, all have a place, and each one receives a small portion of the food which proves as sufficient as the bread and fish in the biblical feeding of the five thousand.

At this point he notices that his "other" becomes critical, while he assumes a positive, affirmative, conciliatory role, the attitude of a well-adjusted consciousness. He distinguishes himself clearly from his shadow. The former positive traits of the shadow can now be assumed by the conscious ego. In his mother's apartment, there is room for all the relatives. All are invited to a shared meal, a "small communion." All, even the small, uninteresting persons among them, are welcome. This last statement indicates a fading of the psychological inflation caused by the unconscious contents. Now the dreamer accepts, not only his shadow-aspect, but the inadequate parts of his being as well. This is important. Both one's own darkness, personified in the shadow, and middle-class narrowness must be accepted. Only that which one forgives in oneself can one tolerate in others. Insight into one's own shortcomings leads to tolerance for the weaknesses of others. Space is created within the dreamer's soul for all that is embodied in his relatives and all that his ancestors have bequeathed upon him. By using the positive, masculine attitude anticipated in the dream of the ancestral picture with the satin dress (Dream Sixty), he is able to distinguish himself from the shadow. Because he has now a more reliable consciousness and a firmer ego, he can, at the same time, accept his unpleasant, petty aspects without succumbing to them.

Three Hungarian refugees with intelligent, noble faces have found shelter in the fourth, smallest room. In the cathedral in which the three great emperors were laid to rest, the *fourth* one was excluded. His mother's domicile offers space to the three refugees in a *fourth* room. We may assume that they represent the fourth, dark side. The collective darkness, or shadow-side of our collective unconscious, cannot be totally accepted. That would be a catastrophe. However, from an excluded *minority,* a few are accepted who embody to an unusual degree the characteristics and values of the other side. The three Hungarian officers, as if coming from the land behind the wooden partition and the other side of the river, are probably an evolved version of the horrid wart-men of Dream Thirty-Eight. Now the threesome is being harbored in the fourth room, the dreamer's personal realm. If we are right in assuming that the three Hungarians evolved from the wart-men, then we may say that the natural human being who developed from the instinctual soul has found access to his mother's home.

This is true even though his mother endeavored to give him an overly rigid, Catholic upbringing. Her critical attitude condemned whatever was at odds with her convictions. Her son was quite attached to her, but he could be around her only for brief periods. She had changed but little during the last few years, but the dreamer's attitude towards her had changed a great deal. Earlier, he dreamed he had visited her, and she had placed a serpent around his neck. The dream made him shudder, but he reminded himself of all that he had learned from his dreams. The serpent represented her instinctual nature which she was unwittingly projecting upon her son. Thanks to this insight, he was able to tolerate her with understanding and empathy during his next visit. His different attitude has led to a change of the image of the mother within him. The feminine-maternal sides of his soul have become more open-hearted, broader and kindly.

At one time the Hungarians, as Magyars, belonged to the North Eurasian horsemen.[244] In admitting these three Hungarians, the dreamer accepts the representatives of a population that has achieved a synthesis of Asiatic and Western culture. The three Hungarians still carry in their blood the Asiatic characteristics that formerly sent the dreamer into a state of panic. What slumbered deep within him as a nomadic-rapacious and gruesome disposition and what, as long as he was not aware of it, appeared to him as a projection upon Asians have now changed and become capable of assimilation. The Hungarian officers, whose noble air the dreamer stresses, seem exceptionally courageous and disciplined. By suffering and self-discipline, they have grown a long way from the wart-men.[245]

Dream Sixty-Two: Betrothal

"My little sister is betrothed to the sultan."

The Hungarian language is related to that of the Turks. The dreamer, having admitted the Hungarian officers to his mother's house, again expands his contacts with the East. One of the daughters from this house is to be married to a sultan and live in an Eastern country. In past centuries the Chinese offered noble, young Chinese women in marriage to the Mongol rulers of adjacent lands.[246] Through these marriages, they were able to appease the wild nomads.

The dreamer's little sister is to be engaged to the sultan. As his closest relative, she approximates his essence. She is an aspect of his rejuvenated Anima which is to be wedded to the sultan. The archetype of the royal wedding, then, is operative here. We may assume that this royal wedding will take place in Turkey, a distant country to the dreamer. It is beyond his native country, beyond his consciousness. In the dream of the riding lesson (Dream Forty-Nine), three imperial couples appeared. In the following dream, these couples were supplemented by an animal couple. Later a flying hart, symbolizing masculine instinctual drive, fell into a large river, returning to the unconscious.

In this dream a *new* masculine, royal being, the sultan, emerges from the unconscious. He is a central figure. Because his bride is not of royal origin, she is subordinate to him. The sultan symbolizes the dreamer's *Self* which gradually, beginning from the unconscious, assumes leadership. Through the betrothal, the Anima is to return from her projection onto the outward world to her proper place, the unconscious. She is to become the dreamer's intermediary to the unconscious and its center, the sultan. As long as the Anima is projected upon nature or upon a woman, a man remains dependent. Part of his soul is outside. By reclaiming the Anima, he becomes free and independent. He gains his Anima, and in the sultan he finds a new center of gravity. The sister-Anima is elevated through her marriage to the sultan. She simultaneously becomes queen as well as one of the many ladies of the harem. Her dual position embodies the goddess and represents the individual life. She is goddess and yet only one of the goddess's thousand aspects.

This dream is strangely laconic. One single sentence remains in the dreamer's memory. Background events barely reach consciousness. The next dream occurred a few weeks later.

Dream Sixty-Three: End of the World

First Part: "I enter a cathedral through a side portal. People are crowding each other inside and outside. They are standing on the steps of the portal in the antechamber. I stand there too. I look around. I see many Catholic fathers from my school. They greet me by nodding. They are standing outside in simple robes and do not officiate as priests. They allow me to go forward to the highest step. I look inside. The archbishop celebrates the mass. The altar should have been to my right in the main nave, but a wall stands in its place. The office consists in the archbishop writing on the wall what he wants to preach. Then he is carried outside, like the pope, on a sort of *sedia gestatoria*. However, it is not high on the crowd's shoulders but much lower, as in a sedan-chair. Before I can get close enough to talk to him, he is already outside, being carried through the crowd."

The dreamer comments: "At one time the sinners who had not received absolution in confession had to remain in these antechambers until they did obtain absolution. I always place myself in the antechambers during a service, as I think of myself as a publican, not a Pharisee. In this particular context, the fathers represent my former teachers, not priests. The dream illustrates my early development. There is no altar, only a wall, an obstacle. The pastoral letters, the revelations, the dogmas are written on it. These words are law. The spiritual leader who writes these words allows no contact or opportunity for questions. The crowd, however, seems to be satisfied. They kneel down as he is carried away. His rank is indicated by the sedan-chair."

Second Part: "From this cathedral I proceed towards a mountain. I reach a village where a festive celebration is taking place.

Students in old costumes with colorful caps and ribbons (some even dressed like Bajazzos in colorful silk dresses) roam through the streets. I wear a simple, ordinary suit. I recognize many former friends from my student days. I call to them, but they do not respond. They don't recognize me. I think that I, too, should wear a student cap. Then they would recognize me."

Dreamer's commentary: "My early development continues. My inner potential leads me from high school to the university. It also leads me from a relative sense of individuality, fostered by my teachers who recognize and greet me, to a collective experience of the student body where I am not recognized as an individual but through badges and color."

Third Part: "I leave this small town and reach a mountain road. Here I see a winding road descend into the valley. Military vehicles with soldiers drive on it. I think of joining them. I hope I know one of them. Maybe we'll go into war. I run downhill and reach a company of foot soldiers. I go to the front of the group where an officer is marching. I walk beside him. He looks at me and says, 'Remain here in front. This is your proper place. You undoubtedly outrank me. We are marching into battle.' While marching we sing, but the song is appropriate to dancing, not marching. I am annoyed, and when we pass through a town with numerous people (similarly as before with the archbishop) I lose my troops in the crowd. When the march and the music do not fit, everything falls apart."

Comments by the dreamer: "After my studies and a brief period of employment, I joined the service where I descended further into a collective situation. I attained a high position, but the military was not my proper ambience. My feelings and my actions no longer coincided, and everything fell apart."

Fourth Part: "I'm climbing a mountain path. I see high mountain peaks and valleys with rivers that glitter in the sun like winding ribbons. I rejoice. Then I see behind me rocky peaks like sheet lightning. The air trembles. I see flashes and feel distant shocks. Are cannons firing in the distance or bombs exploding? Suddenly I realize that it is much worse. It may be an atomic explosion. No, it is even worse. It is the beginning of the end of the world. Horrified, I tell this to the 'second one' beside me. He does not want to believe it, but I'm more and more convinced. The flames in the sky become brighter and brighter. The air trembles. Everything shakes. I suddenly see flames spurt out in the mountains. The peaks tumble upon each other and bury the rivers and valleys below. I recall the passage in Revelations which describes mountains tumbling upon each other. Blue flames spit everywhere from the mountain. They come closer and closer. I turn around to flee. It is useless. No one can escape. Where can I turn? What can I do? In a few minutes I will burn and die. I want to repent my sins, make peace with God, and prepare myself for death. Where can I do this? At that instant, I see the kind of tiny chapel one often finds in the open fields. I run towards it, but when I get there I see that it is nothing more than one column with a picture and a cross above it. I cannot enter for shelter, not even for the few minutes before the catastrophe reaches me. I run on. I see a slightly larger chapel. I know that it is dedicated to the Virgin Mary. Inside its cool walls I will be safe for a few minutes. I will be able to pray and collect myself. Then I make a decision that has become possible only as a result of my development. I think, 'No, I shall not seek a refuge for praying and repenting. In these last minutes, I must *do* something. I must somehow be of help, rather than selfishly think of my own salvation and wait for the end.' I renounce my temporary security and salvation and run on towards the valley, the depths of the erupting inferno. I do so voluntarily. I want to help, to be useful to the very end. I pass an arched court with green arbors and vines (similar to the court of the monastery where, instead of entering the throne hall, I looked for a room of my own). I see a woman. She is my wife. Another feminine being, possibly my daughter, is there along with a boy, who may be my son or myself. I approach my wife who apparently does not understand that a catastrophe is approaching. I embrace her protectively and hide her head against my chest so that she will not see the horror. I could confess and tell her of all my failings, but it seems unimportant. What counts is to spare her and to be with her in death. A wonderful calm comes over me. I'm entirely free of fear. I look forward to death. I don't flee it, because I have overcome it within myself."

The dreamer comments: "I don't know what the end of the

world signifies. The fear in the dream was enormous. The decision to renounce my own safety and to stop being concerned with my own salvation was an act of courage. It was quite similar when the Russians arrived. . . .

Especially interesting is the development in my relation to the church. The early part of the dream with the archbishop is followed by the search for salvation in the first country chapel. This chapel, however, is but a rustic pillar with a picture, almost like the posts erected for Pan in the country-side of ancient Greece. I cannot go *inside,* because there is no inside. The chapel of the Virgin Mary, on the other hand, is a simple structure. It has no pictures, but its dedication to Mary gives it importance. It would offer shelter. Its small size contrasts with the ostentatious cathedral in the earlier part of the dream. For me, size is unimportant. I prefer the Mary chapel with its protective, naked walls. It is limited to the most simple and essential. It reminds me of the simple and concrete theme of the speech about Mary (Dream Forty-Eight): Mary as woman and working person.

At this point, I make the decision to renounce salvation. Finally I reach the woman, my wife, whose health has been my constant concern and whom I have tried to protect from wrongs and insults. The woman may also represent the Anima and the fourth member of the quartet. The message of the dream's finale seems to be: 'One's inner development is crucial even when facing the end of the world. One must eventually be in harmony with the Anima and unite the four figures. If one can achieve that, life is fulfilled. Death is insignificant because it is no longer an interruption of the journey. Inner development is the ultimate task. After its completion, the great peace follows.' I felt as if all heaviness had fallen from me. Inside I experienced a blissful calm. It was completion. As a whole, the dream shows the inner journey of a mortal human being."

There is little to add to the dreamer's comments on the first three phases of the dream. His explanation of the "end of the world," however, is insufficient. It is hard not to desist from interpreting dreams with such powerful, numerous emotions. Who knows what future destinies they anticipate? The inner images are so overwhelming and the accompanying emotions so strong that such a dream is first taken as a presentiment of external events (especially as we have good reason to fear a fiery end of the world caused by atomic explosions). However, once we gain some distance from the dream, we may find an inner, collective and individual meaning. The dreamer can discover analogous motifs in mythology and religious history. One must keep in mind that such an impressive, archetypal dream does not address the dreamer alone. The dream portrays something essential to the transition, reorientation and continuation of our entire culture. The dreamer is thus a carrier of historical developments. He has not chosen this path arbitrarily. After World War II, he had reached a point at which his education, his willingness and his consciousness could no longer help him. He therefore had to listen to his dreams and follow his inner images. Whoever looks within himself encounters the collective unconscious and touches the very course of historical development.

Jung states: "The fantasy of a world holocaust, the catastrophic end of the world, is the projection of the fundamental, original picture of the great, complete change."[247]

In *Odin and Germanic Faith in Destiny,* Martin Ninck describes the Ragnarok, the Germanic twilight of the gods:

> Fate unfolds in unbroken sequence. Battle follows upon battle. Contrasts become more extreme. The most beloved god succumbs. A brief armistice follows the shackling of Loki, but there are increasingly ominous signs. Discontent grows among the giants and human beings. The brood of Loki (the fire) grows alarmingly, frees itself, and storms with the Thurses into the last battle, the destiny of the gods, as the Edda calls it. Even the highest gods are fated to fall and perish. Everything old founders, but out of the womb of destiny a new, more beautiful world arises.[248]

And later: "In the woods of Hoddmimir two human beings hide from the blaze."[249] "Thus there is no end," states Ninck, "no last judgment, no stiffening in the grasp of a motionless eternity. Ragnarok represents the birth-pangs of a world-bearing pregnancy. It is a return, a renewal of the world."[250] This dream seems to anticipate a world holocaust, but it, too, brings renewal along with destruction. It anticipates a peace which the dreamer compares with Nirvana, a fully detached state of eternal happiness.

In the dream, the world ends, as it did in the Ragnarok, in fire.

Flames spurt everywhere from the mountains and ground. We already encountered the fire hidden within the earth in Haggard's *She*.[251] In Haggard's book, the pillar of fire is divine energy which preserves the earth and makes it fertile, a spiritual fire which inspires creative deeds. This magic fire burns all inessential attributes in order to free the pure *being,* the essence, and elevate nature to eternal life and heavenly beauty. This same fire is also the judgment which transforms the haughty She into dust and ashes so that she may reappear in a transfigured shape. Simon Magus speaks of the purifying and spiritualizing force of fire. In the Old Testament, fire is the wrath, the light, the creative and destructive power of God. In Christendom it is the suffering of hell and purgatory as well as the flame of the Holy Spirit. In alchemy, fire is at once the prime matter and driving force of the opus (process). In the earth-fire, the alchemist sees the divine love of God. In the earth-fire, She encounters both creative godhead and substance for matrimonial union, the blending and refounding of the opposing principles: sun and moon, spirit and soul.

The catastrophic end of the world, then, is—like the Ragnarok—a transformation of the gods, the divine powers in the world, and the human beings. An aged world dissolves in the fire of the Creator, so that its quintessence may emerge heightened and transfigured. The erupting flames express those spiritual energies from which the earth and all its creatures originated. They express the spirit that sustains the world and to which, according to Simon Magus, the world is being returned, "as if into a barn." According to Heraclitus, the cosmos continually transforms itself into this fire. In the Apocalypse of John and Henoch, this same fire is purification as well as punishment and annihilation. Even here it is the being of the godhead. In a moment of heightened experience, the dreamer is able to see the energies or the spirit underlying all life. He who had been no match for the low spirit of the brandy is now able, as a psychic-spiritual being, to cope with the panic of the physical person. In the course of the eruption of such cosmic emotions, the human being is in danger of perishing as natural being. He may lose consciousness and reason. Alchemy, however, asserts that through fire, and by means of many fires, the quintessence of gold can be extracted from the prime matter of unconscious life, and human beings can be made to glow as the "stone."

According to the dreamer, this dream is similar to the experience of life passing before a dying person's eyes. The first three parts of the dream can be clearly correlated with three phases of his life: childhood, studies, and years of travel. The fourth part, the great peril and decision, may be a final test. It follows the previous steps and encompasses the development of the dreamer after his wartime experiences. Once more, in heart-rending symbolical images, he lives through a summation of the previous path, in order to be able to give his own conscious, decisive answer.

After leaving the broad military road, the dreamer climbs up a narrow footpath used by mountaineers and shepherds. A rarely frequented path, it offers a wonderful view of high mountain peaks, wide valleys and a winding river. From this elevated path, he can survey his environment and the flow of his life (the ribbon of the river sparkling in the sun). From here he observes new peaks, new spiritual heights. The solitary path does not lead to conformity nor external success, but to himself. One must walk this narrow path alone. At first the sky is sunny and clear. Then distant sheet-lightning announces the storm which assumes frightful proportions. At first the path of internal development seemed pleasant and easy, no more difficult than a hike in the mountains, but then inner danger and shock announce themselves in the storm and in the approaching noise of war.

In Dream Forty the dreamer experienced an atomic explosion. "Nuclear changes" had to occur within the soul in order for the split-off fourth element to be integrated. Once more he sees the dangers he incurred and to which he is inwardly exposed. He had always been driven by an inner fire, a zealous spirit eager for change and transformation. He had always sought in the church refuge from the passions slumbering in his soul. The church protects the human being from the soul's abysses. Even this time he could have fled into the chapel to seek Mary's protection, but he sees the fire's inevitable approach. Sooner or later, it will reach him and everyone else.

Now, when he cannot escape annihilation, he sees clearly that, rather than protect and purify himself, he must act. Thus he no longer runs in order to save himself, but in order to seek those closest to him. He finds his wife and children. When his care and loving concern are turned towards his wife, transformation occurs. Instead of being driven, hunted, and tormented, he is fulfilled. Along his long path of development, he has tried to cope with the dark, dangerous and burning side of his instinctual nature. But now, in the extreme peril, he escapes from anxiety into love. He comments that his wife was simultaneously his inner Anima and that his son was also himself. Those closest to him thus represent the inner figures which complete his four-fold wholeness. The four figures are, as in fairy tales, in two couples, indicating the equalization between masculine and feminine tendencies. In this moment of fulfillment, the contrast between inside and outside is suspended by the coincidence of the inner figures with external reality. Eros who sought fulfillment in a distant country returns home to the family.

Had the dreamer fled to the chapel, he would have found once more protection from himself and from radical changes. Love would have remained for him, as for most men, a religious matter, a concern of Mary, the saints, the priests and women. He would have remained committed to the logos and action. Feeling would have remained unconsciously identified with nature, country and church. However, over a number of years, the dreamer—broadening his understanding of religious contents and the veneration of the mother of God—became aware of the possibility of realizing, in his own life, the aims of religion. The long sought-for transformation has finally occurred in an unexpected way. The fire turns devouring greed and inferior spirit into warmth of heart and light of understanding.

In the dream, the transformation occurs as a result of a single, courageous decision. In actual life many smaller decisions will have to follow, but because reorientation has occurred once, it will be easier for consciousness to follow up on it.

I shall mention five additional, brief dreams, some to show that such an experience of transformation does not automatically set everything straight, others to show the foundation for a new beginning.

Dream Sixty-Four: Arrogance

"A fat and conceited fellow attacks me with arrogant insults. I respond with even greater arrogance. He becomes increasingly angry. I goad him further. Finally, he jumps up, grabs a towel or napkin, and tries to strangle me from behind. A woman beside me screams in terror and he desists."

The fat, conceited fellow is in many legends the hero's shadow-companion. He is a lazy pleasure-seeker whose indolence is disturbed and overtaxed by the hero and his journey. He is the body-person who arrogantly fights the demands of the ego and Self. This arrogance comes from the overtaxed body, from the shadow whose natural needs have not been adequately heeded. Heightened self-control and increased consideration of the outer world would further endanger him. What the dreamer needs is consideration for and indulgence of the weaker one within himself.[252] Respect for the weakness of one's shadow will deflate its arrogance. The Anima saves the dreamer; she does not side with the shadow.

Dream Sixty-Five: Baggage

"We arrived at our destination in an enormous truck. Soldiers were loading and unloading baggage from the oversized vehicle. I had to continue my journey by train. I didn't have far to go. My baggage was light. I was surprised that I had only a knapsack and a handbag. The knapsack had a carrying frame. It was far too large and hindered me in walking because my heels hit its steel pipes. At the lower end of the frame was a round section of human bone, a bundle, and a tuft of dried plants, among them mimosas. I cannot remove these appendages by hand, and I try to rub them off against the ground. The bone and the bundle come off easily, but the dried plants are hard to get rid of. It takes a long time before they are stripped off."

The dreamer's baggage has become light. He carries only a few things. The frame of his knapsack, however, is still too large. He can easily free himself of the attached bones which represent the thoughts of death that still bother him occasionally. On bottles containing poison, crossed bones symbolize death. The second appendage is not defined. The mimosas and his mimosa-like irritability are harder to get rid of. These two difficulties seem to be linked to the oversized frame he continues to carry. Being an extroverted-intuitive person, he recognizes after this dream that he must restrict his outward "frame" even more in order to become free and flexible.

Dream Sixty-Six: The Giantess and Her Child

"In the midst of a crowd I'm sitting in a fine armchair. I discover an acquaintance who was unable to get a seat. I ask him, 'Where is your wife?' I would have given her my seat. He comes closer as he did not understand me. As he approaches, a woman, a well-proportioned and extremely beautiful giantess, is in his stead. She talks to a two- or three-year-old child who is also exceptionally beautiful. The child sits on a cupboard in order to be level with the woman's eyes. I repeatedly draw the attention of a woman sitting in front of me to the giantess's beauty and the child's charm."

The dreamer characterizes his acquaintance as a decent and fair comrade-in-arms who never let his people down. In place of this positive person, the extremely beautiful, gigantic woman and the lovely child appear. The Anima presents herself as a superhuman, semi-divine figure. Her transformation through the fire has elevated and embellished her. The dreamer is related to his family, and she is related to the inner child. The inner union of opposites is to become reality in her child. The child's loveliness is the fruit of the combination of red and white. In the tale of Snow White, the queen wishes for a child as black as ebony, as white as snow and as red as blood. In other words, she wishes for a child who combines the steps of the alchemical process: black, white, and red.

Dream Sixty-Seven: The Oversized Farmer

"On the edge of a freshly plowed and harrowed field with good, black soil stands a healthy, good-looking, and oversized farmer. As I look at him, I think that more men like him are needed to till the field. In that instant my wish is granted, and several oversized men appear on the field. I realize that there are too many now. The first one could have managed the field alone."

The farmer belongs to the same race of giants as the woman in the preceding dream. He is an archetypal man. One is sufficient; more would be superfluous. He is a superman, but not because he feels superior or takes himself too seriously. His large size is not expressed in ambition but in the tilling and tending of an earthly field, that is, in the fulfillment of the simplest duties of life. Significantly, the dreamer no longer identifies with inner figures but conceives of them as the larger ones within himself. Equally important, someone knows how to till the field in this dream. The seed is no longer left to the hazards of nature as it was in the dream of the field on the mountain slope (Dream Thirty-Nine). The sower of the field is not the ego but one who is larger than the ego and who tends to the simple work of this world so that the field of life will not remain unused. One worker can till the entire field. Individual responsibility is required, not spectacular achievement. In an alchemistic treatise titled "Secrets of the Nature of the Large and of the Small Farmer," the farmer himself is a symbol of the alchemical process.[253] He is aware of the union of the white and red lily.

Dream Sixty-Eight: The Oversized Couple

"From the stony bank of a wild river, an oversized, beautiful, blond man and woman [the farmer had had dark hair] board two small boats made of bark. Instead of using paddles, they give themselves up to the current. Full of joy and happiness, they shoot down the river through whirlpools and rapids. They stand, jump, and even squat, but they maintain their balance and master the wildest currents."

The oversized, beautiful couple are reminiscent of the two human beings who, after the fall of the Nordic gods, became the parents of a new human race. From the fire of the world holocaust arises a new generation who surpass their predecessors in size, self-assurance, force and beauty. The couple succeeds the old gods and heroes. They symbolize the reality of spirit and soul in the life of the ordinary human being and the encounter between superhuman and human nature. The two happily balance themselves as they ride on the light boats through the river's whirlpools. They are unencumbered, and the boats have neither paddle nor rudder. They give themselves up to destiny and necessity. They let themselves be carried by the river of life. The stony bank and whirlpools, representing life's difficulties, test their strength and skill. In previous unrecorded dreams, the dreamer was able to abandon his boat just before reaching the rapids where he would have been shipwrecked and drowned. However, after this dream he is able to cope with approaching difficulties and to pass the tests. He no longer needs to be afraid of problems that had seemed insurmountable. The dream's optimism gives him courage.

In conclusion we add a last dream that deals with the dreamer's religious concerns.

Dream Sixty-Nine: The Chapel in the Vatican

"During a trip, I lodged inside the Vatican. Before my departure, I began looking for my baggage. Through a hallway I reached a fairly large room, resembling a chapel, where a woman knelt, praying. In front, near an altar, a bright light was burning. The woman faced the light. The entire room was filled with magnificent, white marble statues of Greek and Roman gods which were turned with their backs towards the entrance. I did not find it disturbing that pagan gods were placed in a Christian room of worship."

The dreamer has recognized ancient gods in the forces of nature. Now this last dream reveals a synthesis of the pagan sense of nature and the Christian spirit. The Anima's worship includes both Christianity's spiritual revelation and an experience of the powers within the natural soul. The dreamer had experienced those powers as both dangerous and helpful. Now he knows that he must respect and accept them. If he tries to avoid them, they will avenge themselves through illnesses and psychological failure. However, once he has become aware of himself and his requirements, and once nature and spirit, consciousness and the unconscious, masculinity and femininity, and present and past are integrated, he finds a new inner peace, a deep understanding of Christian virtues, a live piety, and true, warm human concern. By our accepting and including the natural soul, the barbarian within us is allied with spiritual consciousness, and both are thereby transformed. The poacher became the good-looking, strong farmer who tills his field. The heath-cock became the troll who was transformed into the beautiful, oversized woman with the lovely child. These dream-figures remind one of the ancient gods who were also oversized human beings. Since the beginning—when first vermin, then rats, then whores dressed in red appeared to him menacingly in his dreams—there has been a progressive transformation in the dreamer. With the appearance of these large, luminous figures, a new path into the future has opened up.

Concluding Remarks to the Series of Dreams

We have followed the dreamer on the long, intertwined paths of inner clarification. Through his dreams, we have discussed everything that has affected him: profession, environment, family, ancestors, his own nature, women, the war, his religious education, God. Naturally, many people deal with such problems. They pose questions concerning God and the meaning of life and draw conclusions in accordance with their world views. However, only a few appreciate the importance of consulting their dreams in these endeavors.

The dreamer began his inward path by assessing and clarifying his present difficulties and inadequacies. He then had an intuitive presentiment of a new goal: the search for the royal couple. Insight into his ties to his mother and sister was followed by an experience of his own feminine side. While he explored the light and dark inner figures, he experienced the Anima's ambivalent aspects. Only by differentiating himself from the shadow and the Anima's changing demands and negative moods can a man gain full possession of his masculinity. On the other hand, he reaches the wholeness of his Self only by allowing the Anima to speak and by giving proper consideration to his feelings. True spiritual masculinity develops through conscious questioning of accepted world views.

At first the dreamer felt that his relationship with the Anima should not be mixed with religious questions. He felt the two were different, even opposite topics, but his dreams allowed no such separation. At one time the Anima dressed in dark soul-material was hidden in the tabernacle. At another time, to the dreamer's distaste, a woman officiated as priestess in the church. The queen was acclaimed as heavenly queen thereafter. Mary was discussed as a simple worker. Another dream reveals the Mother Church as the *Magna Mater,* the great mother of the country and the Christian Anima of the world. Only towards the end did the dreamer recognize the interdependence and interconnectedness between the dreams relating to his religious attitude and those dealing with his exploration of and dialogue with the Anima. The Anima mediates the inner images. What arises from the unconscious is represented by or through her first, and assimilated by male consciousness later.

The dreams go beyond the dreamer's conscious intentions. In fact, they frequently act in contrast to his wishes and will (for example, Dream Twenty-Eight, "The Church Collapses," and Twenty-Eight A, "The Bomb"). They also anticipate insights which he has not consciously attained (for example, Dreams Thirty-Four, "The Tabernacle"; Forty-Eight, "Four Speeches"; and Sixty-Three, "End of the World"). Many pose riddles which are solved only by subsequent dreams (for example, Dreams Thirty-Six, "Brandy"; Thirty-Seven, "The Transition"; and Fifty-Nine, "The Flying Hart"). The dreams lead towards a widening of consciousness (for example, Dreams Eleven, "The Heath-Cock"; Twelve, "The Bathing-Suit"; and Thirty, "The Eagle"). They demand a radical reorientation of consciousness (for example, Dreams Twenty, "The Woman-Commander"; Twenty-Five, "The Runner"; and Fifty-Three, "Imprisonment in the Rocky Cliff"). A few aim at restricting the unconscious (for example, Dreams Eighteen, "The Anima Warns Against the Eleven Crows"; Nineteen, "The White Bull"; and Fifty-Four, "The Taming of the Anima"). They also aim at the differentiation of consciousness and at a genuine Christian attitude which can only be attained through slow, patient growth (for example, Dreams Thirty-Four, "The Tabernacle"; Forty-Six, "The Convent with the Throne Room"; and Sixty-Three, "End of the World"). Finally, they offer the foundation for a new spiritual orientation (for example, Dreams Thirty-Three, "The New Church"; Thirty-Four, "The Tabernacle"; Forty-Seven, "The Round Church"; Sixty-One, "The Church of the *Magna Mater* and the Mother's Home"; and Sixty-Nine, "The Chapel in the Vatican").

The dreams brought about profound discussions of the darkest, as well as the highest and holiest, contents of the soul. Gaining insight and knowledge is an important part of the journey, but realizing this insight in everyday life is more important and difficult. One must continually struggle towards this realization. All too often it is at this point that one fails. Once the symbols of the Self—the circle, the royal couple, or the quaternity—approach, there is a presentiment of an inner consolidation. Such inner wholeness, however, must prove itself in actual life. Only through continued effort can one overcome recurring relapses and deficiencies to actualize this wholeness. Relapses which follow truly important, inspiring dreams are especially disappointing, but Jung's comment may serve as consolation:

> The proficient person will constantly find, either because of unfavorable circumstances, technical errors, or seemingly demonic incidents, that the completion of the process is hindered, and that he, therefore, must begin anew. Whoever attempts to establish his security in the everyday world by following an analogous psychological journey, will have similar experiences. More than once he will find that what he has achieved falls to pieces in the collision with reality. However, he must tirelessly examine the inadequacies in his orientation and the blind spots in his psychological visual field. Just as the philosopher's stone, with its wondrous powers, has never been actually produced, so psychic totality will never be reached empirically. Consciousness is too narrow to ever comprehend the full inventory of the soul. We will always have to begin again. The adept in alchemy always knew that it was ultimately a matter of the "res simplex" [the simple thing]. Human beings today will learn by experience that the process will not prosper without the greatest possible simplicity. The simple, however, is also the most difficult.[254]

The dreamer experiences this simplicity at the end of the dream series in the joyful human couple, the tall woman with the lovely child, and the farmer who tills the field. The series dealing with the Anima, then, finds its natural conclusion in these last dreams.

III. Summary

The first part of this book, "Psychological Interpretations of Rider Haggard's *She*," examines a novel of the late nineteenth century. In the second part, the dreams of a contemporary man were analyzed. Through these analyses, we intended to show that Haggard's book is not a unique, solitary fantasy. In fact, it reflects contemporary inner pictures of the unconscious. Starting out from a few introductory dreams, the series grew until it found a natural closure in the dreams of the end of the world (Dream Sixty-Three) and the oversized human beings (Dreams Sixty-Six through Sixty-Eight). That which Haggard imagined was intuited and inwardly experienced over a period of eight years by a modern, professional man. These inward experiences were elucidated in the psychotherapeutic dialogue. They were then integrated with the dreamer's conscious world view.

We find a number of elements shared by the novel and the dream series. The steps of inner development which they describe are largely the same, even though the two men belonged to different periods, religions, countries, and professions.

Differences in form and details may be attributed to differences in time-scales. Haggard wrote *She* in six weeks. The dreams, on the other hand, were experienced and assimilated over a period of eight years. Haggard's novel portrays in one single sketch the mythology latently present in the unconscious and describes it as a manifold event containing various steps. The dreams, on the other hand, are related to daytime experiences and gradually mix events close to consciousness with archetypal motifs from the deep layers of the collective unconscious. In the course of development, these motifs keep changing.

For a Protestant, the archetypal images tend to signal an eruption from the irrational sphere. The mere experience of those images is a powerful event for him. He is, however, in danger of remaining in a state of admiration—for example, in a romantic glorification of antiquity or in a modern paganism.[255] For a Catholic, pictures and symbols represent a familiar world. Today, however, many Catholics and Protestants live on two levels. Their lives are characterized by natural-scientific thought which remains unharmonized with their religious views. Most grow up without a true religious education. Those who had religious training discard it, as religious and natural-scientific thinking appear incompatible.

When the unconscious soul announces itself in dreams or fantasies, it is advisable to pay attention to them. They bring forth the forgotten, original, religious images. These are contents which are necessary for shaping a full life attaining inner wholeness. They contain the remote past and the future. One must reflect upon their meaning and confront and integrate them with traditional, conscious world views. Our dreamer is quite aware of his religious beliefs. When he is preoccupied with the unconscious, he is eager to compare its contents with the great, religious models. This effort leads to a link between the conscious and the unconscious, the development and differentiation of the contents of the unconscious, and a broadening and deepening of consciousness.

Conflicts exist in *She* between the views of the two Englishmen, Leo and Holly, and the views of She. Haggard remains stuck in the conflict. He is unable to bring his Protestant, Victorian ideal of the gentleman into harmony with the Anima's demands.

Although we have pointed out parallels between the developments described in the novel and the dream series, we must emphasize that the inner process can also evolve differently. Each individual's unconscious follows its own path.

Both in the novel and the dream series, we find that the approach to the Anima can take place only after the death of the old ego and a confrontation with animals, that is, the instincts. *She* begins with the death of Holly's friend, Vincey, who represents Haggard's ego. Similarly, the dreamer's ego symbolically dies in the dream of the airplane-crash (Dream Two). In both cases, youthful mastery of the world has reached a limit. In order to progress further, a radical reorientation is required. One must painfully renounce the primary function. As the poet and the dreamer were

intuitive types, they must abandon intuition for a while in favor of such inferior functions as *thinking* and *sensation*. After the renunciation of intuition, several companion-figures who represent the inferior functions are introduced. They are shadow-figures who, however, can intercede helpfully or take on the role of lagging reflection. Holly, the hero's shadow in the novel, is also his reflection and guide. He is later joined by Billali, the old wise man. The dreamer, too, often experiences "another" beside him. The other may be a younger brother; an indefinite, dark companion; a hunting assistant; or an old man who assumes leadership.

As we stated earlier, the approach to the Anima can take place only after one has confronted one's instincts in the form of animals. Leo and Holly hunt the animals which they discover, but we notice that the dreamer, though an eager hunter, gradually manages to refrain from firing his rifle. He gives the animal time for transformation. He is not allowed simply to kill the game. He must listen to it, find a relationship with it, recognize it as part of himself, and humanize it. In the beginning, when the poacher shoots the young hart, he is punished by the dreamer (Dream Thirteen). Only towards the end of his development does the dreamer aim at the heavenly hart because he must now sacrifice his identification with the nature-divinity (Dream Fifty-Nine).

In *She* the Anima announces herself first in the sphinx. The unconscious, feminine nature-soul is contaminated by the animal instincts. Later appears Ustane, a human aspect of the Anima that is still close to nature. Over her stands Ayesha as goddess.

In the dreams, the Anima develops from a heath-cock to a troll; then to an impersonal, female army commander; and, finally, to the heavenly queen. She also appears as the whore-Anima, the opposite of the elegant lady on the upper floor. As sisterly companion, and later as his daughter, the Anima becomes directly related to the dreamer and assists him in his confrontation with the animals. She enables him to grow beyond his blind instinctual ties without needing to kill the animals.

In the novel, first Ustane and then She assists the hero against the savages, the blind affective reactions. Here, defense requires radical means as there were no prior conscious experiences with the instinctual side.

Once the dreamer has found the link with his ancestors and the proper level of emotional relatedness (symbolized by the heart), he

begins to explore the spiritual tradition of the East and, subsequently, his own religion. In the novel, the heroes similarly reach the burial city of Kor (heart), housing previous generations. Here Holly and She have long discussions dealing with spiritual and religious traditions. This broadening of consciousness is a necessary development.

For the dreamer, spiritual discussions are followed by the discovery or reconstitution of spiritual reality. The dream concerning the tabernacle leads the dreamer to a new evaluation of his life. His outward life is likened to the tabernacle and his inner soul-life to the "holiest of holies" within it. Later he obtains from the queen the sapphire ring with the crown of white pearls, the symbol of a purified and spiritualized experience of reality and of love. Through effort and proper devotion, a trans-temporal meaning becomes manifest in one's life.

The white pearls decorating the sapphire ring correspond to the mummy's little foot in *She*. Both ivory whiteness and mummification symbolize the immortal body. The foot itself emphasizes this body's concrete presence. Holly sees in the mummy's foot a portrayal of the eternal life-cycle of the spirit. The body is the temporary residence of the eternally alive spirit. The novel has no symbol which corresponds to the sapphire, the transparent, blue, hard gem. In the novel, new insights are not solidified in everyday life.

Subsequent dreams raise issues concerning *red* and *white*, the alchemical symbols for spirit and soul. The dreamer must now purify, elevate, sacrifice, and transform spirit and soul.

White is dispersed, once more, in the explosion of the white powder (Dream Forty), and red is dispersed in the volcano's eruption (Dream Forty-One). The danger of passionate nature, symbolized by red, manifests itself. The development of white, the soul, takes place in the dream alluding to the sacrifice of Aida, where the Anima is installed as priestess, and later in the humble worship and discussion of various aspects of the heavenly queen. Mary turns into the archetypal image of the human soul. When she is worshiped as simple woman, every woman, as well as every man's humble soul, is elevated through her. The dreamer's mother, too, is a simple woman (Dream Sixty-One, second part). In her modest habitation all the relatives, even the least liked and insignificant ones, as well as three Hungarian delegates from a realm beyond the river, find acceptance. Mary, the queen of all creatures, never turns away anyone who comes to her. Similarly, the mother-Anima, together with her son's soul, admits the split-off fourth in the fourth room. The differentiation of white leads to a stepwise change of the Anima-image and eventually to the sister's betrothal with the sultan, who represents the yet unconscious Self. The youngest sister, as youthful form of the Anima, becomes here the bridelike soul.

The production of red is far more difficult. One cannot simply accept the traditional spirit. The dreamer must search for the raw material of the spirit, primitive emotionality or impulsivity, which in itself is neither good nor evil. It can easily become immoderate and destructive rather than creative. Before he can uncover and purify the red, the dreamer has to meet the unredeemed crowds, the three wart-men, and, later, Mephistopheles. The dreamer must neither identify with evil, with Mephisto, nor with Faust, who represents what the world commonly regards as good. The riding lesson with the princesses and the transformation into a hart establish the dreamer's connection with his nature. Accepting his impulsive-instinctual side requires an increased sense of responsibility and a more differentiated understanding of the shadow. The dreams demand the submission of the ego to an inner judge. Thus, the chthonian figure of the Egyptian is arrested, and the Anima is tamed. Transformation now affects the dreamer quite personally. The sacrifice of the heavenly hart, symbolizing the offering of the instinctual nature, and scaring away the ugly red and blue bird are also essential to the purification of red. In the end, the dreamer must expose himself to transformation in the fire of the world's end.

In the novel, when She drops her dark cloak, she emerges "like a blessed spirit from the grave, like Venus from the waves, like Galathea from the stone." She is the *white* queen who shines like a light. With her Leo seeks the fire of life that glows in all colors and glitters like lightning. The pillar of fire is the *glowing red spirit* of nature which works within the earth's womb. Leo is to unite himself with this creative spirit, but this union fails because there has been no prior testing and actualization in life.

It is important that Leo does not allow himself to be carried away by the Anima's intoxication with power. The novel ends with She's sacrificial death. Only as a result of the unintentional self-sacrifice of the Anima does the reverse aspect of the fire, the danger inherent in passionate, creative seizure, become manifest.

The dreamer, on the other hand, endangered by the threatening flames, is able to go beyond his fears and to think of others. He succeeds in confronting the flames with a conscious decision. As a result, he is transformed and capable of experiencing wholeness. He compares the peace that overcomes him with the experience of Nirvana. The quiet which fills him he calls "fulfillment." The wedding to which he had been invited did not take place the first time. Later, it occurred on several different experiential levels. Now, in face of the fire, it is experienced again, when he lovingly and protectively turns towards his wife and, simultaneously, his inner Anima. Ultimate despair suddenly changes into profound, inward peace. By caring for those nearest to him, he accepts his Anima as the capacity for loving relatedness and as inner reality. Since he goes beyond his ego and commits himself wholly, he experiences himself as a whole.

This extreme experience is followed by a descent towards everyday life. The human being is and remains the same in terms of his talents and shortcomings. He cannot escape being the psychological type he is. However, the environment to which he returns is closer to his heart now because he has been linked to the three figures, represented by his wife and children. In addition, he is able to handle external and internal problems with more self-assurance. He finds the *inner* causes of his errors with greater ease. What previously caused him despair is now an occasion to test the wholeness he has experienced.

At the end of the dream series, the Anima is no longer an animal or whore. She is an oversized woman accompanied by a lovely child (Dream Sixty-Six). She has become mother. In his novel *Ayesha*, Haggard also envisions the Anima's motherhood in a picture within a volcanic temple. The last dreams show the Anima as *companion and mother* (Dreams Sixty-Six and Sixty-Eight). The circle is complete. The man's feminine soul was awakened and influenced by the mother. If he is to mature, the son must separate from the mother in order to find his life's companion in his beloved. When his young wife becomes a mother, he is compelled to withdraw once more the projection of his soul image in order to experience his own soul independently of wife and mother. It is a long journey of exploration aimed at freeing the soul from the unconscious and from projections. He is to transform the Anima's two aspects, goddess and nixie, into a capacity for human relatedness within the concrete world. His own soul is to become capable of relating and mothering.

The arch-image of the soul always retains the rank of goddess. She stays "She-who-is-to-be-obeyed," the superior, benevolent and abysmal mistress soul. Our consciousness experiences and grasps only a small fraction of her unlimited disguises, among them, earth- and death-mother, Anima Mundi, Sophia, and heavenly queen.

In the search for the Anima, both the soul and the masculine aspect are changed. The latter meets the dreamer in the guise of two inner figures who, like Holly and Leo, represent two different functions. One is the farmer patiently tilling the earthly field (Dream Sixty-Seven); the other is the oversized man with the little boat made of bark (Dream Sixty-Eight) who portrays the courageous, independent spirit of enterprise confidently entrusting itself to the stream of life. In these two figures we may recognize transformations of Faust and Mephistopheles. The earthbound farmer uses the instinctual nature and practical knowledge of Mephistopheles. He satisfies his needs with his own strength. The boatman adopts Faust's zeal for research in a way which does not ignore human relationships. We may view the four oversized figures as the fruit of the transformation. They combine superhuman strength, assuredness, and freedom.

In the second volume of the novel *(Ayesha),* an altar picture hangs high above the priestess in the temple. It portrays the winged great mother, Isis, and her child. Similarly, we find in one of the last dreams (Dream Sixty-Six) the exceedingly lovely child who sits, remarkably, on a ledge at the height of the giantess's eyes. In both situations, the child points beyond what has been achieved to an inner unity where the opposites of mother and companion, doing and thinking fuse into the individual oneness of being. That the child is seated at the height of the giantess's eyes may indicate that the center of consciousness is to be at this level.[256] In the novel we also find that the altar image is elevated. Jung points out that, in the end, Faust becomes a "blessed boy" whose "astonished seeing" replaces the previous need to possess.[257] At this point, one might also mention the frequently misunderstood words of Christ in

Matthew (18:3): "Unless you turn around and become as young children, you will by no means enter the kingdom of heaven."

The dream series ends with the inner child who is a promise of the future. Based on a widened consciousness and a sharper sense of responsibility, this child embodies a return to life's spontaneity, to the kind of immediacy that feels obligated both to the unconscious and the superpersonal spirit. This obligation includes the task of delving deeper into the meaning of Christian tradition and God's image. The child represents the beginning of a new inner attitude that must be experienced, affirmed and fought for. While the dreams speak of a live child, the child in the novel appears in an altar picture. In the dreams, the symbol for inner integration is close to life; in the novel, it is an unattained ideal image.

Both in Haggard's *She* and the dream series, the search for the soul is depicted as a human being's confrontation with nature and divine powers. The approach of human consciousness to the great figures of the unconscious leads to the birth of an inner divine child. However, as instrument or carrier of this process, the human being must, more than ever, be conscious of his/her limits. He must strive for the narrow region between the opposites, identifying with neither side. Otherwise, he becomes prey to a subhuman or superhuman state. If he seeks to maintain the human middle between the inner opposites and respects the inner structure, he can mature towards becoming a whole human being. This inner completeness can never be reached fully and permanently during one's lifetime. It remains a goal that must be constantly striven for, but which, at times, can be happily and serenely experienced.

A Note to the Reader

Not only the text of this book but also all quotations from German-language works have been translated into English by Julius Heuscher and David Scott May. The reader is being referred, not to C. G. Jung's English-language *Collected Works,* but rather to the text of his German writings, for the most part collected in *Gesamtausgabe,* ed. Marianne Niehaus-Jung, 16 vols. (Olten, Switzerland: Walter, 1971). For the sake of brevity, references to this opus are abbreviated as follows: Jung, *CW* volume number, inclusive paragraph numbers.

Otherwise in the endnotes, if a title is given first in German, then with an English translation in parentheses, an English edition of that work may not be available. In those cases where we could locate an English edition, we have supplied that bibliographical information following the German.

The poem by Andrew Lang printed below was omitted in error from the text of this book. It should have appeared on page 31.

Spring Publications

SHE!

To H.R.H.
Not in the waste beyond the swamp and sand,
The fever-haunted forest and lagoon,
Mysterious Kor, thy fanes forsaken stand,
With lonely towers beneath a lonely moon.
Not there does Ayesha linger—rune by rune
Spelling the scriptures of a people banned,
The world is disenchanted! Oversoon
Shall Europe send her spies through all the land!

Nay, not in Kor, but in whatever spot,
In fields, or towns, or by the insatiate sea,
Hearts brood o'er buried loves and unforgot,
Or wreck themselves on some Divine decree,
Or would o'erleap the limits of their lot—
There—in the tombs and deathless—dwelleth SHE!

Notes

1. "Soul-images, Anima and Animus are, respectively, the complementary aspects of the feminine nature in the unconscious of the man and of the masculine nature in the unconscious of the woman. We meet her countersexual personifications of the unconscious in the shape of a semi-bestial or semi-divine woman in the man, and in the shape of analogous masculine figures in the woman. Just as men and women have masculine as well as feminine genes, so they also have masculine as well as feminine traits. Of these, however, one portion is not lived consciously. Within the unconscious experience of man the Anima portrays through her personal aspect unconscious feelings, emotions, moods and inclinations, and through her archetypal aspect she represents the integrated mother-woman-image. Within the unconscious experience of the woman, the personal aspect of the Animus portrays affects, enthusiasms and opinions of the man, while the archetypal aspect represents mankind's multilayered condensation of father-man-images. When they are lifted to the conscious level, these contents and images give up some of their autonomy and thereby become mediators between the deeper levels of the unconscious and consciousness. The Anima becomes the inspiring woman—for example, Dante's Beatrice—the Animus becomes a 'logos spermaticos,' a creative word, who uncovers new spiritual dimensions of time." Kurt V. Sury, *Wörterbuch der Psychologie* (Vocabulary of Psychology), 2d ed. (Basel/Stuttgart: Benno Schwabe, 1958), 358.

2. Jung felt constrained to make a conceptual distinction between *soul* and *psyche*. By *psyche* he means "the totality of all psychological processes, whether conscious or unconscious. . . ." By soul, on the other hand, he means "a specific, delineated matrix of function which is characterized best as 'personality.'" "As far as the character of the soul is concerned, one can say that . . . the general thesis is valid to the extent that the soul is all in all *complementary* to the external character. The 'unconscious' soul tends to contain all those universal qualities which are lacking in the conscious orientation." Jung, *CW* 6, §§877, 884.

3. Jung, *CW* 9, ii, §41.

4. See also Esther Harding, "She: A Portrait of the Anima," in *Spring 1947*: 59–93.

5. Jung, *CW* 15, §§51–53.

6. Intuition or the ability to surmise is, according to Jung, one of the four

basic functions: thinking, feeling, sensation, and intuition. During one's youth it is the most easily developed function that is commonly used, whereby arises, for example, the "intuitive functional type." Introversion designates an attitude which tends to orient itself primarily in relation to inner psychic processes, in contrast to the extroverted attitude which is interested principally in external events. Cf. Jung, CW 6, §834.

7.   This presentation of H. R. Haggard's life is based upon his autobiography written in 1912, The Days of My Life, 2 vols. (London: Longmans, Green and Co., Ltd., 1926), as well as on the biography, The Cloak That I Left (London: Hodder and Stoughton, 1951), which was published by his daughter Lilias Rider Haggard.

8.   L. R. Haggard, The Cloak, 24.

9.   H. R. Haggard, Days of My Life, I: 17. Once, when the youngest of the brothers wished to travel to Egypt, the father invited him for leave-taking to his club in Pall Mall. Then he took leave from him at the door. As the son was walking away, he suddenly heard the father call loudly, "Arthur, Arthur." To avoid drawing excessive attention from the bystanders, the son started to walk faster. Now the father called him even more loudly. Arthur began to run and the people became startled. One exclaimed, "Stop the thief!" But Arthur kept running, followed by the crowd and a policeman until the guard at Marlborough House stopped him. Finally he gave up and allowed the crowd to accompany him back to the Oxford and Cambridge Club. At a distance he still heard his father yell, "Don't forget to greet mother!" The father then disappeared laughingly into his club, and Arthur proceeded to the railroad station, from whence he departed, via Bradenham, to Egypt.

10.   An unconscious tie of son or daughter to the mother. Sury, Wörterbuch der Psychologie.

11.   Jung, CW 9, i, §§161 ff.

12.   Jung, CW 6, §726. See also above, n. 6.

13.   Myers, Human Personality (London: Longmans, 1906), I: 7.

14.   Gurney, Podmore and Myers, Phantasms of the Living.

15.   L. R. Haggard, The Cloak, 268.

16.   Bernhard Fehr, Englische Literaturgeschichte des 19. & 20. Jahrhunderts (History of English Literature of the 19th and 20th Centuries) (Leipzig: Tauchnitz, 1934), 314.

17.   See also Jung, CW 11, §619.

18.   This had come about in the following way: the English declared Cetewayo, a Zulu chieftain, to be king. This proclamation created difficulties, however, since Cetewayo did not wish to be appointed by England. Eventually a way was found to save the situation. The Zulu chieftains announced in a large meeting that the spirit of Chakas, the great barbaric, bloody Zulu king, had entered Sompseu (which was the African name of Shepstone), whereupon he was entitled to perform the coronation of Cetewayo. As a result of this, Shepstone gained innocently the reputation of being possessed, which stood in strange contrast to his benevolent, responsible, and prudent personality. Throughout the period of Shepstone's administration there was hardly one black rebellion to speak of. H. R. Haggard, Days of My Life, I: 70–71.

19. *Days of My Life,* I: 104: "I thank my father Sompseu for this message. I am glad that he has sent it, because the Dutch have tired me out and I intend to fight them once, and once only, and to drive them over the Vaal. Kabana [name of messenger] you see my impis [armies] are gathered. It was to fight the Dutch; I called them together; now I will send them back to their homes."

20. L.R. Haggard, *The Cloak,* 218.

21. The first relay (on the journey to one's self) leads to the experience of the shadow, which symbolizes our "other side," our "dark brother" who invisibly belongs inseparably to our wholeness. Jolande Jacobi, *Die Psychologie von C. G. Jung* (1959), 165; English edition: *The Psychology of C. G. Jung,* trans. R. Manheim (New Haven: Yale University Press, 1959).

22. By the term "Anima" Jung understands the feminine soul of the man. See discussion of Rider's mother-complex, pp. 5–7 above, and Jung, CW 7, §§297 ff.

23. *Jess* is one of Haggard's most likeable books. It takes place in the beginning of the Boer war, on the English side; yet it was well-liked even by the Boers and was found even in their trenches.

24. H.R. Haggard, *Jess* (1887), I: 265–66.

25. Ibid., 272.

26. Jung, CW 9, ii, §20.

27. H.R. Haggard, *Jess,* I: 886: "But it was a lie, and they both knew it was a lie."

28. H.R. Haggard, *Days of My Life,* 292.

29. For example, Winston Churchill.

30. H.R. Haggard, *Days of My Life,* II: 96.

31. Ibid., 103.

32. H.R. Haggard, *Allan and the Ice-Gods: A Tale of Beginnings,* ed. R. and D. Menville (Tauchnitz: Reginald Ayer Co., 1976), 188.

33. L.R. Haggard, *The Cloak,* 277–78.

34. H.R. Haggard, *Days of My Life,* I: 245–46.

35. Pronounced: E'scha.

36. In Rider's early youth there lived in the wall-closet of his room a rag doll with unusually frightening features: shoe buttons for eyes, black wool for hair, and a spooky smile on the painted face. As a child, Rider viewed the doll as a fetish and was terribly scared of it. L.R. Haggard, *The Cloak,* 28.

37. H.R. Haggard, *Jess,* I: 265.

38. By primary function, Jung means the one of the four functions (thinking, feeling, intuition, and sensation) which is most developed and relied upon most often, usually to the exclusion of the other three.

39. The ferryman of the dead in the underworld of antiquity.

40. Helmuth Jacobsohn, "Das Gegensatzproblem im Altaegyptischen Mythos" ("The Problem of Oppositions in the Myths of Ancient Egypt") in *Studien zur analytischen Psychologie C. G. Jungs* (Studies Concerning the Analytic Psychology of C. G. Jung) (Zürich, 1955), II: 192.

41. Ibid., 190: "Wherever difficult or dangerous situations occurred for the gods or for the human beings, Thoth was at hand. Because of this he also was in the deepest sense the Psychopompos. Thus he helped in the resurrection of Osiris during the drama of the Egyptian Gods, and he helped the Ba-like Osiris NN in

his ascent to Heaven."

42. Jung, CW 8, §§131 ff. Of the four functions (sensation, thinking, feeling, and intuition), the least developed and "inferior" one remains most closely linked with the unconscious. If later in life this inferior function is given increasing attention, it succeeds in establishing a relationship between unconscious contents and consciousness. Jung, therefore, named it the transcendent function, not in a theological but in a psychological sense, because it is capable of catching and integrating contents that are beyond consciousness, that otherwise are barely perceived motions of the unconscious.

43. By "quest" is meant the journey as a mystical search. Such "quests" are a recurrent concept in the medieval epics.

44. Jung, CW 9, §281.

45. Larousse, Mythologie Générale, 18.

46. Jung, CW 5, §566: "At Siegfried's birth Sieglinde dies, as anticipated. The foster mother, however, is not a woman, but a cripple-like dwarf, belonging to the gender that renounces all love (cf. Grimm, Myth. I, p. 314). This dwarf is exemplified by Mime or Mimir, a colossal being of great wisdom, an earlier Nature-god of the Ages. . . . Just as Wotan goes to a wise woman for advice, so Odhin goes to Mimir's fountain, where wisdom and prudent council are kept. . . . Mimir's fountain points unequivocally to the mother-image. In Mimir and his fountain, mother and embryo are fused. At the same time, in the guise of mother, Mimir is the source of wisdom and art. Just the way Bes, the dwarf and educator, is an extension of the mother-goddess, so Mimir is an extension of the maternal spring. . . . They are mythological Animus figures. The Egyptian god of the Netherworld, the crippled shadow of Osiris, who celebrates a sad resurrection in Harpocrates, is the educator of Horus, who must avenge his father's death."

47. Just as the man's Anima embodies his eros, his ability to relate, so does a woman's Animus (or the mother's Animus) represent her logos, her spiritual and intellectual abilities.

48. Jung, CW 16, §421, n. 19.

49. Jung, CW 5, §265; and K. Kerényi, Die Mythologie der Griechen (Zürich, 1951), 56; English edition: The Gods of the Greeks, trans. Norman Cameron (London: Thames and Hudson, 1951).

50. H. Jacobsohn, "Die dogmatische Stellung des Königs in der Theologie der alten Aegypter" ("The Dogmatic Position of the King in the Theology of Ancient Egypt"), in Aegyptische Forschungen, Heft 8 (Glueckstadt und Hamburg, 1939).

51. Ibid., 51.

52. H. Jacobsohn, "Das Gegensatzproblem," II: 176. "Originally the Ka is the Mana power that flows from the creator-god Ptah or Atum or Horus, through which the god disperses himself in the world and the living creatures: the power that acts upon and within the world. In the 5th Dynasty the Ka became the Creator Spiritus, the spirit of the Sungod grown conscious of his creativeness and fatherliness, the spirit in whom the son, the god-man, was conscious of being one with the father. It became the spirit by means of which the father was creative in the world and in human beings through his son. The last manifestation, the final stage of the creativeness of the Ka, was the god Osiris (the 'Ka of Horus'), the god who, for the time being, is completely attached to the world and its materiality."

53. Margarete Riemschneider, *Augengott und Heilige Hochzeit* (Eye-God and Holy Marriage) (Leipzig: Koehler, 1953), 230.

54. Margret Ostrowski, "The Anima in the Prometheus Books of Carl Spitteler," lecture given in the Psychology Club, Zürich, 1957.

55. Jung, *CW* 16, §421.

56. Kerényi, *Die Mythologie,* 224.

57. Ibid., 265.

58. S. Hurwitz, *Die Gestalt des Sterbenden Messias* (The Figure of the Dying Messiah) (Zürich, 1958), 211–12.

59. Riemschneider, *Augengott,* 1 ff.

60. Alfred Hildebrandt, *Lieder des Rgveda* (Songs of the Rgveda) (Goettingen, 1913), I, 118: 5—"May the virgin, the daughter of the sun be pleased, as she joins you in your chariot, oh Asvins. . . ."

61. According to Jung, the first approach to the collective unconscious during an analysis frequently manifests itself in dreams of water. See also Part II, Dream Five, of this book.

62. See Jung, *CW* 12, §31, for a discussion of quaternity as wholeness.

63. Erich Neumann, *Die Grosse Mutter* (Zürich, 1956), 212; English edition: *The Great Mother,* trans. R. Manheim (Princeton: Princeton University Press, 1964).

64. M.-L. von Franz, "Die Passio Perpetuae," in C. G. Jung, *Aion* (Zürich, 1951), 467 ff.; published in English as *The Passion of Perpetua,* trans. Elizabeth Welsh (Dallas: Spring Publications, 1980).

65. Jung, *CW* 14, ii, §383.

66. Jung, *CW* 9, ii, §14.

67. *Jess* had been sitting beside a bush with reddish blossoms when she became aware of her love. And legend has it that the coffin with Osiris, drifting down the Nile River, was stopped by a tamarisk, which also carries reddish flowers.

68. Jung, *CW* 12, §518.

69. Jung, *CW* 12, §240: Illustration III of the figurine of Lambspringk of the *Musaeum Hermeticum* (Frankfort, 1625).

70. Riemschneider, *Augengott,* 224, 283.

71. Jung, *CW* 5, §415.

72. Kaigh, *Witchcraft and Magic of Africa* (London, 1947), 13.

73. Hercules overcame both serpent *and* lion!

74. Laurens van der Post, *Das dunkle Auge Afrikas* (Berlin, 1957), 50; English edition: *The Dark Eye of Africa* (London: Hogarth Press, 1955).

75. In Jung's conception, the Self is the goal of the process of individuation, of the subjective development. The Self embraces the entirety of the human being, consciousness and the unconscious, both personal and collective data. This is in contrast to the ego which forms the center of consciousness. As such, the archetype of the Self transcends consciousness. It is not an intellectual concept but rather an irrational concept. It manifests itself in various symbols of wholeness. For example, it is in circular drawings which enclose contrasting tendencies of the personality, in the rose, in the lotus blossom, or as we find in Master Eckhart, in the small circular castle within the soul. See also Jung, *CW* 12, §247.

76. Kerényi, *Die Mythologie,* 84.

77. Inasmuch as we focus in this book upon the Anima, that is, on the unconscious, emotional side of the man, we must leave undone the description of the Animus and the opinionatedness with which the wife may torment the husband. The account of guilt in marital difficulties is fairly evenly divided between the sexes. Esther Harding writes about the woman's Animus in *Der Weg der Frau,* 4th ed. (Zürich); English edition: *The Way of All Women* (New York: Harper & Row, 1975).

78. In various sites of Africa, relics of earlier Mediterranean cultures can be found. In *Das dunkle Auge Afrikas,* 47–48, van der Post states, "The bushmen in the Calahari desert still live like in the beginning of our civilization. Visiting there recently, I had the opportunity to observe them in their natural, innocent, communal life. The man still performs his ancient love-ritual with the bow of Cupid which up to then had been for me no more than a picture on an old Greek vase. At the foot of the large, high mesa, where the sleeping sickness is endemic, I saw black people with beautiful bodies. They unexpectedly appeared and approached me joyfully with garlands of wild flowers around their necks. They played on flutes that resembled those of the god Pan. I had also known them from the pictures of old Greek vases."

79. Neumann, *Die Grosse Mutter,* 54.

80. Jung, *CW* 13, §170.

81. Jung, *CW* 9, ii, §334.

82. Ibid., §344.

83. Jung, *CW* 5, §438.

84. Mandalas are circular drawings made for cultural purposes to represent the wholeness that is the seat and temple of the deity. They are found predominantly in India and in Tibet. See Jung, *CW* 12, §§122 ff.

85. *Handwörterbuch des Islam,* 29.

86. Ibid.

87. Margaret Smith, *Rabi'a the Mystic* (Cambridge, 1928), 120.

88. Ibid., 121.

89. Erwin Rouselle, *Eranos Jahrbuch—1933,* 170: "The spinning woman sets in motion. . . ."

90. Pierre Benoit, *L'Atlantide* (Paris: A. Michel, 1919), 98–99.

91. Ibid., 109.

92. Edmund O. Lippmann, *Entstehung und Ausbreitung der Alchemie* (Origin and Dissemination of Alchemy) (Berlin: Springer, 1919), 5 and 34.

93. *Gilgamesch* (Insel Buecherei), no. 203, p. 25: "You shall have to hear of all your shameful actions. I shall settle with you: Year after year you caused bitter suffering to Tammuz, the youthful lover, the god of spring. You fell in love with a colorfully dressed shepherd-boy; you broke his wing. . . ." Thus Gilgamesh settles with Ishtar in regard to her lovers' fates.

94. Benoit, *L'Atlantide,* 313.

95. Ibid., 167–68.

96. Jung, *CW* 5, §83.

97. M.-L. von Franz, lecture concerning St. Exupéry's *The Little Prince,* held before the Psychology Club, Zürich.

98. Arthur Avalon, pseud., *Die Schlangenkraft* (Berlin: Wilmersdorf, 1961), 207; English edition: *The Serpent Power* (New York: Dover, 1974).

99. In this respect he is different from Saint-Avit, the hero in Benoit's novel.

100. These are the same words as used in *Jess*.

101. Caminada, *Die Verzauberten Taeler, Kulte und Braeuche im alten Raetien* (The Bewitched Valleys, Cults and Customs in Old Romansh Areas) (Olten, Switzerland, 1961), 75 ff., and Frazer, *Der goldene Zweig* (Leipzig, 1928), 933 ff.; English edition: *The Golden Bough* (New York: St. Martin's Press, 1980).

102. Riemschneider, *Augengott*, 223 ff.

103. Neumann, *Die Grosse Mutter*, 255.

104. M. Eliade, *Schamanismus und archaische Ekstasetechnik* (Zürich, 1957), 103 ff. and 152; English edition: *Shamanism: Archaic Techniques of Ecstasy*, trans. Willard R. Trask (Princeton: Princeton University Press, 1964).

105. Gen. 6: 2 f.

106. Jung, *CW* 6, §810: "I distinguish, therefore, between Ego and Self, inasmuch as the Ego is only the subject of my consciousness, whereas the Self is the subject of my entire psyche, including its unconscious part. Thus the Self would be viewed as an ideal magnitude that contains the Ego within itself. In unconscious fantasies the Self tends to manifest itself as a superordinate or ideal personality such as, for example, Faust in Goethe, or Zarathustra in Nietzsche. Yet for the sake of the ideal, the archaic traits of the Self are occasionally presented as separate from the 'higher' Self in Goethe's *Faust....*"

107. Plutarch, *De Iside et Osiride,* quoted from Neumann, *Die Grosse Mutter,* 211: "I'm everything that was, that is, and that shall be, and there never was a person who lifted my veil." Neumann says of her: "She keeps the key of the fertility-goddesses, the key to the doors of the womb and the netherworld, to death and rebirth."

108. Eliade, *Schamanismus,* 445 ff.

109. Ibid., 448–49.

110. Ibid., 195 ff.

111. Jung, *CW* 14, i, §§149 ff.

112. Jung, *CW* 13, §273.

113. Jung, *CW* 5, §659.

114. Ibid., §528.

115. K. H. De Jong, *Das Antike Mysterienwesen* (The Ancient Mysteries) (Leiden: Brill, 1909), 22; quoted by Jung in *CW* 5, §528.

116. Wilhelm Nestle, *Die Vorsokratiker* (The Presocratic Thinkers) (Jena: E. Diederichs, 1929), 120.

117. Ibid.: "The fire is the treasury of all things perceived physically or spiritually, which Simon Magus calls the hidden and the visible things.... Whatever part of the world is preserved, is thus divine; what is corporeal is consumed in the world-fire. Yet inasmuch as the fire is the force of god, the burning of the world means also the world's complete dissolution in the godhead. Already in the Orphic mysteries we find this purifying and deifying force of fire: 'Each night Demeter holds Baubo's child that has been entrusted to her into the fire, in order to burn off the mortal part of its being and to make it divine.'"

118. Riessler, *Altjuedisches Schrifttum: Henochbuch, aegyptisch* (Ancient

Hebrew Texts: Book of Enoch), 18: 11 ff.

119. Dante, *The Divine Comedy,* Purgatory, 27: 10 ff.

120. "Introitus Apert.," in *Mus. Herm.* (1678), 654, cited by Jung, CW 13, §§256, 257.

121. "Gloria Mundi," in *Mus. Herm.,* 246, cited by Jung, CW 12, §446.

122. For example, in the symbols of Lambspringk (*Mus. Herm., 372*)—cited by Jung, CW 12, §446.

123. "Aquarium Sapientium," in *Mus. Herm.,* cited by Jung, CW 13, §§256, 257.

124. Jung, CW 14, i, §42: "Of the three essences."

125. Kees, *Des Götterglaube im Alten Aegypten* (The Faith of Ancient Egypt) (Leipzig, 1941), 95 ff.

126. Ibid., 97.

127. Ibid., 129.

128. Ibid., 98.

129. Eliade, *Schamanismus,* 251 ff.

130. Ibid., 260.

131. Neumann, *Die Grosse Mutter,* 268, 270.

132. Ibid., 210.

133. Ibid., 234.

134. Hegemonius, *Acta Archelai VIII* (Leipzig: Beeson, 1906), 11. This citation was kindly given to me by Prof. Jung.

135. Quispel, "Zeit und Geschichte im Antiken Christentum" (Time and History in Early Christianity), in *Eranos Jahrbuch—1951,* 122; as well as Eliade, *The Myth of the Eternal Return,* trans. W. R. Trask (Princeton: Princeton University Press, 1954).

136. Kerényi suspects that the proclamation in Eleusis contained the news that the goddess of Death had borne a child inside the fire, as a guarantee of rebirth after death. *Die Mysterien von Eleusis* (Zürich, 1962), 99; in English, see: *Eleusis: Archetypal Image of Mother and Daughter,* trans. Ralph Manheim, Bollingen Series 65/4 (New York and London, 1967).

137. L. R. Haggard, *The Cloak,* 129.

138. Jung, CW 16, §504.

139. Jung, CW 11, §351.

140. Jung–Kerényi, *Einführung in das Wesen der Mythologie* (Zürich, 1951), 199; English edition: *Essays on a Science of Mythology,* trans. R. F. C. Hull, Bollingen Series 22 (Princeton: Princeton University Press, 1969).

141. H. R. Haggard, *She and Allan* (Tauchnitz), 255.

142. Ibid., 254.

143. Plato, *Das Gastmahl* (The Symposium), trans. Kurt Hildebrandt (Leipzig, 1934), 129 ff.

144. H. R. Haggard, *Wisdom's Daughter* (Tauchnitz), 267.

145. Jung, CW 16, §494, illustr. 9 of Rosarium.

146. The primary function is the one of the four (sensation, thinking, feeling, and intuition) which is most easily developed and through which adjustment to life is accomplished most easily.

147. The "shadow" is "the inferior personality"; it is the sum of all those per-

sonal and collective psychological dispositions which are not being lived on account of their irreconcilability with the consciously lived way of life; thus they group themselves in the unconscious as a relatively autonomous, partial personality with contrary tendencies. "The dreamer and the figure of the shadow that appears in dreams are of the same sex. As a fragment of the personal unconscious the shadow belongs to the Ego; as the archetype of the antagonist it belongs to the collective unconscious." Sury, *Wörterbuch der Psychologie.*

148. Individuation—becoming a Self; becoming whole; realizing one's own being.

149. Jung, *CW* 6, §§681 ff.

150. *The Egyptian Book of the Dead,* trans. Wallis Budge (London, 1928), 4, n. 2, concerning Khepera: "He is an aspect of the rising sun and has his place in the boat of the sun-god. He is the god of matter in transition from inanimateness to life, as well as of the dead body in the instant in which a spiritual, glorified body emerges from it. His symbol is the beetle."

151. Jung, *Bericht über das Seminar von Prof. Hauer* (Report about Prof. Hauer's Seminar) (Zürich: Seminardruck, 1932), 120.

152. Jung, *CW* 14, ii, §§1 ff.

153. Andreae Johann Valentin, *Chymische Hochzeit Christiani Rosencreutz* (Berlin, 1922), 2; English edition: *The Hermetick Romance: or, The Chymical Wedding,* written in High Dutch by Christian Rosencreutz, trans. E. Foxcroft (London: A. Sowle, 1960).

154. See Part I of this book: "Psychological Interpretation of Rider Haggard's *She.*"

155. Andreae, *Chymische Hochzeit.*

156. Jung, *CW* 12, §§332 ff.

157. Andreae, *Chymische Hochzeit,* 2.

158. Jung, *CW* 16, §461.

159. Martin Ninck, *Wodan und Germanischer Schicksalsglaube* (Odin and Germanic Faith in Destiny) (Jena: E. Diederichs, 1935), 257 ff.

160. Emma Jung, "Die Anima als Naturwesen," in *Studien zur analytischen Psychologie C. G. Jungs* (Zürich, 1955), II: 78–79; in English: "The Anima as an Elemental Being," trans. Hildegard Nagel, in *Animus and Anima* (Dallas: Spring Publications, 1957/1985).

161. Eric Graf Oxenstierna, *Die Goldhoerner von Gallehus* (The Golden Horns of Gallehus) (1956), 155.

162. Jung, *CW* 14, i, §§181, 182.

163. Ninck, *Wodan,* 282–83.

164. Ibid., 34 ff. "Berserk" originally meant "bear-skinned."

165. The contents of the collective unconscious are in themselves morally indifferent (as is nature itself). It is, however, imperative that a human being consciously distinguish between the positive and negative, healing and dangerous aspects of these contents in order to prevent the irruption of the collective shadow.

166. Jung, *CW* 18, ii, §§1692 ff.

167. Jung, *CW* 9, ii, §§43 ff.

168. See also Part I of this book, concerning the crater as mandala.

169. Jung, *CW* 12, §13, and *CW* 9, i, §693 and *CW* 9, ii, §59, concerning the foursomeness and rotation of the mandala.

170. Ninck, *Wodan,* 37.

171. Ibid., 174.

172. Basil Ivan Rakoczi, *The Painted Caravan* (S'Gravenhage, 1954), 47.

173. Linda Fierz-David, *Der Liebestraum des Poliphilo* (Zürich, 1946), 77; English edition: *The Dream of Poliphilo,* trans. Mary Hottinger, Bollingen Series 25 (New York: Bollingen Foundation/Pantheon, 1950).

174. Goethe, *Faust,* Part I.

175. See Part I of this book: "Psychological Interpretation of Rider Haggard's *She.*"

176. Gilles Quispel, *Gnosis als Weltreligion* (Gnosis as World-Religion) (Zürich, 1951), 61–62. B. Leisegang, too, points out in his *Gnosis* that Simon Magus saw in Helen of Troy the incarnation of the divine Ennoia (2d ed., 66). Ennoia means "constancy of consciousness, representation, thought, concept, and reflection." K. Kerényi told me that Helen was venerated as a goddess in Sparta.

177. Jung, *CW* 18, ii, §§1692 ff.

178. Jung, *CW* 5, §354.

179. H. Jacobsohn, "Die dogmatische Stellung," 19.

180. In Switzerland the immense "bull of Uri" is a silvery-white male calf raised exclusively on cow milk for nine years. It had to be led daily to a certain place by a pure virgin. K. Gisler, *Geschichtliches, Sagen und Legenden aus Uri* (Historical Facts, Sagas and Legends from Uri) (Altdorf: Buchdruckerei Altdorf, 1911), 88.

181. H. Jacobsohn, "Die dogmatische Stellung," 62.

182. Communication from Mary Elliot.

183. The "Asian commander" has the same role as She in the second volume of *Ayesha,* where She attempts to spread her rule from Central Asia to China and the entire world. See Part I of this book, 110–12.

184. See Part I of this book. There we find Billali as the executor of She's orders.

185. Avalon, *Die Schlangenkraft,* verses 28–29, and picture 6, pp. 233–38. "Chakra" means wheel.

186. Jung, *Seminar von Prof. Hauer,* 133–34.

187. Jung, *CW* 9, i, §449 and *CW* 16, §425.

188. Ninck, *Wodan,* 11.

189. Jung, *CW* 13, §350.

190. Herrigel, *Zen in der Kunst des Bogenschiessens* (Munich: Planegg, 1953); English edition: *Zen and the Art of Archery* (New York: Random House, 1971).

191. In this connection, see *Die Philosophie des I-Ging,* trans. Richard Wilhelm (Dusseldorf, 1960); English edition: *The I Ching, or Book of Changes* (London: Routledge and Kegan Paul, 1950).

192. Edgar Hennecke, "Hirt des Hermas," in *Neutestamentliche Apokryphen* (1904), 235 ff.; also published in *New Testament Apocrypha* (Philadelphia: Westminster Press, 1966).

193. See also Dream Eighteen of the eleven crows.

194. Jung, *CW* 12, illustr. 4.

195. Jung, *CW* 13, §420.
196. Ibid., §355.
197. Ibid., §403, n. 158.
198. Mary Elliot kindly drew my attention to this nursery rhyme:

> I had a little nut tree and nothing would it bear
> But a silver apple and a golden pear.
> The Queen of Spain's daughter came to visit me.
> All on account of my little nut tree.

199. In the alchemical garden one finds not only Mercury, representing the earth, and the sun- and moon-tree, but also the other planets, Saturn, Mars, Jupiter, and Venus. The gardener's strong brother, who recognizes the necessity to dig, seems to correspond to the "gardener Saturn." In the blackness of depression, the latter conveys insight into the inadequacy of the current condition. It seems justified to assume Mars and Jupiter to be the other two male figures, and Venus to be the fourth, feminine, helpful person. See Jung, *CW* 13, §355.
200. According to the dictionary, *tabernaculum* is the Latin word for "tent."
201. Jung, *CW* 13, §459.
202. Ibid., §321.
203. See Jung, *CW* 14, ii, §419, on the *"coelum"* or "air-colored liquid."
204. Jung, *Seminar von Prof. Hauer*, 133.
205. Jung, *CW* 16, §§516 and 517.
206. See Jung, *CW* 14, ii, §362.
207. In the following, we refer to Jung, *CW* 11, §§309 ff. and 381 ff.
208. Ibid., §384.
209. Jung, *CW* 11, §§269–72.
210. In *She,* the old wise man, Noot, has been dead for two thousand years. The conflict between Leo, Holly, and She fails because this leader-figure is lacking. Haggard was compelled to repeat this symbolical story in numerous variations because of this lack. Only in his last novel, *Queen of the Dawn* (published in the last year of his life), does the old wise man re-emerge as a positive figure and as teacher of the Anima.
211. Robert Graves, *The White Goddess* (New York, 1948), 77.
212. Jung, Kerényi and Radin, *Der Gottliche Schelm* (The Divine Rogue) (Zürich: Rhein-Verlag, 1954), 191; Jung, *CW* 9, i, §§465–66.
213. Jung, *CW* 18, ii, §§1692 ff.
214. Jung, *CW* 13, §268.
215. See part I of this book: "Psychological Interpretation of Rider Haggard's *She.*"
216. Andreae, *Chymische Hochzeit*, 64.
217. For the significance of "the fourth" see Jung, *CW* 11, §§250–52.
218. In Negro spirituals we find an expression of this piety of black people.
219. Jung, *CW* 9, ii, §342.
220. Briffault, *The Mothers*, 3 : 184 ff., cited in Esther Harding, *Frauen-Mysterien* (Zürich, 1949), 85–87; English edition: *Women's Mysteries* (New York: Harper & Row, 1976).

221. Ernesto Buonaiuti, *Maria in der Christlichen Ueberlieferung* (Mary in the Christian Tradition) (Zürich, 1938), 396–97.

222. A lasting identification with an animal would indicate a danger. In this dream, however, the hart transforms back to a human being.

223. See Jung, *CW* 9, i, §449.

224. Andreae, *Chymische Hochzeit*, 59; Jung, *CW* 14, i, §31; and von Franz, "Die Passio Perpetuae," 463 ff.

225. In *Ephesians* 4 : 1–2, Paul states: "I, therefore, the prisoner in [the] Lord entreat you to walk worthily of the calling with which you were called, with complete lowliness of mind and mildness, with long-suffering. . . ."

226. Cited from Ninck, *Wodan*, 299.

227. Von Franz, *Die Visionen des Niklaus von Flue* (The Visions of Nicholas from Flue) (Zürich, 1959), 41 ff.; reprinted by Daimon Verlag (Zürich).

228. Jung, *CW* 5, §§659 ff.

229. Such a fate befell Hölderlin and Novalis. The former was driven early into permanent insanity; the latter died in his twenties.

230. In German, red horses are called "foxes."

231. *The Complete Grimm's Fairy Tales* (New York: Pantheon Books, 1972), 244.

232. For example, Pu Sung-Ling, *Gaukler, Daemonen und Fuechse* (Jugglers, Demons and Foxes) (Basel, 1955).

233. *Grimm's Fairy Tales,* 272.

234. See also Jung, *CW* 9, i, §§422 ff., dealing with the tale "The Princess on the Tree."

235. Ninck, in *Wodan*, 256, speaks of the bird "griff" as the "clawing wrath."

236. See Part I of this book, 41.

237. "According to C. G. Jung, 'synchronicity' is a meaningful coincidence of an inner and an outer experience which cannot be attributed to a causal relationship. This phenomenon exists apart from causality and seems to rest on an archetypal basis." See Sury, *Wörterbuch,* and Jung, *CW* 8, §§849–50.

238. Oxenstierna, *Die Goldhoerner,* 155.

239. Waldemar Fenn, *Grafica Prehistorica* (Mahon, 1950), 166, fig. 153.

240. Ibid., fig. 23, rock painting of the cave of Arce (Cadiz).

241. Graves, *The White Goddess,* 261.

242. Jung, *CW* 9, ii, §44: "I wish to mention that the Ego approaches the Self more and more as it assimilates meaningful contents of the unconscious. This approach will invariably create an inflation of the Ego, unless one is able to discriminate between the Ego and the unconscious figures. Such a discrimination, however, is successful only if one is able to gain reasonable, human limits to the Ego and accord a certain amount of autonomy and reality to the figures of the unconscious, especially the Self, the Anima, the Animus and the Shadow."

243. Jung, "Der Geist der Psychologie," in *Eranos Jahrbuch*—1946, 485, and *CW* 8, §§835–36 on synchronicity.

244. Michael de Ferdinandy, *Historia Mundi,* V: 208.

245. Von Franz, *Niklaus von Flue,* 59. Reference to an analogous visionary experience of St. Nicholas from Flue in which three noble men of pagan origin visit the saint, furthering in him the development of a new, comprehensive per-

sonality.

246. Mabel Smith Waln, *Im Lande der schnellen Pferde* (In the Land of the Fast Horses) (Wiesbaden, 1958).

247. Jung, *CW* 5, §681.

248. Ninck, *Wodan,* 190–91.

249. Ibid., 217.

250. Ibid., 312.

251. In connection with the following remarks, see Part I of this book about the pillar of fire, 98–99.

252. We already mentioned this need to limit one's consideration of the outer world in our discussion of the transition dream (Dream Thirty-Seven). See also Jung, *CW* 13, §§433–34.

253. Jung has kindly directed my attention to this treatise: "Geheimnis der Natur des grossen und des kleinen Bauers," in *Gresshoff nach Ferguson,* ed. Walch (1731).

254. Jung, *CW* 14, ii, §§413–14.

255. As was the case during the Hitler period.

256. Avalon, *Die Schlangenkraft,* 240, referring to tantra yoga.

257. Jung, *CW* 18, ii, §§1692 ff. and *CW* 9, i, §268.

Recent and New Titles from Spring

PAGAN MEDITATIONS   Ginette Paris

An appreciation of three Greek Goddesses as values of importance to our twentieth-century collective life: Aphrodite as civilized sexuality and beauty; Artemis as solitude, ecological significance, and a perspective on abortion; and Hestia as warm hearth, security, and stability. This contribution to *imaginative* feminism addresses both the meditative interior of each person and the community of culture. (204 pp., ISBN 0-88214-330-1)

HERMES: *Guide of Souls*   Karl Kerényi

The famous mythographer, classicist, and friend of Jung here presents a beautiful, authoritative study of the great God whom the Greeks revered as Guide of Souls. Chapters on Hermes and Night, Hermes and Eros, Hermes and the Goddesses illuminate the complex role of Hermes in classical mythology, while also providing an archetypal background for the guiding of souls in psychotherapy. (104 pp., ISBN 0-88214-207-0)

ANIMA: *An Anatomy of a Personified Notion*   James Hillman

Anima and Eros, Anima and Feeling, Anima and Feminine, Mediatrix of the Unknown—ten succinct chapters, accompanied by relevant quotations from Jung (on left-hand pages facing Hillman's essay), which clarify the moods, persons, and definitions of the most subtle and elusive aspect of psychology and of life. (188 pp., ISBN 0-88214-316-6)

"In spite of the stimulating complexity of this analysis, this book captures and retains the fascinating and living quality of the anima."—*Choice*

A CELTIC QUEST
Sexuality and Soul in Individuation   John Layard

This classic Welsh tale of heroic youth in search of soul finds a master equal to its riddles in John Layard, Oxford anthropologist and Jungian analyst. The quest proceeds as a boar hunt, encountering giants and dwarfs, bitch-dogs, helpful ants, the Witch Hag, until the soul is won. Brilliant appendices, together with scholarly apparatus and a full index, have established this volume as the standard interpretative psychological text of Celtic legend. (264 pp., ISBN 0-88214-110-4)

COMMENTARY ON PLATO'S SYMPOSIUM ON LOVE
                                    Marsilio Ficino, trans. Sears Jayne

Marsilio Ficino, the head of the Platonic Academy in Renaissance Florence and the first ever to translate the complete works of Plato, also wrote this Latin essay on love. Popular in European court-circles for almost two hundred years, this book influenced painters such as Botticelli and Michelangelo, and writers such as Spenser and Castiglione. Jayne's English translation, based on Marcel's edition, includes an introduction. (213 pp., ISBN 0-88214-601-7)

"Jayne's translation is eminently readable, copiously annotated, and contains a bibliography of particular value."—*Choice*

Spring Publications • P.O. Box 222069 • Dallas, TX 75222